THE ROSARY AND
THE MICROPHONE

Studies in Popular Music

Series Editors: Alyn Shipton, lecturer in jazz history at the Royal Academy of Music, London, and at City University, London; and Christopher Partridge, Professor of Religious Studies, Lancaster University

From jazz to reggae, bhangra to heavy metal, electronica to qawwali, and from production to consumption, *Studies in Popular Music* is a multi-disciplinary series which aims to contribute to a comprehensive understanding of popular music. It will provide analyses of theoretical perspectives, a broad range of case studies, and discussion of key issues.

Published

Do You Want to Know a Secret?: The Autobiography of Billly J. Kramer
Billy J. Kramer with Alyn Shipton

Dub in Babylon: Understanding the Evolution and Significance of Dub Reggae in Jamaica and Britain from King Tubby to Post-Punk
Christopher Partridge

Falco and Beyond: Neo Nothing Post of All
Ewa Mazierska

Global Tribe: Technology, Spirituality and Psytrance
Graham St John

Heavy Metal: Controversies and Countercultures
Edited by Titus Hjelm, Keith Kahn-Harris and Mark LeVine

Nick Cave: A Study of Love, Death and Apocalypse
Roland Boer

Open up the Doors: Music in the Modern Church
Mark Evans

Send in the Clones: A Cultural Study of Tribute Bands
Georgina Gregory

Technomad: Global Raving Countercultures
Graham St John

*The Lost Women of Rock Music:
Female Musicians of the Punk Era* (second edition)
Helen Reddington

The Northern Soul Scene
Edited by Sarah Raine, Tim Wall and Nicola Watchman Smith

THE ROSARY AND THE MICROPHONE

RELIGIOUS IMPULSE IN U2'S MEDIATED BRAND

NICHOLAS P. GRECO

SHEFFIELD UK   BRISTOL CT

Published by Equinox Publishing Ltd.

UK: Office 415, The Workstation, 15 Paternoster Row, Sheffield, South Yorkshire S1 2BX
USA: ISD, 70 Enterprise Drive, Bristol, CT 06010

www.equinoxpub.com

First published 2019

© Nicholas P. Greco 2019.

All rights reserved. No part of this publication may be reproduced or transmitted in any form or by any means, electronic or mechanical, including photocopying, recording or any information storage or retrieval system, without prior permission in writing from the publishers.

British Library Cataloguing-in-Publication Data
A catalogue record for this book is available from the British Library.

Library of Congress Cataloging-in-Publication Data
Names: Greco, Nicholas P., 1973- author
Title: The rosary and the microphone : religious impulse in U2's mediated brand/ Nicholas P. Greco.
Description: Sheffield, South Yorkshire ; Bristol, CT : Equinox Publishing, 2019.
  | Series: Studies in popular music | Includes bibliographica references I and index.
Identifiers: LCCN 2018052165 (print) | LCCN 2018052652 (ebook) | ISBN 9781781795569 (ePDF) | ISBN 9781781795545 (hb) | ISBN 9781781795552 (pb)
Subjects: LCSH: U2 (Musical group) | Rock music--Religious aspects--Christianity.
Classification: LCC ML421.U2 (ebook) | LCC ML421.U2 G74 2019 (print) | DDC 782.42166092/2--dc23
LC record available at https://lccn.loc.gov/2018052165

ISBN: 978 1 78179 554 5   (hardback)
       978 1 78179 555 2   (paperback)
       978 1 78179 556 9   (ePDF)

Typeset by CA Typesetting Ltd.

To Serafina Persephone Greco, who probably got the idea of her "LEMONADE PLNET" lemonade stand from my *PopMart* tour t-shirt.

J.M.J.T.

Contents

	Acknowledgements	ix
	Preface	x
	Introduction	1
1	From Underground to Overground: U2 from *Boy* to *Rattle and Hum*	17
2	U2 and the Blinding Lights of the City	37
3	Beautiful Day: Technological Optimism, Gesture and Intimacy	62
4	The Irish in America: Nationalism and Politics on Tour	88
5	The Rosary and the Microphone: Social Justice and the Stage	113
6	*Linear*: A Way Forward	145
7	*Songs of Innocence* as Barthes' Ideal Novel	171
	Conclusions: A Cosmopolitan Christianity	188
	Bibliography	199
	Index	209

Acknowledgements

This book would not have been possible without the support of my family. My partner Antonella and my daughter Serafina have listened to a lot of U2's music and watched more than their share of video footage featuring the band. I am not sure that there are many young children that know as much about Bono and his ideas as Serafina. Both of you: all my life, I will worship you, and the ground beneath your feet.

My colleagues at Providence have been more than helpful, especially in the last push of much of this material. I must acknowledge Dr Michael J. Gilmour. This book emerged from a sort of wager – without money – as to who would be able to secure a book contract more quickly. He certainly won the wager (which got him absolutely nothing but a large amount of stressful work, though it also resulted in an excellent book on C. S. Lewis and animals). I am still indebted to him, as he continues to allow me to bother him with quotes and ideas, and I continue to invite him to treat me to the same.

Jerrad Peters has been a faithful companion on this journey. He has both mocked me and has given me encouragement throughout the writing process. He knows what the writing "grind" is like, and I thank him for his support and for his true and deep kinship. I admit that I should always take his advice the first time around.

Providence allowed me to run a senior-level course on U2 in the winter of 2018, and I must acknowledge the work of two students, Alena Collier and Naaman Sturrup. Their participation in the class encouraged me to bring forward strange, complex ideas on a band about which they knew only a little. They pushed me to think about the band in new ways, and I appreciate the role that they had in the creation of this work. Thank you, Alena and Naaman: just like in the song, don't *ever* let the bastards grind you down.

I do not know either Bono, The Edge, Larry Mullen Jr or Adam Clayton personally. But what I do know is that the world would be a worse place without them in it. U2 present a world that could be, or that should be. And that is what makes them special.

St. Teresa Benedicta of the Cross, pray for us.

Preface

In the spring of 2018, I presented a public lecture at a local bookstore in Winnipeg, Manitoba, Canada, during which I introduced some of the overarching thoughts that inform the analyses that appear in this book. I made the general point (as I do in the following pages) that Bono and U2 draw on a particularly Christian religious impulse that finds its expression in the band's presentation in concert, music video and so forth. In other words, U2 show this religious impulse in their mediated brand.

In the question-and-answer period at the end of the lecture, a member of the intimate audience mentioned, near tears, how Bono (through the music of U2) helped her work through the death of her father in light of the difficult relationship Bono had with his own father. Another attendee mentioned how U2's music was fundamentally good, even in their (apparent) complicity with what might be called corporate or market forces and commercial interests. Still, for this school teacher, the band's music brought people together. Finally, another person suggested that a band (or corporation) cannot be as commercially successful or have a global reach as big as U2 do without being in some way complicit with, for instance, market forces. The person likened U2 to the fitness brand Nike which has been criticized for using low-wage labourers. But the company has also been commended for its innovation and global focus, for instance for creating a dedicated *hijab* for use by Muslim women in sport.

One attendee at my lecture questioned whether Bono's concerns with social justice might be characterized as simply humanist rather than Christian. Similarly, Joshua Rothman writes, "While secular listeners tend to think of U2's religiosity as preachy window dressing, religious listeners see faith as central to the band's identity. To some people, Bono's lyrics are treacly platitudes, verging on nonsense; to others, they're thoughtful, searching, and profound meditations on faith".[1] This is the tension in which U2 sit, and a tension that can make the band both annoying (to some) and interesting (to many) at the same time. They annoy because they do not *fit* the categories into which rock bands are generally assigned, and they are interesting for that very same reason. Of course, this is just one reason why the band annoys (and interests). The general discourse around the band would suggest that people are also annoyed at Bono's propensity to "preach" from a higher moral position – with a condescending tone – not to mention the discomfort of a performer who seems to tout the punk music origins of a (now) very successful band. The band sell themselves as "authentic" while employing, for instance, a keyboard player in the "underworld" beneath the stage. Utilizing session keyboardist Terry Lawless under the stage explicitly demonstrates the artifice of the "live" presentation. Furthermore, Bono fraternizes with the rich while advocating for the poor, and invests his fortune while employing corporate practices to avoid paying more taxes than absolutely necessary. Also, one can argue that U2 promote no real activism but facilitate the participation in what is called "slacktivism", an engagement with social media involving social justice ideas rather than any meaningful action. Describing how the members of U2 themselves tried to navigate those tensions, Rothman writes that the band almost broke up early in their career "because the twin demands of piety and rock stardom could not be reconciled". They did not break up, nor could the twin demands be reconciled. Rothman continues to suggest that the band's "thin ecclesiology has become thick", and that they have a "philanthropic arm", something that makes U2 sound much more like a corporation than a rock band.[2]

My memories of my first experiences with U2 are fuzzy. Even consulting with my sister, I am no closer to figuring out these details. It was my sister who first introduced me to the band, I think, and when I ask her about it now, she mentions the song, 'A Sort of Homecoming' as the one she remembers, the one that "started it". I recall that my cousin, who was only a few years older than me, was practising to become a drummer. Sometime in the mid-1980s (certainly before *The Joshua Tree*), my family visited his family, and my cousin and I ran downstairs to his basement where he proceeded to show me how he had improved in his drumming. He played his drum kit along to songs from *The Unforgettable Fire*, the vinyl record spinning on his turntable. I remember he had shown my sister and me his *The Unforgettable Fire* record which had a pencilled stick figure playing a stick drum kit on the label, which was, at the time, my cousin's "signature". I remember that my sister had listened to a lot of *The Joshua Tree*, and I remember going to the music store in the local mall waiting for a new U2 album to come out (the album was probably *Achtung Baby*). But I was waiting for it for my sister, not for myself, at least as far as I can remember.

For some reason, my own personal engagement with U2 came later. I only became a fan of U2 when I was in my last years of high school and first years of university in the early 1990s. I was not a fan of the band's early music until much later: the first album that I remember having – that was my own – was *Achtung Baby*, bought at a Walmart on a road trip to a Christian music festival in the United States. It was a compact disc in a paper package, and I remember doing my best to preserve the rather fragile packaging as much as I could (I could not). I remember a friend in my youth group who, it was said, had a copy of *Rattle and Hum* on vinyl, which she destroyed in a fit of pietism, in order to rid her home of any "secular" music. She bought the album on compact disc a few years later. I remember during the year I attended a Christian college, my roommate was critical of my choice of music as I played *Achtung Baby* in my dorm room. He was not appreciative of Bono's use of the word "bastard" in the song 'Acrobat'. He suggested that, as my spiritual life became deeper and as I became closer to Christ, my tastes in music would change. This did not happen. I also remember the colleague in the dorm room across from mine who claimed that 'Acrobat' was the song that ultimately ushered him to a place of conversion to Christianity. This young man's mantra was the popular one that God works in mysterious ways. My roommate had little appreciation for the idea that a song like 'Acrobat' would be a conduit for Christian evangelism, or that it would lead someone onto the path to Jesus.

I saw U2 in concert for the first time during the *PopMart* tour in 1997. I went to the Olympic Stadium in Montréal with a group of friends from my church youth group (though, at this point, I was in my early twenties). During that concert, I remember marvelling at the spectacle of that huge screen. I remember how the large space of the Olympic Stadium was transformed into one of the most amazing clubs or discothèques I had ever been in (this was a truly immersive experience for me).

I saw U2 twice during the *Elevation* tour, again in Montréal. It was clear that they could fill a stadium of some sixty thousand people with throbbing sound and immersive lights, but in that arena in Montréal, I realized that the band could also bring us to church, so to speak. I realized that a U2 show was a spiritual experience; I did not yet understand all of the social justice action and world change that U2 were proposing, but I certainly experienced first-hand the idea of the creation of a potential world, and the transformative power and feeling of transcendence into a new world that happens in concert. This feeling continued when my partner and I saw the band at the same arena venue during the *Vertigo* tour. That night, we were certain that we would have had a chance to meet Bono, whose car had arrived at the arena venue for the concert moments before we arrived to that entrance. We sheepishly watched as people walked from the scene giddy with the knowledge that they had seen the star. Many of them seemed to be holding onto pieces of paper signed by Bono, or so we thought. We never saw the papers closely enough to know that these were signed pieces or simply some other collectible. For that matter, people could have seen a sports star. The concert venue was a hockey arena after all, and Montréal is a city eternally under the allure of that sport. But I remember that moment clearly; there was a charged atmosphere between me and my partner, thinking that we were that close to greatness (a greatness that goes by the name "Bono"). We never did find out if he had been close by.

I saw the band in Winnipeg during the *U2 360°* tour, this time with some friends from the university where I work. I remember the moment when the band began to perform 'Zooropa', a song that I did not remember the band performing in any of the shows that I had attended prior. I remember the joy that I felt at hearing that song, and at the thought that maybe there were those in attendance at this concert who had never heard the song before, in any context. I remember jubilantly shouting, "Let's go overground!" along with Bono under the telescoping television screens on that visually-impressive round stage.

The U2 that I find most compelling is U2 in live performance, and this might be why the band in concert make so frequent an appearance in this book. This is where U2 live, at least for me. I have sometimes wondered whether U2 would ever stop touring and become a studio band. Their days with Brian Eno in the 1990s, and the emergence of the recording studio itself as a musical instrument during that time, makes me think that perhaps they would choose the studio as their primary mode of expression. There, they would be able to break new musical ground, to marshal all of their talents and use them to their full potential without worrying how an album would sound or be received in the context of a world tour. But then, fans would lose out on so many awesome experiences, both in terms of attending a live U2 concert performance, and the opportunity of experiencing the band in the context of a live concert film. There is absolutely nothing that can measure up to U2 in live performance, and there is no doubt that something special happens during a U2 concert. Is a U2 concert a sacramental event? This book is implicitly trying to answer that question, and I think the answer is *towards* yes. A U2 show changes you, experiencing U2 in their many mediations changes you and, if you receive their message, they make you better.

This book is a love letter to U2. It should be clear that I am a fan-scholar, and so I am biased to look at the band positively. Even so, the goal of this book is not to be completely uncritical. There is a sense that the band are complicit with corporate interests, and those that hold that view would not be wrong. As the listener at my lecture mentioned, when an entity becomes so big, there is no way that it cannot be complicit, wrapped up completely in the popular music and celebrity machine.

In a way that I never expected at the onset of this project, this book is also a love letter to French theorist Roland Barthes. Barthes seems to be the thread that holds this study together, and hopefully the reader will find the use of his theory justified. I do not think that Barthes would have enjoyed the music of U2 (he has not written at all about popular music, though he was an amateur musician himself, in the form of a classical pianist). However, Barthes would have surely appreciated the spectacle of U2. While popular music performance is not the same as the made-up sport of professional wrestling (that Barthes did write about), Bono's character of The Fly is a made-up rock star, and Mr MacPhisto is a made-up villain that the audience loves to hate. I could only imagine what Barthes would have to say about these characters and the mythologies that the band play with, reinforce and introduce. Again, these personae point to the complicity of U2: they are playing with the ideas that they are pushing against.

The majority of this book, I feel, is filled with the act of following threads. What I mean by this is that the book attempts to map common threads or ideas throughout the career of the band. In exploring how U2 present themselves through their concert performances throughout the years, or exploring how they perform a particular song over various tours, or the band's presentation through music video, I hope to show that the band's central message – global care – continues to be part of their mediated message, even with the band's many external transformations and new ways of doing things. U2 use the noise to lobby for the quiet.

Notes

1. Joshua Rothman, "The Church of U2", *The New Yorker* (16 September 2014); available from https://www.newyorker.com/culture/cultural-comment/church-u2 (accessed 28 August 2017).
2. Ibid. To be fair, the band do introduce Lawless during the keyboard solo during the song 'Unknown Caller' in the *U2 360° Live at the Rose Bowl* concert film.

Introduction

Consider the scene: an outdoor stadium is filled with people waiting for a popular music performance by a critically and commercially acclaimed band. In fact, some have spent significant amounts of money and invested much travel time in order to attend this concert. At one end of the stadium, towards which all of the attendees are facing, there is a stage. The stage seems to be in a state of incompleteness, and appears to have been set up haphazardly. The sides of the stage are covered in scaffolding, and, as music blasts through the speakers, black-clad stagehands finish putting musical equipment into place. Work lights illuminate the stage; high on the scaffolding is a flickering set of neon letters spelling out "ZOO TV": the "T" and "V" are placed within the two "O"s, like the logo of some new and unknown television network. Hip hop music echoes out of the speakers. The lights in the stadium are dimmed and huge video screens on either side of the stage begin to show the image of the horn of a trumpet, accompanied by its sonic complement. The image changes to a boy playing a large drum, interspersed with what looks to be archival footage of women stretching (as if preparing for physical exercise). As the display of various disparate images continues, other voices come through the sound system: "What do you want?", one of the voices asks.

More video screens are activated, each displaying more disjointed images. Then, Beethoven's 'Ode To Joy', from his Ninth Symphony, begins to play as the crowd starts to cheer more loudly. Then, the symbols which are featured on the flag of the European Union – twelve yellow stars on a blue field – appear on one of the video screens. But something is wrong: a star becomes unstuck and falls while a human figure emerges from underneath the stage. The figure appears in front of the blue of the video screen, but is seen only in silhouette. A spotlight does not yet illuminate him. The figure begins to prance around in front of the screen, raising his arm in a gesture that appears to be a Nazi salute, and march in goose step.

That is the scene at the very start of the *Zoo TV: Live from Sydney* concert film, a recording of a concert from the *Zoo TV* tour, which ran from 1992 to 1993. It deftly embodies what U2 had become in the previous decade, complete with politics and spirituality: the energy of their punk-inspired early years, the sincerity of *The Joshua Tree* and the albums they released in the 1980s, and the veiled statements and embracing of technology of the 1991 release, *Achtung*

Baby. The tour either constitutes U2 at their prime, or it shows U2 at their least authentic, sold out to commercial interests and slaves to postmodern drivel and crass spectacle.

U2 are not a rock band. U2 are a corporation. U2 are an institution that makes music and goes on tour. They are a lobbying force, but not really a charitable organization. U2 can be thought of as an educational institution, an entertainment company and a transportation and logistics leader. The music – and all that goes with it – is only a single part of a multifaceted project in which the receiving of monetary revenue is also important. Music for U2 is not an afterthought, but it is also not an end.

This book is about U2 and how they develop their "star image" through the various media that they utilize to portray themselves and to communicate with their audience and the outside world. The religious impulse is the driving force that informs and runs throughout their mediated brand, sometimes explicitly and often implicitly.

First, about the title of this book: the image of the rosary and the microphone is one that explicitly refers to a particular moment in U2's live concert performance. During a performance of the song '40' at the very end of the *Vertigo 2005: Live from Chicago* concert film, Bono places a rosary that was hanging around his neck on to the microphone as the band plays the closing strains of the song. He dedicates the performance to a Roman Catholic priest from the University of Notre Dame. The moment is a poignant reminder of the close relationship that Bono – and by extension, the band – has with institutional religion. Beyond that, though, it points to a particular religious sensibility on the part of the band, and a willingness to engage with ideas outside of the conventional rock celebrity context.

Second, the definition for social justice herein is somewhat limited: here, social justice refers to a general sense of what can be described as "outward attention", the awareness and concern for events happening outside of the concert venue, outside of the context of the concert machine and popular music industry as a whole, and a concern for the wellbeing of those experiencing oppressive circumstances and difficulties. An example of U2's social justice project includes awareness of the plight and struggle of refugees from Syria's civil war, and those from surrounding regions, who are looking to Europe for accommodation and safety, as made clear in the Paris concert during the *iNNOCENCE + eXPERIENCE* tour.

Third, the term, "cosmopolitanism", is also used in a limited sense. Cosmopolitanism here refers to a sort of "global care", a concern that is free from local prejudice, and rather focused outward, that is, globally (a sense of a global social justice). In the case of U2, this concern stems from local experience (the Irish conflicts that informed much of the band's upbringing) but is transformed throughout their career into a global impulse. Even though the band focus on localized concerns, be it the political situation in Myanmar, the religious and cultural tensions in Ireland or environmental issues surrounding nuclear power generation in the United Kingdom, the greater idea is that of the cultivation of a general global good. Through various means, the band negotiate their place in the world as a global, mediated brand. U2 communicate a kind of cosmopolitanism, or global care, and desire for far-reaching and inclusive social justice initiatives.

U2 are a politically engaged band that sit at the intersection of a particular brand of Christianity and the band's mediation in a global context and for a global audience. U2's brand is heavily informed by a Christianity embodied by Bono and his own personal religious formation. This brand is expressed by a global concern, or cosmopolitanism, that looks outward and seems to draw others to do the same. The religious impulse finds its expression in what is called here U2's "Christian cosmopolitanism", an outward view of Christianity that is linked to the lived experience of individuals in a connected and interdependent world. Through the primarily semiotic study of U2's various mediations, this book maps the band's strategies for negotiating its place in the world as a global band – and mediated brand – and as a proponent of a kind of cosmopolitanism, or global care. The book explores U2 in live performance, through music videos and in unique media offerings, such as the feature-length music video *Linear*.

This book takes what might be called a "Barthesian" approach to the study of U2's signs. There are a few reasons why this is the appropriate approach here. First, Roland Barthes writes about nostalgia and loss, especially in relation to his mother. Much of his late writing – after his mother's death – explores themes of loss, nostalgia and memory. All of these themes also exist, in some form, in the band. Bono also struggles with the death of his mother, a figure that informs him throughout his career (and, in a special way, in the band's later music). Second, like the band, Roland Barthes implicitly expresses a religious tension. Barthes' Protestant upbringing is at odds with a primarily Roman Catholic France; his own homosexuality is at odds with the Protestantism of his childhood. As noted by Emma Mason, Barthes' family was made up of a Roman Catholic father (whom he did not know, as his father died when Barthes was very young), a Protestant mother and a half-brother from a Jewish father.[1] Mason claims that, though Barthes seemed not to hold closely to any religious belief himself, he would have been familiar with religious language, and with the Bible. Tiphaine Samoyault, in her biography of Barthes, recounts how he and his mother would spend Sunday evenings with a personal friend of his mother's that was a pastor. That friend would share with them both supper and the biblical text:

> They often stayed with the pastor Louis Bertrand ... [He] had, until 1919, been pastor in Bayonne, which explains his connection with Henriette Barthes: he most probably baptized Roland Barthes ... What Barthes remembered of Louis Bertrand was essentially the slow way he read the Bible. "The Bible is read so slowly at every meal that we sometimes miss the train if we are leaving that evening".[2]

His recollection of the evenings with Bertrand does not seem altogether positive. The dinners might have been nourishing but the readings seemed nothing but a bother and simply an obstacle or waste of time for the young Barthes. Nevertheless, Barthes seemed to keep these early experiences in mind: they were truly formative for him, and in turn, informed his work, especially later in his life.

The tension between this seemingly innate (sense of) Protestantism emerges towards the end of his life. Even in terms of Barthes' exploration of Christian grace in grieving (upon the death of his mother), it seems that he oscillates between the two Christian faith traditions of (familial) Protestantism and (national) Roman Catholicism. Generally, in Protestantism, sin is inherent in human nature but is covered by grace through the act of faith and of believing in Jesus Christ and his redemptive act for humanity. In Roman Catholicism, grace is continually dispensed through the sacraments. Emma Mason writes,

> on the one hand, [Barthes'] "new life" [that is, his late-in-life project, *Vita Nova*] is intended to be one of continuous writing, a habitual rule of life to replace that "silent dailiness" once shared with his mother; on the other, he seeks an epiphanic grace akin to that described by Augustine on reading the Psalms, "I was inwardly pricked" and so commenced "the purpose of a new life".[3]

It is interesting that Barthes was receptive to the ideas of religious life – and a broad sense of Christianity that seemingly spans sectarian divisions – though he seemed not to be religious himself.[4]

Like Barthes, U2 also sit at the intersection of religious – particularly Christian – tension, at the intersection of Protestantism and Roman Catholicism, not only in terms of the obvious sectarianism rife in the Ireland of their youth. Specifically, U2 live within their own historical tensions at the intersection of a broadly defined evangelical Christianity and the "secular" realm of popular music and rock music in particular. Furthermore, they live with the tension of being commercially successful, playing music that might be perceived as focusing on superficial love and sexuality rather than anything of an esoteric or religious importance, or anything of the numinous or spiritual. Also, like any band in post-World War II Western popular music, U2 rely on their mediated image in order to create the "star image" of the band. In turn, each member of the band carefully constructs personae in order to cultivate and maintain their celebrity status: they exhibit inauthenticity in the guise of authenticity. Roland Barthes did something similar: Samoyault describes how Barthes was continually concerned with his image as he grew into adulthood. His transformation from possessing a slender physique as a boy into having a body that he describes as "plump" was concerning: "I had the morphology of someone *super-slim* for my entire youth, and in fact I wasn't accepted for military service because I wasn't the right weight. And at that time I always lived with the idea that I'd be slim, for ever and ever". Samoyault suggests that Barthes did as those in religious orders would do, that is, *control* his body.[5] Such control of the body is in the realm of the cultivation and maintenance of celebrity.

Of course, this is not to suggest that Barthes was a celebrity in the same sense as Bono or the other members of U2. Rather, Barthes made an effort to create and maintain what he later refers to as an "image-repertoire", a way of perceiving himself in his mind in relation to others – an internal "reality" which might or might not be an accurate portrayal of himself in the context of actual relationships.[6] In *Roland Barthes by Roland Barthes*, he expresses his dissatisfaction with this "image-repertoire", a sort of mirror in which the truth of the image is contested.[7] In a telling passage, he writes (referring to himself in the third person): "he imagines, each time he writes something, that he will hurt one of his friends – never the same one: it changes".[8] It is clear that he is concerned with his mediated image. And, as Samoyault points out, he works hard to *maintain* it, to document his weight, for instance, and to carefully control his writing. In fact, Barthes does a particularly celebrity-like thing: Adam Phillips, in his Foreword to *Roland Barthes by Roland Barthes*, writes,

> Barthes's favorite motto, he tells us on several occasions, was, *Larvatus prodeo* (I advance pointing to my mask). There is in Barthes's writing an ironic self-consciousness that knows that it can't always see what it is showing other people, but is always acutely aware of the audience, and of the reader as part of an audience, as sociable rather than solitary.[9]

Furthermore, Barthes' project is represented in the following aphorism: "One writes in order to be loved".[10] U2 seemingly respond to the French theorist with 'Do You Feel Loved?' from their album *Pop*, as if the band are in conversation with him.

It might seem strange to populate a book on an Irish band and their contemporary, mediated, image with constant references to Roland Barthes, a dead French theorist about whom many U2 fans might know little. Many U2 fans might not mind the fact that they know little about him. But Barthes is a keen observer of the world around him. As a semiotician, he finds value and deep meaning in items of the everyday: commodities that are bought and sold; literature that both carries explicit meaning and value (nationalistic and otherwise); as well as items of what might be deemed of limited worth. As a band firmly entrenched in the commodity world of contemporary popular music – and drivers of the industry of buying and selling their own product – U2 understand themselves to be the commodity that they themselves promote.

Finally, in her book on translation, Kate Briggs (herself a translator of Barthes' lectures on how to make a novel) writes about the nature of language and Barthes' own approach towards the creation of haiku in particular. Quoting Adrienne Ghaly, Briggs writes,

> *how*, exactly, one might go about doing this, engaging with the actuality, the real-life practice of doing this [that is, how to write] – is, for Barthes, a way of asking about "language's power to disrupt dominating, classifying and appropriating stances to which certain kinds of language use commit us". It is a way of asking how to write (and thus also how to make?) the world differently.[11]

Like U2, then, Barthes understands the power of discourse to change the world.

Evangelicalism

Some clarification is needed in order to situate U2 at the intersection of often sparring religious viewpoints. Of course, the band are heavily informed by "The Troubles" in Northern Ireland, a set of sectarian conflicts that occurred over thirty years, and continue to be felt in parts of the region. "The Troubles" are considered to have begun during a civil rights march in the city of Derry (Londonderry) in October 1968. Inspired by the civil rights movement in the United States, in which the minority black population was looking for equality with the majority white population, the Derry Housing Action Committee and the Northern Ireland Civil Rights Association organized a civil action in order to demand equality for the Roman Catholic minority in Northern Ireland, a civil rights movement that began officially in 1967. On 5 October 1968, Northern Irish nationalist politician Ivan Cooper demanded equality in terms of housing, employment and what he felt were personal freedoms of speech and assembly that were being constantly curtailed. What was initially a civil rights march became the catalyst for a much wider conflict along religious and nationalist lines, between Nationalist/Republican Roman Catholics and Unionist/Loyalist Protestants. Northern Ireland's population in the 1960s consisted of a majority of Protestants with a minority Roman Catholic population, who felt that they were subject to discrimination, particularly in the form of a lack of public housing provisions. Further violence led to what was supposed to be a brief intervention by the British Army in order to relieve local police forces. The British Army's involvement in Northern Ireland lasted until 2007.

"The Troubles" were not limited to Northern Ireland; violence erupted in Dublin and Monaghan on 17 May 1974. In the song 'Raised by Wolves' from *Songs of Innocence*, Bono recounts that he would have been physically close to the second of three bombs in Dublin that day, on Talbot Street. In a *Rolling Stone* interview, Bono states, "It was a real incident that happened in our country where three car bombs were set to go off at the same time in Dublin on a Friday night, 5:30 … On any other Friday I would have been at this record shop, just down the corner, but I cycled to school that day".[12]

Bono was raised by parents who were Christian. But Bono's parents were of different Christian faith traditions, a Protestant mother and Roman Catholic father, which would have put him in the middle of Irish sectarian conflict. Early on in their career, most of the band members explored what evangelical Protestantism had to offer. Generally, evangelical Protestantism is a different "flavour" of Christianity than even mainstream Protestantism, and can be thought of as almost anathema to traditional Roman Catholic belief and practice. David Bebbington clarifies what Evangelicalism generally means. There are four "priorities" that make up the "quadrilateral" of Evangelicalism, according to Bebbington. They are: "*conversionism*, the belief that lives need to be changed; *activism*, the expression of the gospel in effort; *biblicism*, a particular regard for the Bible; and what may be called *crucicentrism*, a stress on the sacrifice of Christ on the cross".[13]

Bono's childhood home was free from any Christian symbols or elements in order to avoid additional conflict; the home was a neutral site in terms of sectarian Christianity in the Irish context. While being raised in such an environment without any particular religious figures or symbols, Bono did seemingly vacillate between a brand of evangelical Christianity and a later sympathy with Roman Catholicism. Bebbington's characteristics of Evangelicalism do find their equivalents in Roman Catholicism. For instance, in the *Catechism of the Catholic Church* (paragraph 1427), it states, "Jesus calls to conversion. This call is an essential part of the proclamation of the kingdom … In the Church's preaching this call is addressed first to those who do not yet know Christ and his Gospel". As for crucicentrism, the death of Christ is central to the practical theology of Roman Catholicism, in that the Eucharist – that is, the body and blood of Christ broken and shed for sinners – is acknowledged and revered. That sacrament – or means of grace – is celebrated at every service (or "mass") in the Roman Catholic Church. In terms of biblicism, Roman Catholicism takes a divergent view: the Bible (a particular canon of writings that were collected and esteemed through Church tradition) does not stand alone. The Catechism states (in paragraph 82), "Both Scripture and Tradition must be accepted and honoured with equal sentiments of devotion and reverence". Ironically, reading of the Sacred Scripture takes a central place in the Mass.

The last point, regarding activism (or, to use Bebbington's words, "the expression of the gospel in effort"), the Catechism is clear, whereas, generally, evangelical Christianity is not. Consider paragraph 2420: "In the moral order she [the Church] bears a mission distinct from that of political authorities: the Church is concerned with the temporal aspects of the common good because they are ordered to the sovereign Good, our ultimate end".

In addition to adhering to Bebbington's "quadrilateral" of belief (to varying degrees), the Canadian lobby group Evangelical Fellowship of Canada considers Evangelicalism a historical movement: Evangelicalism includes "those denominations or churches growing out of the eighteenth century revivals".[14] This is perhaps where U2's own faith formation meets with the tenets of Evangelicalism. That is, their brief formation in Evangelicalism was perhaps less about the individual tenets of the movement. They still seem to be very much followers of the "activist" and, perhaps at the time of their formation, "biblicist" aspects of Evangelicalism. But the association of U2 with evangelical Christianity is not so much about the other aspects (of "conversionalism" or "crucicentrism"), but rather, simply, that they were part of a movement that called itself "evangelical" and was somehow rooted in those spiritual awakenings or revivals.

Like all such movements, Evangelicalism is not homogeneous or monolithic. It would be safe to suggest, though, that Evangelicalism of the sort that informed U2 early on in their career would share some of the characteristics with which Bebbington (and others) identify. Further, U2 fight against themselves, in a way, as they confront the policies and ideas of a mostly white, mostly Republican population. This group constitutes a politically and socially conservative side in the United States, and demonstrates the political power of the "Religious Right", the site of a conflation of political clout and religious belief. This evangelical base both supports U2 and provides for them an enemy. While such a characterization might be strong, it is also apt: consider a story later in which Bono's alter ego Mr MacPhisto encounters a Birmingham "squeaky" (as in "squeaky clean"), an evangelical that would not be out of place among the caricatures of American evangelical Protestants.

In the United States, it is commonly misconstrued that Evangelicalism is defined by race (being white) and by political view (primarily Republican). But Leith Anderson and Ed Stetzer suggest that the categories by which evangelicals are defined are unfixed; they suggest that there are those who do not call themselves evangelicals but still hold to evangelical beliefs, while there are those who call themselves by the label but do not hold the same beliefs as evangelicals.[15] But there are an additional four statements that Anderson and Stetzer formulate in order to identify Americans as evangelical (though it could be also extrapolated that answering in the affirmative to all of these questions contributes to the evangelical impulse in global evangelicals). The four statements are:

> The Bible is the highest authority for what I believe; It is very important for me personally to encourage non-Christians to trust Jesus Christ as their savior; Jesus Christ's death on the cross is the only sacrifice that could remove the penalty of my sin; Only those who trust in Jesus Christ alone as their Savior receive God's free gift of eternal salvation.[16]

These statements do not move so far from Bebbington's "quadrilateral", but they seem to make things a little bit more nuanced, while completely removing the "activist" element. Anderson and Stetzer acknowledge that Bebbington is attempting to understand what evangelicals believe and how they have acted in history. These statements are meant to "distinguish between a self-identified Evangelical, a person affiliated with an Evangelical denomination, or someone with classic Evangelical beliefs".[17] The statements – and the differing ways that the survey group answer them, or how affirming they are of particular statements over others – determine how people understand who they are, and allow outside observers to further understand who they are as well. Brian Stiller adds the following: "A helpful way to understand Evangelical is to follow David Bebbington's definition with one addition: ... 5) trusting in the empowering work of the Holy Spirit".[18]

Where does U2 fit, then, in this religious context, and in the tension between such "flavours" of Christianity? U2 provide a sort of middle ground in the tension between Protestantism (particularly evangelical Protestantism) and Roman Catholicism. It would appear that the band are not particularly interested in the notion of conversion, at least in terms of the intentional setting apart that some Christians enter into after deciding to follow Christ. For U2, the conversion is ongoing and progressive, perhaps aligning more closely with Roman Catholic Christianity. The band certainly fit into a "historical" Evangelicalism, becoming members of the evangelical Shalom Fellowship early in their career, though it is unclear how closely the Shalom Fellowship followed the tenets put forward by Bebbington. It is clear, though, that the Shalom Fellowship certainly held the Sacred Scripture in high regard, and seemed to encourage a sort of holiness – a setting apart of its members from the rest of the world and its behaviour. It is clear that, for U2, the Bible takes a more prominent place than Sacred Tradition; clearly the members of U2 are not followers of traditional (or Traditional) Christianity, even if Larry Mullen Jr was raised firmly in the Roman Catholic Church. About the Bible, in 2006, Bono told *Rolling Stone*, "It sustains me ... It's a plumb line for me. In the Scriptures, it is self-described as a clear pool that you can see yourself in, to see where you're at, if you're still enough". Furthermore, Bono's Christianity seems to acknowledge the centrality of Christ's death and resurrection. At least, he affirms the first part of the traditional creeds (as in the Apostle's Creed), "I believe in Jesus Christ, his only Son, our Lord. He was conceived by the power of the Holy Spirit and born of the Virgin Mary". Again, to *Rolling Stone*, he states, "That this scale of creation, and the unfathomable universe, should describe itself in such vulnerability, as a child [that is, Jesus, whom Christians believe to be God incarnate]. That is mind-blowing to me. I guess that would make me a Christian". And yet he states,

> I'm wary of faith outside of actions. I'm wary of religiosity that ignores the wider world. In 2001, only seven percent of evangelicals polled felt it incumbent upon themselves to respond to the AIDS emergency. This appalled me. I asked for meetings with as many church leaders as would have them with me. I used my background in the Scriptures to speak to them about the so-called leprosy of our age and how I felt Christ would respond to it. And they had better get to it quickly, or they would be very much on the other side of what God was doing in the world.

Bono, then, acts as a sort of prophet – a voice of God – instructing the Church on how to act in the world. In the same interview with *Rolling Stone*, Bono says something striking: "The music that really turns me on is either running toward God or away from God. Both recognize the pivot, that God is at the center of the jaunt".[19] Thus, conceivably, God is at the centre of U2's "jaunt". Even the least "Christian" of the band members (that is, Adam Clayton, the single member who is not a Christ follower, at least according to the discourse that surrounds this facet of the band) acknowledges the band's project in the world, making reference to the need for a solution to the refugee crisis and further response from the European Union in particular, in the name of the greater global good (clearly indicated in an interview with Leona Graham of Absolute Radio in late 2017). So, of the four elements of evangelical Christianity (and their equivalents in Roman Catholicism), the most important seems "activism" or "social justice", and it is much more central to Roman Catholicism than it is to Evangelicalism, even if Bebbington identifies it as a distinctive. Evangelical Protestant Christianity seems often to manifest itself as an individual religion, focused on the salvation of the individual, a spiritual concern rather than one focused on the physical *present* world. The activism comes in the form of evangelism, telling others about Jesus Christ and his work of salvation from sin. Roman Catholic Christianity, while always looking forward to the life in the Kingdom of Heaven after death, does seem to encourage the care of the world while humanity is waiting for Christ's return.

The central tenet that seems to inform U2's project in the world is as follows:

> For the Lord your God is God of gods and Lord of lords, the great God, mighty and awesome, who is not partial and takes no bribe, who executes justice for the orphan and the widow, and who loves the strangers, providing them food and clothing. You shall also love the stranger, for you were strangers in the land of Egypt (Deuteronomy 10:17-19).[20]

A secondary tenet, that is perhaps not as explicit in their later career, is expressed by Jesus' words in the New Testament:

> He said to him, "'You shall love the Lord your God with all your heart, and with all your soul, and with all your mind'. This is the greatest and first commandment. And a second is like it: 'You shall love your neighbour as yourself'. On these two commandments hang all the law and the prophets" (Matthew 22:37-40).

These are the guiding principles of the band. Larry Mullen Jr states,

> We all have views on what our Irishness means to us. Two members of the band were born in England and were raised in the Protestant faith. Bono's mother was Protestant and his father was Catholic. I was brought up Catholic. U2 are a living example of the kind of unity of faith and tradition that is possible in Northern Ireland.[21]

The beginning of U2

The story of U2 begins with a note posted by Larry Mullen Jr on the Mount Temple Public School bulletin board in autumn 1976. The handwritten note (by a fourteen-year-old Mullen) stated, "Drummer seeks musicians to form a band". Writing for the *Irish Times*, Brian Boyd recounts the story that the group was to be called the "Larry Mullen Band" with auditions taking place on Saturday, 25 September 1976, in the drummer's kitchen.[22] Mullen Jr was born to a devout Roman Catholic father, and was the only member of the band who was well-trained on his instrument early in his life. He used to practise drumming while watching *Top of the Pops* (the English music television programme) in 1973 and listening to Roxy Music and David Bowie.[23] Adam Clayton (the future bass player for the band) was born in England. His father was an Air Force officer and moved to Dublin and then settled in Malahide, a small but affluent town north of Dublin on the east coast. According to Eamon Dunphy, Malahide was comfortable and peaceful, without the religious sectarianism prevalent in the larger cities.[24] Clayton went to Mount Temple after having disciplinary trouble at a previous school. He once wore sunglasses to class, which was prohibited. When the headmaster asked him why he was wearing sunglasses when it was not permitted, Clayton answered, "Why not? I need them to protect my eyes".[25]

Northern Ireland (part of the United Kingdom) shares a border with U2's Ireland. The sectarian conflict of the neighbour country informs much of U2's music. Deep divisions existed (and continue to exist) between nationalist Roman Catholics, who were for an independent Northern Ireland (independent from the United Kingdom), and Unionist Protestants. Paul Hewson was born of a Roman Catholic father and Protestant mother, and was raised as a Protestant. He was later known as Bono, so named after a hearing-aid store in their neighbourhood called "Bonovox"; he was called "Bonovox of O'Connell Street".[26] In his formative years, Bono would attend church services with his friend Derek Rowen, otherwise known as "Guggi", in Bono's circles. In a 2005 interview in *Rolling Stone*, Bono recalls Guggi's spiritual influence: "His parents were not just Protestant, they were some obscure cult of Protestant. In America, it would be Pentecostal. His father was like a creature from the Old Testament. He spoke constantly of the Scriptures and had the sense that the end was nigh – and to prepare for it".[27]

Dave Evans (later dubbed by Bono as The Edge) was brought up as a Presbyterian by his Welsh parents (he moved to Ireland from England at the age of one). Clayton was also raised as a Protestant. Noel McLaughlin mentions that drummer Mullen Jr is most representative of what he calls "'orthodox' Irish identity": born in Ireland to Roman Catholic parents. He concludes, "Much also has been made of all four band members' education at Mount Temple Comprehensive in Dublin, Ireland's first non-denominational school".[28] If the band came from disparate religious backgrounds, coming together across sectarian lines in the broader Irish context, Clayton seemed the opposite, *without* the religious (and certainly sectarian) awareness of the others.

Back to the posting by Mullen Jr in 1976, Dave Evans agreed to meet with Mullen Jr and others. He brought along his guitar-playing brother Dick and met with Paul Hewson (who also brought a guitar) and another fellow student named Ivan (also with a guitar). Boyd recounts how Clayton "swanned in later wearing a full-length Afghan coat".[29] After playing together for a short time, the band began to gel. Hewson and Clayton were not as proficient in their instruments as Evans and Mullen Jr, and no one wanted to be lead singer. Dunphy suggests that Hewson had conviction and Clayton had confidence, which balanced the musicianship of the other two. With Dick Evans and the other guitarist preferring to leave the group, U2's membership was pretty much set (though they had yet to settle on that name, instead beginning as Feedback, and The Hype, before U2).[30] Paul Hewson decided to sing.

Though the band were formed in Ireland, the sectarian concerns of the Northern Irish neighbours was still a cause for concern. The religious affiliations of the individual band members must not be forgotten or overlooked. While their individual affiliations were not an instigator of violence in their Dublin neighbourhood context, nevertheless, the band acted as a site for the unification of these religious factions, a living out of a neutral Christianity, flavoured, of course, by the nominal religion or religious upbringing of many of the band members. This changed, though, as the band began to embrace a "lived" Christianity, a much deeper sense of commitment to a mostly unfamiliar kind of religion.

Chapter overview

Chapter 1, "From Underground to Overground: U2 from *Boy* to *Rattle and Hum*", consists of an overview of the critical reception of the band's releases, identifying the types of discussions that continue to revolve around the band. The chapter maps out the career of the band, pointing out relevant events and defines the "outline" of the band's mediated image, by setting out the band's various developments through time. Through this brief survey, it is interesting to note that the band's penchant for activism has not always been well-received.

Chapter 2, "U2 and the Blinding Lights of the City", explores how U2's music and stage presentation use the image of the contemporary city as a site for exploring the utopian and dystopian aspects of contemporary life. The ways that U2 approach the urban experience also point to the complicity of the band, as they express both a powerful utopian idea (social change and human progress) and dystopian problem (being complicit with market forces; being drenched in irony or postmodern flux).

Chapter 3, "Beautiful Day: Technological Optimism, Gesture and Intimacy", explores the promotional video for 'Beautiful Day', and how the band nurture a sense of the intimate with their audience while attempting to foster a sense of optimism in the face of the dehumanizing contemporary world. Horace Newcomb's discussion of television aesthetics is useful in order to understand what U2 are doing in their televisual presentation. Finally, a pair of music videos are analysed in order to demonstrate how the band foster an awareness of the need for empathy and outward concern.

Chapter 4, "The Irish in America: Nationalism and Politics on Tour", takes a detailed look at U2's presentation in concert during the *Elevation* tour and after the events of 11 September 2001. The band broaden their identity from being solely Irish to being a world brand, moving from focusing on local concerns to global problems. It is during their *Elevation* tour that they manifest a sort of global reach. An analysis of U2's concert film, *Elevation 2001: Live in Boston*, is central to this chapter.

Chapter 5, "The Rosary and the Microphone: Social Justice and the Stage", takes as its basis the idea that the stage itself is a site of meaning-making. In all of its various iterations, the stage becomes a sort of "global platform", a site for display which literally travels the world, and a strong semiotic marker for the band's agenda. It is through stage design and lighting that the band communicate their message, including that of outward care. Furthermore, the stage is the site of the manifestation of Bono's many personae, performances that serve to attract attention to social issues, and deflect criticism of the band's complicity.

Chapter 6, "*Linear*: A Way Forward", focuses on *Linear*, a full-length promotional video for the album *No Line on the Horizon*. The chapter embarks on a unique sustained analysis of this rare visual artefact. The full-length promotional video seems to represent a "way out" from the oppression of the state to a utopian "beyond". The band are a "guide" throughout the film, suggesting a new way forward, a way that points to coexistence as a goal. As a theoretical framework, the analysis uses Roland Barthes' lectures on how to live together. The long-form video illustrates how one might live *with* others in a polarized world, through the employments of idiorrythmy, or living in solitude with regular interruptions.

Chapter 7, "*Songs of Innocence* as Barthes' Ideal Novel", explores the notion of U2's later work as an example of Barthes' *Vita Nova*, a new sort of novel. Roland Barthes' desire to write a novel late in his life is ultimately a story of conversion, a decision to move in a direction different from what he was doing in the past. U2's album, *Songs of Innocence*, is an imperfect example of Barthes' ideal novel: it expresses both passion and intimacy, while conveying a loss of innocence. This chapter is particularly heavy in terms of Barthesian philosophy; his ideas on mourning and grace arguably permeate through U2's music inasmuch as U2's music expresses Bono's own struggles in negotiating grief and death in his own family.

"Conclusions: A Cosmopolitan Christianity" consolidates the various threads in order to solidify the idea that the band signifies a cosmopolitanism that has as its driving force a particular "flavour" of Christianity. Primarily, the conclusion explores what cosmopolitanism might mean for U2 in contemporary society, and briefly considers *Songs of Experience*, released at the end of 2017.

Through all of these permutations, manifestations and *mediations*, the band illustrate how that religious impulse, from an early experience of the conflation of two warring "flavours" of Christianity and spurred on by the band's early experience with Evangelicalism, informs the band's message. They want to make their audience aware of the need for global care and empathy, and to understand how others feel, and they also seem to believe that, in understanding the fate and feelings of others, their audience will be changed. In turn, the world will change as well.

Notes

1. Emma Mason, "Punctive Grace: Reading Religion in Barthes' *Mourning Diary*", *Textual Practice* 30.2 (2016): 341 n. 7.
2. Tiphaine Samoyault, *Barthes: A Biography*, translated by Andrew Brown (Cambridge: Polity Press, 2017), 54.
3. Mason, "Punctive Grace", p. 332. Mason is quoting from St Augustine, *Confessions*, translated by Albert C. Outler (Grand Rapids: Christian Classics Ethereal Library, 1955), 138; available from http://ccel.org/ccel/augustine/confessions.pdf (accessed 24 March 2018).
4. He mentions in his writings how the religious life – Christianity, in particular – did not suit him, precisely because of his homosexuality. In *Mourning Diary*, Barthes remarks that he hopes to find a kind of enlightenment, perhaps in the form of a religion that he saw (solely, it seems) in the life of his mother: one that is "without violence (without militarism, without proselytism)" (252).
5. Samoyault, *Barthes: A Biography*, 121–22. Note that Barthes would look to primarily Roman Catholic Christian tradition for inspiration.
6. Roland Barthes, *A Lover's Discourse: Fragments*, translated by Richard Howard (New York: Hill and Wang, 2010), 180.
7. Roland Barthes, *Roland Barthes by Roland Barthes*, translated by Richard Howard (New York: Hill and Wang, 2010), 44.
8. Ibid., 49.
9. Ibid., x.
10. Ibid., 104.
11. Kate Briggs, *This Little Art* (London: Fitzcarraldo Editions, 2018), 274. Briggs is quoting Adrienne Ghaly, "Cultural Theory on a Micro-Scale: Roland Barthes's Lectures at the Collège de France", *L'Esprit Créateur* 55.4 (Winter 2015): 48. Ghaly continues: "The importance of unravelling what the haiku's 'novelistic' writing is doing, and discovering how to recreate its modes of relational thought, returns us to a crucial aspect of a rhetorical

view of language: enunciative acts can have a profound and potentially lasting effect on the world. Barthes's purpose is both avowedly utopian and practical in application, even if consciously fragmentary. The haiku is not a separate or 'higher' sphere of the aesthetic away from the fray of most aspects of life. The form offers ways of thinking relationally that we can carry with us as we move through the world" (48).

12. "Exclusive: Bono Reveals Secrets of U2's Surprise Album 'Songs of Innocence'", *Rolling Stone* (9 September 2014); available from https://tinyurl.com/U-20140909 (accessed 14 January 2018).

13. D. W. Bebbington, *Evangelicalism in Modern Britain: A History from the 1730s to the 1800s* (London and New York: Routledge, 1989), 2–3.

14. "What is an Evangelical?", *Evangelical Fellowship of Canada*; available from https://www.evangelicalfellowship.ca/About-us/About-Evangelicals (accessed 23 January 2018).

15. Leith Anderson and Ed Stetzer, "A New Way to Define Evangelicals", *Christianity Today* 60.3 (April 2016): 54.

16. Ibid., 55.

17. Ibid.

18. Brian Stiller, "To Be or Not to Be an Evangelical", *Christianity Today* (31 March 2018); available from http://www.christianitytoday.com/edstetzer/2018/march/to-be-or-not-to-be-evangelical.html (accessed 17 April 2018).

19. Jann S. Wenner, "Bono: The Rolling Stone Interview", *Rolling Stone* (3 November 2005); available from https://www.rollingstone.com/music/news/bono-the-rolling-stone-interview-20051103 (accessed 18 February 2018).

20. The Scripture quotations are from the New Revised Standard Version.

21. Neil McCormick, *U2 by U2* (London: HarperCollins, 2006), 351.

22. Brian Boyd, "U2 Hit 40: The 'Drummer Seeks Musicians' Note that Started It All", *Irish Times* (21 September 2016); available from https://www.irishtimes.com/culture/music/u2-hit-40-the-drummer-seeks-musicians-note-that-started-it-all-1.2799922 (accessed 18 June 2018).

23. Eamon Dunphy, *Unforgettable Fire: Past, Present, and Future – The Definitive Biography of U2* (New York: Warner Books, 1987), 52–54.

24. Ibid., 36.

25. Ibid., 43.

26. Ibid., 75.

27. Wenner, "Bono: The Rolling Stone Interview".

28. Noel McLaughlin, "Bono! Do You Ever Take Those Wretched Sunglasses Off?: U2 and the Performance of Irishness", *Popular Music History* 4.3 (2009): 314.

29. Boyd, "U2 Hit 40".

30. Dunphy, *Unforgettable Fire*, 61.

1 From Underground to Overground: U2 from *Boy* to *Rattle and Hum*

U2's career can be divided into four periods. The first period follows their establishment as a band, their building of a fanbase and the "breakthrough" of both critical and widespread fan acclaim. This phase begins with their debut three-song release, *Three* (1978), followed by *Boy* (1980), *October* (1981), *War* (1983) and the live album recorded during the following tour, *Under a Blood Red Sky*. Next came *The Unforgettable Fire* (1984), and then *The Joshua Tree* (1987) and the *Rattle and Hum* (mostly) live album and its accompanying theatrical film (1988). Interestingly, other than the debut EP, the first period of U2's career fits into the decade of the 1980s. U2 themselves seem to define their first phase differently. In the U2-produced book, *North Side Story: U2 in Dublin 1978–1983*, published in 2014 (produced by the Irish music magazine *Hot Press*, but for U2.com fan-subscribers), "phase one of the U2 project" is closed out by the band's first live album, *Under a Blood Red Sky*; the dividing line seems to come before the successes of *The Unforgettable Fire* and *The Joshua Tree*.

The second period follows their "reinvention" after the huge successes of *The Joshua Tree* and *Rattle and Hum*. In 1991, U2 released an album that expressed the first massive change to their sound, *Achtung Baby*. This was followed by the experimental *Zooropa* (1993). In 1995, the band collaborated with Brian Eno and released *Original Soundtracks 1* as the band Passengers. *Pop* was the final album of this period, released in 1997. While the 1990s have been considered (by fans) as a hugely important time for the band, they released only four albums during this time. Of the four, only two are proper studio albums: *Zooropa* was a project that was birthed during the tour for *Achtung Baby* and Passengers was a collaboration, resulting in an album that cannot be defined as being strictly by U2 (though all the members of U2 are part of Passengers). It was during the 1990s, though, that U2's status as a "touring" band – as a band interested in live spectacle, particularly – was firmly established.

The band's third period emerges, again, with the change of decade, beginning with *All That You Can't Leave Behind* (2000), *How to Dismantle an Atomic Bomb* (2004) and *No Line on the Horizon* (2009). Between each of these albums, the band released important concert films: *Elevation 2001: Live from Boston*

(2001); *U2 Go Home: Live from Slane Castle, Ireland* (2003); *Vertigo 05: Live from Chicago* (2005) and *Vertigo 05: Live from Milan* (2006); and, finally, *U2 360° at the Rose Bowl* (2010).

The new releases, *Songs of Innocence* in 2014, and its tour concert film, *U2 iNNOCENCE + eXPERIENCE: Live in Paris* (2016), along with 2017's *Songs of Experience*, begin a tentative fourth period (as of yet, it is difficult to ascertain whether a new period or phase has begun, or whether these new albums simply continue the third period of the band). Certainly, the fertile nature of the band's first full decade, the 1980s, has not been replicated in any of the subsequent decades. That is, they released more albums in the 1980s than they have in any subsequent decade. This is probably due to the demands of global touring on release schedules; in fact, *Zooropa* seems an anomaly in that it came out of the context of touring. Since the 1990s, a pattern of releases has been established: the band have released an album and then gone on a major tour, during which a live show has been recorded and subsequently released in the form of a concert film.

These third and fourth periods are mostly the focus of the various analyses in this present work. A brief survey through the critical reception of the band's releases reveals that U2 have always been a political band; that is, U2 have seemingly put social issues and local (and global) concerns at the forefront of their presentation. With *The Joshua Tree*, the band experienced global success, both monetary and critical. The album is rife with explorations of the horrors of war (funded by domestic agents – primarily the Reagan administration) on foreign soil, and the experiences of civilians in the midst of conflict, the not-so-sure promise of the American dream, and the acknowledgement of atrocities committed by dictatorial governments. For instance, 'Mothers of the Disappeared' refers to a group of women whose children were forcibly taken by the governments of El Salvador and other Central and South American countries in the early 1980s. With U2's global success came a global awareness. While *Achtung Baby* does not necessarily address the political issues of its moment (as do some of the stronger pieces from *The Joshua Tree*), it emerges from a deeply politicized context: a newly reunified Germany, with the fall of the Berlin Wall, was a recent event at the time of its creation and release.

If the 1980s was a period of movement for U2 from a sort of inward reflection of local conflict (and their place within – or without – it) to a reflection of global conflict in the Americas specifically, more broadly than simply continental, then the 1990s were different altogether. The period of the band in the 1990s certainly showed the band looking towards the global: there was little "local" about the band's presentation at the time. They seemed just as comfortable to criticize American president George H. W. Bush as they were willing to point out the fragility of the European Union, all the while evoking German Fascism. During the *Zoo TV* tour, and as clearly displayed on the cover of the 1994 concert film, *Zoo TV: Live from Sydney*, the band wore blue military-esque uniforms, complete with berets, epaulettes and stylized letter Z's on their collars, not unlike the stylized "SS" of Nazi *Schuttzstaffel*.

In 1998, the band continued this global criticism. But the band's outward-facing criticism became more subversive. *PopMart: Live from Mexico City* features the band being generally critical of themselves, creating a stage that basically erases the band with a mediated copy, dwarfing the musicians with their televised selves transmitted on a 165-foot screen. One of the shirt designs (for shirts sold at the *PopMart* concerts) features a shopping cart orbiting a planet resembling a lemon, foregrounding the band's global fame (or even a "planetary" or "galactic" infamy) and the consumerist nature of the popular music industry and celebrity machine. For their encore during tour performances, members of the band emerged from a giant motorized spinning mirrored lemon (akin to a disco mirror-ball) mounted on a moving platform: the top of the lemon opened to allow the members to walk down a staircase to the stage below, where they began to perform the track, 'Discothèque', transforming the stadium into a dancehall complete with booming bass and swirling lighting throughout.

All of the spectacle of the 1990s did not exactly go away in the 2000s – U2's stage shows were still considered spectacles and "not to be missed" by fans – but the spectacle was presented differently. For instance, at the start of shows on the *Elevation* tour (in support of *All That You Can't Leave Behind*), the band emerged onto the stage with all of the arena "house" lights on. In other words, the band delayed the explicit artifice of the concert experience until the middle of the first song. At that point, the lights suddenly turned off and the show more closely resembled a traditional popular music concert, with the band being the solely lit element in the arena. The later *U2 360°* tour featured U2 in the centre of the stadium. This functioned in two ways. First, and most obviously, it allowed the band to sell more tickets. This was a strategy that U2 began in the early 2000s when tickets from behind the stage were made available. This also meant, though, that the band could not use a giant screen or elaborate stage, as such a construction would interfere with sight lines for those seated behind the stage. Tickets purchased for seats behind the stage during the *Elevation* tour were clearly marked as such. It was also a strategy to put the band *in the middle* of the crowd, to allow the crowd to both focus on the band, and have the band act as a unifying principle. The band remained the (literal) centre of the experience but the crowd had equal access with the band in their midst.[1]

The *U2 360°* tour ended in the summer of 2011 and *Songs of Innocence* was released in 2014, with the supporting tour running throughout 2015. The band went on tour to celebrate the thirtieth anniversary of *The Joshua Tree* in 2017, during which the band returned to the idea of a large screen, thus obstructing seats at the back of the stage, and therefore disallowing their sale. In December 2017, *Songs of Experience*, a companion to *Songs of Innocence*, was released, and the accompanying tour began in early 2018.

Critical reception

As early as 1978, U2 was being described as a "band to be noticed". In April of that year, Bill Graham writes, "They impress as articulate, aware and hard-working individuals who are prepared to weigh up others' advice as they embark on their vocation". Certainly Graham recognizes that the then-youngsters were not yet in a place to actually name their life-long vocation; he mentions that they are "currently studying for their Leaving Certs.", referring to their state-run finishing exams for secondary school graduation.[2] Nevertheless, Graham uses terminology that suggests a sense of life-long calling. Niall Stokes describes this vocation – in its very early stages – as made manifest in the creation of "Lypton Village" (Dunphy calls this group "The Village"), a make-believe social group, in which they could separate from "the compromises of their parents' generation, the violence that was raging in Northern Ireland, and the conventional, low expectations in relation to work and careers that likely lay just around the corner unless they found a different way".[3] Dunphy puts it as follows:

> The Village was a state of mind, subconscious as well as conscious rejection of the stereotypes of young Irish manhood on offer. Having rejected cultural identity, they proceeded to adjust their personal identities as well. They invented names for each other, names that would be truer to their real personalities than the names their parents had given them.[4]

Names like "Bono" for Paul Hewson and "The Edge" for Dave Evans stuck (Dunphy suggests that, though The Village gave Evans a name, he was not a member).[5]

With their discovery of a real-life manager in the form of Paul McGuinness, the band signed a record deal with Island Records and recorded *Boy* (released in October 1980) after a three-song EP entitled *U23* or *Three* (released in September 1979). Island was a company primarily built on the reggae music of Bob Marley at that point, and was considered an outsider to the corporate industry of rock music. The band's first EP consisted of three songs (as per the title), two of which were rerecorded for the follow-up full-length *Boy*. Stokes writes that the EP's "crucial strength is its startling uniqueness: you have never heard anything before to which 'Out of Control' or 'Boy/Girl' or 'Stories for Boys' can be remotely reliably compared".[6] Reviewing *Boy* for *Rolling Stone*, Debra Rae Cohen cautiously writes, "Hopefully, U2 may yet justify Island's hyped-up optimism ... U2 is talented, charming and potentially (they're all still under twenty-one) exceptional. But as a new Next Big Thing, they're only the next best thing to something *really* new".[7] Not even Declan Lynch of Ireland's *Hot Press* is completely supportive of the album, or the band's larger project, responding to the band's use of the terms "innocence" and "spiritual": "The record [referring to the "public record" rather than *Boy*] shows that rock'n'roll went sour when it became a vehicle for 'self-awareness', and when people started seeing God in guitar solos".[8] He continues with a startling statement, at least in retrospect: "I wouldn't worry about U2 selling out because I know they will". Lynch suggests the band's "selling out" as inevitable as the band become more popular, but hopes that listeners will hold the group to some sort of "authenticity", stating that "they are as important or as trivial as you want to make them".[9]

At this point in their career, the band's Christianity was very important to them. And with this importance came responsibility. There were to be no random women loitering about or made available for sexual dalliance, and no abuses of alcohol or other controlled substances: Mullen Jr made sure of it. But Clayton was being increasingly alienated in this strict moral environment. Were they to be a Christian band, espousing obviously Christian ideas for a presumably Christian audience? If so, Clayton had little interest.

In 1981, the band released *October*, an album that was explicitly expressive of the band's Christian faith of the time, a thread that was only implicit in some of the songs on *Boy*. It was U2's most Christian album, and a commercial success as well. Neil McCormick writes that *October* "is a Christian LP that avoids all the pedantic puritanism associated with most Christian rock, avoids the old world emotional fascism of organized religion and the crusading preaching of someone like born-again Bob Dylan".[10] McCormick recognizes a more inclusive "spirituality" evoked in the band's music even at this stage. According to Dunphy, the band's religious convictions were informed by a specific brand of evangelical Christianity not associated with any one institutionalized church. In 1979 (well before *October*), the band were invited to the Shalom Fellowship, which was an evangelical Charismatic Christian group led by a man named Dennis Sheedy. The Edge was from a similar Protestant background, so he was happy to go to the meeting. Mullen Jr's mother had just recently died, and he was encouraged to attend. Bono was willing, but would take some time before attending, while Clayton declined, as religion was not something that interested him. The three found something in those meetings that was different from the organized religion in Ireland and the conflict that seemed to come with it. They seemed determined to live out their newly found (or, more accurately, freshly revived) Christian values. About the group, Bono states,

> They were expectant of signs and wonders; lived a kind of early-church religion. It was a commune. People who had cash shared it. They were passionate, and they were funny, and they seemed to have no material desires. Their teaching of the Scriptures reminded me of those people whom I'd heard as a youngster with Guggi. I realize now, looking back, that it was just insatiable intellectual curiosity ... But it got a little too intense, as it always does; it became a bit of a holy huddle. And these people – who are full of inspirational teaching and great ideas – they pretended that our dress, the way we looked, didn't bother them. But very soon it appeared that was not the case. They started asking questions about the music we were listening to. Why are you wearing earrings? Why do you have a mohawk?[11]

As an unbeliever, Clayton was not at all part of that group. When asked by Bill Flanagan about Clayton's place in the band at the time (informed by an observation of Clayton being physically out of the circle of the rest of the band on the cover of *October*), The Edge responds, "We never considered firing Adam ... But I think Adam did feel kind of isolated, marginalized during that period".[12] The Edge's use of the word "marginalized" is interesting: Clayton was not simply on the outskirts of the band's goings-on or often glossed over in their activities, but he was seemingly treated as insignificant or on the outside. This might speak to why the band are concerned with communities and groups within global society that do not have a voice, or whose voice has been taken away: there was once a voiceless member among them. Clayton was not a part of the spiritual revival within which the other band members were finding some sort of positive formation, and was thus treated as the "odd guy", as The Edge characterizes Clayton during that time. It is out of that spiritual revival – and the band's misconduct towards Clayton in the midst of it – that perhaps pushes and *convicts* the band to act differently and actively for the marginalized.

The Shalom Fellowship believed in social justice grounded in a certain biblical hermeneutic. Dunphy describes the group as being of the "charismatic variety".[13] This probably means that they practised glossolalia, the "speaking in tongues" first described in the biblical passage, "All of them were filled with the Holy Spirit and began to speak in other languages, as the Spirit gave them ability" (Acts 2:4). Being part of a "charismatic" evangelical Christian movement also suggests a high view of biblical text: Dunphy says, of the group, "The word of God was simple and true".¹⁴ By the release of *War*, Mullen Jr had changed his views and had decided to leave the community because of its "holiness" mandate, that is, the impulse to be separated from the world, while being critical of it.¹⁵ This was not to be U2's way; they need to be *in the world, while being critical of it*. But, for Bono, the group had provided something important that he did not get from any other source. Dunphy puts it this way:

> Christianity moderated his raging, questing ego, provided a focus for his massive reservoir of spirituality. All his objections to the religious institutions of his childhood, whose dogma had separated his family every Sunday, were resolved by this simple concept of people meeting God in a suburban front room. "Where two or three are gathered together in my name I am present", Christ had vouched. *That* you would never believe looking at the divisions among the established Churches.¹⁶

This sentiment has stayed with Bono through the years. In a 2013 television interview, Bono says, "Whenever you see religious people, where their faith is more important than love, they've got it the wrong way round in my view".¹⁷ In a 2003 interview, Bono states,

> I just go where the life is, you know? Where I feel the Holy Spirit… If it's in the back of a Roman Catholic cathedral, in the quietness and the incense, which suggest the mystery of God, of God's presence, or in the bright lights of the revival tent, I just go where I find life. I don't see denomination. I generally think religion gets in the way of God.¹⁸

As an album, *October* was a statement from members of a band in the midst of a sort of personal Christian revival, a group hoping to take on and change the world around it. But McCormick characterizes at least one song on the album as "cartoon world U2", not a particularly empowering comment for a group trying to enact change from a place of sincere religious conviction.¹⁹ Jon Pareles, writing for *Rolling Stone*, fails to recognize the religious impulse at all; instead, he writes, "It's impossible to take U2 as seriously as they take themselves".²⁰

In fact, as hinted at by Mullen Jr's discomfort with what he felt at the time were religious constraints, tensions also existed on the side of the Shalom Fellowship: "We were getting a lot of people in our ear saying: 'This is impossible, you guys are Christians. You can't be in a band. It's a contradiction and you have to go one way or the other …' [The Edge responds,] 'Okay, it's a contradiction for some, but it's a contradiction I'm able to live with'".²¹ Interestingly, The Edge states, "During the early days, when the rest of us were at the height of our Christian fervour, Adam was actually the most Christian in his tolerance and humanity".[22]

War was released in 1983. The cover features Peter Rowen, the younger brother of "Lypton Village" colleague "Guggi". The younger Rowen was featured on the covers of both *Three* and *Boy* (*October* featured the band on the cover). Liam Mackey celebrates the record with the following:

> It's against this blood-soaked backdrop [of world-wide conflict] that U2 release their third album, a record which bears witness to its time and context with a mixture of fear, courage and hope. In the face of prejudice and deep-rooted embitterment, whose physical language is expressed in the bomb and the gun, this record waves a white flag, not of toothless surrender, but of sanity.[23]

In 2014, Mackay makes an observation of an ideological shift in the band's outlook: "*October* had that kind of introspective, inner searching kind of feel about it. It threw some people because of the spirituality around it – but by the time they got to *War* they were clearly looking out into the world. They were addressing the issues of the day and it had that quality from the off".[24] About the album, J. D. Considine writes,

> U2 may not be great intellectuals, and *War* may sound more profound than it really is. But the songs here stand up against anything on The Clash's *London Calling* in terms of sheer impact, and the fact that U2 can sweep the listener up in the same sort of enthusiastic romanticism that fuels the band's grand gestures is an impressive feat. For once, not having all the answers seems a bonus.[25]

However lofty the final version might have been, *War* was a difficult album to start. For Mullen Jr, the Shalom Fellowship had gone too far in their requirements for "holy" living. The Edge was in conflict with himself and his role in the band, and thought of leaving. Bono had just married his long-time romantic interest, Ali. Dunphy states: "Edge had discovered, figured out, reasoned, a philosophical proposition: that you couldn't detach the mind from the spirit. That Christianity without life was as empty as life without Christianity. That those who sought to force a choice, who demanded you sacrifice one for the other, were wrong".[26]

Out of this conflict, the band wrote 'Sunday Bloody Sunday'. The song can be interpreted as a reference to incidents in Irish history and "The Troubles": "Bloody Sunday" refers to the events of Sunday, 21 November 1920, in Dublin, during which thirty-two people were killed. The day began with members of the Irish Republican Army shooting and killing fifteen members and affiliates of the Royal Irish Constabulary (the Unionist faction). Later in the day, the Royal Irish Constabulary (Auxiliaries) opened fire at a football game between the Dublin Gaelic and Tipperary football teams at Croke Park. Fourteen civilians were killed along with over sixty injured. "Bloody Sunday" also refers to Sunday, 30 January 1972, also known as the "Bogside Massacre", in which twenty-eight civilians were shot by British soldiers, resulting in the deaths of fourteen, during a peaceful march in Derry, Northern Ireland. And, of course, the "war" was still occurring in Northern Ireland when the song was written.

Songs like 'Sunday Bloody Sunday' came to define U2's unique sound. Flanagan explains:

> Adam often plays with the swollen, vibrating bottom sound of a Jamaican dub bassist, covering the most sonic space with the smallest number of notes. Larry, who taught himself to drum and consequently got some things technically wrong, plays with a martial rigidity but uses his kit in a way a properly trained drummer would not. He has tom-toms [that is, drums without a snare] on either side of him, and has a habit of coming off the snare onto them that is contrary to how most percussionists use those drums.[27]

So every time Mullen Jr hits the snare, he comes off and hits the tom-tom drums. Tom-toms are traditionally used for drum fills and embellishments, and not commonly used for the actual main drum beat. Here, the tom-tom drums fill out the sound, contributing to a more complex and exciting musical texture. It is the rhythm section of Clayton and Mullen Jr that supports The Edge's guitar. He uses a delay pedal, which allows a certain played figure to echo and repeat at any predetermined rate or for a predetermined length of time, while continuing to play the guitar. The technique makes the sound much fuller than would a normal chording style. Henrik Marstal argues that The Edge's guitar sound contributes to what he calls "a fabric of other spiritual components", at least in the band's earlier music: the bell-like tones of The Edge's playing marks the band as both spiritual and Irish.[28]

From *War* came U2's most gruelling tour up to this point. Towards the end of the American leg of the tour, the band decided to film a concert from Denver at the Red Rocks Amphitheatre. The audio from the concert was released as *Under a Blood Red Sky*, and U2's first concert video, called *U2 Live at Red Rocks: Under a Blood Red Sky*.

After working with David Bowie and Tony Visconti on the Berlin trilogy of albums (*Low*, *"Heroes"* and *Lodger*), singer, producer and keyboardist (formerly a member of the band Roxy Music) Brian Eno collaborated with U2 for five albums and a tour unlike any conducted previously, and became an architect of

U2's sound in the 1980s and 1990s. Eno, with co-producer Daniel Lanois, produced U2's *The Unforgettable Fire, The Joshua Tree, Achtung Baby* and *Zooropa*. Eno and Lanois continued to collaborate and produce U2 projects into the 2000s, with *All that You Can't Leave Behind, How to Dismantle an Atomic Bomb* and *No Line on the Horizon*. In a 1984 television interview (from a broadcast called *U2: Egos & Icons* that aired in the late 1990s on Canada's music video television network MuchMusic), The Edge speaks of the stage the band was at with regard to commercial success and artistic integrity:

> Our goals as a group have always been creative ones, never commercial ones. And I think, because of that, the whole basis of the band is far more stable than a lot of groups. We haven't achieved our goals at this stage – I don't think we ever will, but ... I can't remember who said it but, it's not arriving that's important, it's the footsteps to arriving that's [sic] important, and that's certainly the way this band operates.[29]

Brian Eno is known to stress the importance of process over the final product, and this notion is reflected in The Edge's words. The journey is important, not the end.

U2 are known now for the extensive use of technology in their music and live concerts, a trend which finds its roots in the production of *The Unforgettable Fire*. Bill Flanagan quotes Bono commenting on the challenges of being progressive in the field of rock music: "How does a three-piece [band] be polyrhythmic? You have to have another thing. On [*The*] *Unforgettable Fire* Brian's contribution was to find little tape loops for us to play off. So that's how this technology thing came together".[30] Later in Flanagan's book, The Edge responds to the claim that *The Unforgettable Fire* stands completely out of time. He states that, in fact, the band had discussions to attain timelessness with the recording, making the point to *not* fix the work in time, balancing "relevance" (being *in* time) with "timelessness" (being *out of* time).[31] The recording process that resulted in *The Unforgettable Fire* is documented by Stokes, who describes how Clayton was playing a sliding bass figure during a break in recording, for what ultimately became the track '4th of July'. Unbeknownst to Clayton or The Edge (who had joined him on guitar), Eno had begun recording their playing. Eno applied a treatment originally destined for Bono's vocals to the guitar part. Subsequently, the result was recorded to stereo "master" tape rather than to the twenty-four-track machine (which would have been the more conventional thing to do). Committing the musical ideas to stereo tape meant that the result could not be corrected or even remixed: it was fixed as a live performance, removed from time and reified as an artefact.[32]

For a song entitled, 'Elvis Presley and America', Eno and Lanois reduced the speed of the backing track for another song on the album and encouraged Bono to improvise a melody and lyrics over it, without revealing just where the backing track originated. This challenged Bono to rethink his approach to the recording process. In the past, Bono's various vocal takes would be spliced together in order to create the desired vocal track, whereas Eno wanted, when possible, to record the vocals in a single take. For Eno, the performance (that is, the process to the final recording) was most important, no matter what flaws might exist within it.

Like *War*, *The Unforgettable Fire* dealt with political issues, such as the continuing struggle for black emancipation in the United States and the work and influence of Martin Luther King Jr. Nevertheless, *Rolling Stone* was not impressed with the album: Kurt Loder writes, "*The Unforgettable Fire* seems to drone on and on, an endless flurry of chinkety guitar scratchings, state-of-the-art sound processing and the most mundane sort of lyrical imagery (barbed wire is a big concept)".[33] Reviewing the release of the 2009 deluxe version of the album, Will Hermes calls the album a "transitional, hit-or-miss set ... When things click, it bridges that record's [that is, *War*] fight-the-power arena rock with the texture fetishism of its follow-up, *The Joshua Tree*".[34] In other words, Hermes calls the album a transition between *War* and *The Joshua Tree*. *The Unforgettable Fire* is an album that seems to have difficulty standing on its own, its one important characteristic being that it is the debut for the production work of Eno and Lanois. Liam Mackey makes the following observations regarding the band's choice of producers:

> Clearly conceived as a challenge for the band – and indeed for Eno who by his own admission was largely unfamiliar with the band's work prior to this – it gave credence to Bono's post-Phoenix Park [a concert in Dublin on 14 August 1983, in front of an audience of some eighty thousand people] declaration that that memorable concert had brought to a close the first full cycle of U-2 [sic].[35]

For many, *The Unforgettable Fire* functions as a transition. This idea of the album as transitionary is supported by Bill Graham's review of the previous live album, *Under a Blood Red Sky*. In his review, Graham writes, "[With *Under a Blood Red Sky*,] the camera pans on a victor's lap of honour. This album closes accounts, clears unfinished business. For their next, will U-2 [sic] change the colour of their skies?"[36]

The "change of colour" ultimately came with the release of *The Joshua Tree* in 1986. In a July 2017 interview with Zane Lowe,[37] Bono makes the point that a performance – U2's "homecoming" – at Dublin's Croke Park on 29 June 1985 (with over fifty thousand fans in attendance, a performance that Niall and Dermot Stokes call "Beyond extraordinary. Only believable because it happened with all those witnesses!!") was the marker of the band's "conquering" of Ireland.[38] But the band would quickly move to conquer the world.

"Live Aid" took place in London on 13 July 1985 at the massive Wembley Stadium. U2 had just been named "Band of the '80s" by *Rolling Stone* magazine (arguably somewhat early for such a distinction in 1985), and they had recently released their third album. Nevertheless, they were a relatively young band, certainly used to a smaller crowd than the one gathered at Wembley that day. U2 was given 15 minutes to perform three songs: Bob Geldof, organizer of the event, had made a rule that no fan would be able to reach the stage. There was a "no fan zone" between the audience and the stage (this would have also facilitated the televising of the event, as space was needed to be made for the free passage of photographers and cameras). Without introduction, U2 began their set with 'Sunday Bloody Sunday' and then went immediately into 'Bad'. The band seemed to have claimed the audience with the song, and Bono decided to do something unplanned. He chose a woman from the audience and beckoned her to come towards the stage. Backstage, band manager Paul McGuinness was wondering what Bono was going to do: the band were only on their second song, and they were running out of time for a third. Meanwhile, Bono continued to sing 'Bad', extending the song well beyond its original length. The woman reached the partition of open space between the crowd and the stage as Bono leapt down into it. Security personnel scrambled to try to contain the crowd closest to the stage as Bono and the woman reached each other. With the help of the concert security staff, the two embraced.

With the embrace at the edge of the crowd, Bono disappeared from the sight of most of those in attendance that day, save the few security personnel there. But, crucially, he was visible to the vast television audience. The symbolic gesture of a performer bonding with an audience member seemed to work as an authentic gesture, though it could easily have been perceived as a gimmick, an intrusion or even a breach of the spirit of the event. As Dunphy suggests, the difference between manipulation and great performance can be dependent upon the performer's confidence in what they are doing. The incident turned out to be a sign of U2's confidence as a true stadium band.[39]

The "Live Aid" performance was witnessed by an audience of over seventy thousand at Wembley Stadium and an estimated television audience of 1.9 billion viewers worldwide. Graham Jones writes:

> This was the moment which assured the band its place in history. In what seemed an endless 12-minute rendition of 'Bad' (with bits of the Rolling Stones and Lou Reed thrown in) Bono – somewhat uncomfortably dressed for a hot day in black coat, black leather

trousers and knee length black boots – vaulted down into the photographer's pit to dance with a young girl fan.[40]

This performance, with its defining moment of Bono seemingly leaving the context of the stage and invading the life of (at least one member of) the audience, was the marker of the band's "conquering" of the world, a global audience. Nevertheless, in the discussion with Lowe, Bono was not happy with that performance, mainly because of the long rendition of the song 'Bad', which was so long that the band were not able to perform the last of the three-song set, 'Pride (In the Name of Love)', which Bono calls their "big song".[41]

The Joshua Tree was released in March 1987. For *Rolling Stone*, Steve Pond writes,

> *The Joshua Tree* is U2's most varied, subtle and accessible album, although it doesn't contain any sure-fire smash hits. But in its musical toughness and strong-willed spirituality, the album lives up to its namesake: a hardy, twisted tree that grows in the rocky deserts of the American Southwest. A Mormon legend claims that their early settlers called the Joshua tree "the praying plant" and thought its gnarled branches suggested the Old Testament prophet Joshua pointing the way to the Promised Land. The title befits a record that concerns itself with resilience in the face of utter social and political desolation, a record steeped in religious imagery.[42]

Bono and the band seem to agree with Zane Lowe when he suggests that the album is not the beginning of a new phase for the band, but rather a companion piece (Lowe calls it a sibling) to *The Unforgettable Fire*, made clear even by the album art: both albums feature gold framing lines around black and white photography. Pond adds: "*The Joshua Tree* is an appropriate response to these times, and a picture bleaker than any U2 has ever painted: a vision of blasted hopes, pointless violence and anguish".[43]

With their "Live Aid" set, U2 had proved that they were a band able to handle a crowd of thousands, and a television audience of millions. Some have argued that the "Live Aid" concert was the defining moment when U2 became one of the biggest bands in the world (Dunphy recounts Paul McGuinness thinking that "his band could [now] play anywhere").[44] With *The Joshua Tree*, the band were now singing songs of America. These were songs *against* America (such as 'Bullet the Blue Sky'), but they were also songs that sounded *like* America: rootsy and loud. Bono had been listening to folk music and the blues, and the result was U2's most commercially successful album. The political side of U2 was evident on the album, though the band's Christianity showed itself less confidently: Bono was clear that he still hadn't found what he was searching for.

Eno took a less prominent role in producing *The Joshua Tree*. The first track on the album, 'Where the Streets Have No Name', took the band weeks to complete. Stokes recounts the culmination of Eno's frustration and resentment during the recording sessions, which resulted in the popular tale that Eno wanted to erase the multitrack recording while the band were away from the studio. The Edge claims that the assistant engineer insisted that Eno not erase the tape, physically standing between Eno and the equipment. The Edge states:

> At one stage he became so frustrated at the amount of time being devoted to 'Where the Streets Have No Name' that he wanted to erase the multi-track. "That's right", The Edge recalls. "We weren't in the studio at the time and he asked the assistant engineer to leave the room. He'd actually decided to do it. But the assistant engineer wouldn't go. He stood in front of the tape machine saying, "Brian, you can't do this". And so he didn't. But it was close.[45]

The Joshua Tree went on to sell some 25 million copies worldwide, winning Grammy Awards for both "Album of the Year" and "Best Rock Performance by a Duo or Group with Vocal".[46] Lowe refers to the band's acceptance speech for "Album of the Year" in the 2017 interview, suggesting that the band did not seem altogether comfortable as "biggest band in the world", making that fact clear from the stage. In the acceptance speech, Bono humorously suggests that it is hard – but enjoyable – work saving the world, and suggests that U2 wanted to make "soul music", not marked by race or instrumentation (as one might expect when speaking of the soul music genre), but the choice to "reveal or conceal". Assumedly, Bono is suggesting that soul music is more "authentic" than other popular music genres. In the speech, Bono takes the opportunity to call attention to both Prince and Bruce Springsteen, apparently both soul music creators without whom U2 would not exist. The band's place as "Rock's hottest ticket" was established with their appearance on the cover of *Time Magazine* on 27 April 1987: Bono is quoted as saying, "We don't think we're that good, really … We think we are overrated, and though we're concerned about living up to people's expectations, it scares us even to live up to our own expectations".[47] It should be noted that this article now appears in full at U2's own official website. From what many fans know of Bono (and, to a lesser extent, other members of the band), these words seem to ring hollow. Though the band are being quoted in the relatively early days of their existence (the article came out less than a decade after the band's formation), the quote seems to betray an ingenuous Bono in the face of what is presented in the *Rattle and Hum* film, a Bono full of swagger and confidence, if not still somewhat baby-faced. Nevertheless, the band seems to solidify their position at the intersection of religion, social conscience and popular music: "Clayton talks worriedly about some fans turning to the band 'needing to be healed', and Bono says, 'I would hate to think everybody was into U2 for "deep" and "meaningful" reasons. We're a noisy rock-'n'-roll band. If we all got onstage and instead of going "Yeow!" The audience all went "Ummmm" or started saying the rosary, it would be awful'". To add to the somewhat saccharine nature of the article, author Jay Cocks quotes a fan from New Jersey saying of the band, "First they opened my mind to their music. Then their music opened my mind to the world".[48] Articles like the *Time* cover story do nothing to assuage the notion that the members of U2 are egotistical; the members of the band can suggest otherwise, but the flaming "U2" on the cover (obviously indicating their "hotness"), and the suggestion that social justice is at the forefront of a project which, in turn, generates millions of dollars for band members (that allows Bono and his family, for instance, to live in a castle, at least for a time) counter that.

The Joshua Tree has sold three times more copies than *The Unforgettable Fire*. The next album, *Rattle and Hum*, sold 14 million copies, making it their second most successful album of the 1980s. The band then decided to make a theatrical film, *Rattle and Hum* (with Paramount Pictures), mixing concert footage and documentary material (amounting to something more akin to the Bob Dylan film, *Don't Look Back*, from 1967) rather than a conventional concert film.

About 1988's *Rattle and Hum*, Anthony DeCurtis writes, "In its inclusiveness and rollicking energy, *Rattle and Hum* caps the story of U2's rise from Dublin obscurity to international superstardom on a raucous, celebratory note. At the same time, it closes off none of the options the band might want to pursue for its next big move – and, possibly, the album even opens a few doors".[49] Here, DeCurtis writes of U2 "in motion and transition", which makes sense, but does so more clearly once the listener hears what comes next; *Rattle and Hum* does not seem a departure from *The Joshua Tree*, but it certainly marks a transition, and one that is more than simply musical.

Writing in the *New York Times*, Jon Pareles suggests that there is not much depth to the album, in stark opposition to *The Joshua Tree*: "[The previous album] swirled together images of love and suffering and apocalypse, of private yearning and global prophecy, in lyrics that made Biblical imagery seem personal and heartfelt. On *Rattle and Hum*, some songs are summed up by their titles".[50] Pareles calls the album a "mess" and "embarrassing", and concludes, "What comes across in song after song is sincere egomania". None of this would be encouraging to the band, and certainly shows the tensions that the band were (and continue to be) working through.

Janet Maslin is more kind. Regarding the *Rattle and Hum* concert film, Maslin states that it has "a sinuous black and white style that superbly showcases the simplicity and directness of the group's performing style, and he [director Phil Joanou] has the good sense to stay with it". She continues, "If anything, the camera might have lingered longer in closeup on the musicians as they play, since they are at their best when the camera's intensity matches their own".[51] While the band should not be excused for it, Mullen Jr suggests when speaking to Zane Lowe that he and the other band members were under a lot of pressure during this time – on a national tour and recording an album while making a documentary/concert film.

Steve Pond writes of the band in 1989, after the release of the *Rattle and Hum* film on home video. He suggests that thinking of U2 as tiring and tiresome is not a new sentiment:

> After years of favorable fan and press reaction to the band's music; years of dramatic stage performances; years in which underground credibility turned into mass success; years of articles based on intense conversations with a hyperbolic, socially minded lead singer and his three more retiring band mates; years of grainy black-and-white photos of deadly serious, brooding faces, growing from dewy-cheeked youth to bestubbled adulthood; after all that, the U2 backlash has set in.[52]

Over twenty years later, Steven Hyden reminisces: "By November 1988, when *Rattle and Hum* was released, the media regarded U2 more like distinguished statesmen than like a rock band ... A backlash was inevitable, and *Rattle and Hum* unwittingly played into the perception that a metric ton of bullshit had been affixed to the bottoms of Bono's cowboy boots in the wake of *The Joshua Tree*'s success".[53] In 1989, Pond summarizes the tensions inherent in U2 at this point in the band's career: that, since the beginning of their career, they made it clear that "they are dead serious, extraordinarily ambitious and convinced of the importance of what ... they are trying to achieve"; that "these three young Christians and the token nonbeliever" wanted their music to matter; and that the band had a frontman in Bono who "originally sounded ingenuous and endearing [but] slowly became problematic". And then, with *The Joshua Tree*, they became one of the biggest rock bands in the world.[54] Pond suggests that Adam Clayton is the "token unbeliever", though that idea might be uncharitable. The inclusion of Clayton in the band – and the maintenance of that friendship – is part of U2's project of openness. If Clayton is a token, he is an important one. Clayton can be thought of as the "everyman" (Adam, from the biblical Hebrew *adamah*, meaning "ground" or "earth"). Clayton is similar to the Freudian "Id" that needs to be controlled by religion. But Clayton can also be thought of as a sort of feminine figure, a counter to the conventional rock swagger of the other members (incidentally, Clayton dresses particularly well, a fact that is often pointed out in the press and clear in band photographs). After all, the profane needs the sacred in order to exist – not a popular statement in the context of traditional Christianity, which often attempts to put to death the profane to be replaced by the sacred. But Clayton fulfils that role: the band's version of Christianity cannot exist without him. And that inclusivity is key: his "English secularism" is key to the existence of the Irish Roman Catholic sensibility of the band. His "playboy" ways need to be there for the "Pope-ishness" of the rest of the band to shine through. The relationship between Clayton and the rest of the band points to inclusiveness, openness and accommodation.

Rattle and Hum was not well-received by the critics, but was a commercial success. For many, U2 was at the top of their game, at the most successful point of their career. But the tour and publicity for *The Joshua Tree* and *Rattle and Hum* took its toll. While the band did tour from September 1989 to January 1990 (on what was called the *Lovetown* tour – ironically, a tour in support of the tour release, *Rattle and Hum*), they were having trouble. For instance, Bono experienced some difficulty with his singing voice and battled with illness, causing the band to cancel or postpone some of the shows. During a concert performance towards the end of the tour, on 30 December 1989, from Dublin, Bono famously proclaimed, "I was explaining to people the other night, but I might've got it a bit wrong – this is just the end of something for U2. And that's why we're playing these concerts – and we're throwing a party for ourselves and you. It's no big deal, it's just – we have to go away and just dream it all up again".

In November 1998, the band released a compilation album called *The Best of 1980–1990*; the companion video compilation ends with a video recording of a live performance of 'One Tree Hill' that was cut from the *Rattle and Hum* concert film. The video recording begins with some visual static that appears to be from the source tape, and features digital numbers across the bottom of the screen: these are digital time codes for video editors, markers which indicate that the video is unfinished and raw. This video points to both the past (those other music videos in the compilation, roughly covering the decade of the band's development) and looks to the future of *Achtung Baby* and the *Zoo TV* tour, a tour that is also marked by raw footage and digital interference in the transmission of the images on the various screens on stage. The 'One Tree Hill' footage is inundated with marks of its mediation: the viewer is experiencing the band *through* the video footage, presented in a seemingly genuine fashion as *raw material*.

There was a transition, then, to a different U2: some might characterize the 1990s as (what is later here referred to as) "complicity". Bono states, "[Sometimes] we need to throw off a bit of moral baggage – which we got to do on

Zoo TV. The duality, which has always been there in us, just came out more in the Nineties. And then, it's fair to say, the sensory overload may have started to take over".[55] Here, Bono is pointing to (or trying to describe) what the duality – or complicity – *looks* like. It is the sensory overload: the 'One Tree Hill' clip features not only Bono and the band but also the time stamps and static, more information than a viewer needs in order to understand what is going on. Instead, the viewer is shown behind the façade of the performance spectacle, to see the technical aspects of editing, and the very medium (or videotape) upon which the footage resides.

Notes

1. It is difficult to separate this notion of stage design from the post-Second Vatican Council idea of the altar moved to the centre of the worship space in Roman Catholic liturgy.
2. Bill Graham, "Yep! It's U2", in *The U2 File: A Hot Press U2 History 1978–1985*, edited by Niall Stokes (Dublin: Hot Press, 1985), 7. The 2014 U2.com subscriber-only title, *North Side Story: U2 in Dublin 1978–1983*, also by Niall Stokes, states that Graham's article was first published in December 1977.
3. Niall Stokes, "Introduction", in *North Side Story: U2 in Dublin 1978–1983* (Dublin: Hot Press, 2014), 9.
4. Eamon Dunphy, *Unforgettable Fire: Past, Present, and Future – The Definitive Biography of U2* (New York: Warner Books, 1987), 75.
5. Ibid., 84.
6. Niall Stokes, "Boys in Control", in *The U2 File: A Hot Press U2 History 1978–1985*, edited by Niall Stokes (Dublin: Hot Press, 1985), 20.
7. Debra Rae Cohen, "U2: Boy", *Rolling Stone* (16 April 1981); available from http://www.rollingstone.com/music/albumreviews/boy-19810416 (accessed 4 July 2016).
8. Declan Lynch, "The Boy Can't Help It", in *North Side Story: U2 in Dublin 1978–1983* (Dublin: Hot Press, 2014), 131.
9. Ibid., 132.
10. Neil McCormick, "Autumn Fire", in *North Side Story: U2 in Dublin 1978–1983* (Dublin: Hot Press, 2014), 174.
11. Jann S. Wenner, "Bono: The Rolling Stone Interview", *Rolling Stone* (3 November 2005), available from https://www.rollingstone.com/music/news/bono-the-rolling-stone-interview-20051103 (accessed 18 February 2018).
12. Bill Flanagan, *U2 at the End of the World* (New York: Delta, 1996), 48.
13. Dunphy, *Unforgettable Fire*, 134.
14. Ibid.
15. Ibid., 203.
16. Ibid.,151.
17. Valerie Robinson, "'I nearly quit U2 before we found fame' says Bono", *Irish Times* (26 June 2013); available from https://tinyurl.com/IT-2013-06-26-news (accessed 6 July 2017).

18. Cathleen Falsani, "Bono's American Prayer", *Christianity Today* (1 March 2003); available from http://www.christianitytoday.com/ct/2003/marchweb-only/2.38.html (accessed 6 July 2017).

19. McCormick, "Autumn Fire", 174.

20. Jon Pareles, "U2: October", *Rolling Stone* (4 February 1982); available from http://www.rollingstone.com/music/albumreviews/october-19820204 (accessed 6 July 2017).

21. Flanagan, *U2 at the End of the World*, 48. The Edge's comments to Flanagan are widely quoted, for instance, by Steve Stockman in *Walk On: The Spiritual Journey of U2* (Lake Mary, FL: Relevant Books, 2001), 30–34, and by Christian Scharen in *One Step Closer: Why U2 Matters to Those Seeking God* (Grand Rapids, MI: Brazos Press, 2006), 163.

22. Neil McCormick, *U2 by U2* (London: HarperCollins, 2006), xiv. For a more recent account of "Lypton Village" and the Shalom Fellowship, see Michael R. MacLeod and Timothy Harvie, "'In God's Country': Spatial Sacredness in U2", in *U2 and the Religious Impulse: Take Me Higher*, edited by Scott Calhoun (London: Bloomsbury, 2018), 135–37.

23. Liam Mackey, "Blood on the Tracks", in *North Side Story: U2 in Dublin 1978–1983* (Dublin: Hot Press, 2014), 227.

24. Ibid., 230–31.

25. J. D. Considine, "Album Reviews: *War*", *Rolling Stone* (31 March 1983); available from https://www.rollingstone.com/music/music-album-reviews/war-105402/ (accessed 30 July 2018).

26. Dunphy, *Unforgettable Fire*, 205.

27. Flanagan, *U2 at the End of the World*, 208–209. Flanagan and Dunphy disagree on the facts: Dunphy suggests that Mullen Jr was formally trained on the drums.

28. Henrik Marstal, "'Edge, Ring Those Bells': The Guitar and its Spiritual Soundscapes in Early U2", in *U2 and the Religious Impulse: Take Me Higher*, edited by Scott Calhoun (London: Bloomsbury, 2018), 12, 16–18.

29. Brian Clark, "U2 – Egos and Icons '97 – Part 1 of 7", *YouTube* (9 February 2008); available from https://www.youtube.com/watch?v=zqlft_5U_lU (accessed 31 July 2018).

30. Flanagan, *U2 at the End of the World*, 25.

31. Ibid., 49.

32. Niall Stokes, *Into the Heart* (London: Carlton Books, 1996), 57, 60.

33. Kurt Loder, "U2: The Unforgettable Fire", *Rolling Stone* (11 October 1984); available from http://www.rollingstone.com/music/albumreviews/the-unforgettable-fire-19841011 (accessed 7 July 2017).

34. Will Hermes, "U2: The Unforgettable Fire (Deluxe Reissue)", *Rolling Stone* (26 October 2009); available from http://www.rollingstone.com/music/albumreviews/the-unforgettable-fire-deluxe-reissue-20091026 (accessed 7 July 2017).

35. Liam Mackey, "Light a Big Fire", in *The U2 File: A Hot Press U2 History 1978–1985*, edited by Niall Stokes (Dublin: Hot Press, 1985), 110.

36. Bill Graham, "It's a Celebration!", in *The U2 File: A Hot Press U2 History 1978–1985*, edited by Niall Stokes (Dublin: Hot Press, 1985), 109.

37. Beats 1 on Apple Music, "U2 and Zane Lowe on Beats 1", *YouTube* (20 July 2017); available from https://www.youtube.com/watch?v=vsKZ3YrF_3Q (accessed 30 July 2018).

38. Niall Stokes and Dermot Stokes, "All Ireland Champions!", in *The U2 File: A Hot Press U2 History 1978–1985*, edited by Niall Stokes (Dublin: Hot Press, 1985), 151.

39. Dunphy, *Unforgettable Fire*, 1–4.
40. Graham Jones, "Live Aid 1985: A Day of Magic", *CNN.com* (6 July 2005); available from http://edition.cnn.com/2005/SHOWBIZ/Music/07/01/liveaid.memories/index.html (accessed 4 August 2017).
41. Beats 1 on Apple Music, "U2 and Zane Lowe on Beats 1".
42. Steve Pond, "U2: The Joshua Tree", *Rolling Stone* (9 April 1987); available from http://www.rollingstone.com/music/albumreviews/the-joshua-tree-19870409 (accessed 5 August 2017).
43. Ibid.
44. Dunphy, *Unforgettable Fire*, 4.
45. Stokes, *Into the Heart*, 63.
46. Adam Sherwin, "New U2 album No Line on the Horizon given lukewarm reception", *The Times* (3 March 2009); available from https://www.thetimes.co.uk/article/new-u2-album-no-line-on-the-horizon-given-lukewarm-reception-df8h3cgmht9 (accessed 6 August 2017).
47. Jay Cocks, "U2: Band on the Run", *Time* (27 April 1987); available from http://www.u2.com/news/title/rocks-hottest-ticket-time-magazine/news/ (accessed 6 August 2017).
48. Ibid.
49. Anthony DeCurtis, "U2: Rattle and Hum", *Rolling Stone* (17 November 1988); available from http://www.rollingstone.com/music/albumreviews/rattle-and-hum-19881117 (accessed 9 August 2017).
50. Jon Pareles, "RECORDINGS; When Self-Importance Interferes with the Music", *New York Times* (16 October 1988); available from http://www.nytimes.com/1988/10/16/arts/recordings-when-self-importance-interferes-with-the-music.html (accessed 11 August 2017).
51. Janet Maslin, "Review/Film; U2 Hits the Road in 'Rattle and Hum'", *New York Times* (4 November 1988); available from http://www.nytimes.com/movie/review?res=940DE3DC1639F937A35752C1A96E948260 (accessed 11 August 2017).
52. Steve Pond, "U2: Now What?", *Rolling Stone* (9 March 1989); available from http://www.rollingstone.com/music/features/now-what-19890309 (accessed 9 August 2017).
53. Steven Hyden, "Searching for Sugar Men", *Grantland* (13 May 2013); available from http://grantland.com/features/a-look-state-rock-documentaries-25-years-u2-rattle-hum/ (accessed 9 August 2017).
54. Pond, "U2: Now What?".
55. Wenner, "Bono: The Rolling Stone Interview".

2   U2 and the Blinding Lights of the City

In autumn 1990, U2 reconvened to begin their next studio project. The recording of the album that became *Achtung Baby* began in Berlin (at that time, in the democratic West Germany), just as the Berlin Wall was falling, and the beginning of the end of communism in Eastern Europe and the fall of the Soviet Union. The Berlin Wall was a massive border barrier that covered around 96 miles, some of that through the city of Berlin. It had been built by the communist East Germany beginning in 1961, as a deterrent to emigration from East Germany to the democratic West Germany. After such great success with *The Joshua Tree*, but only a mediocre reception to *Rattle and Hum*, the band began to "chop down the Joshua Tree"[1] (Larry Mullen Jr in the Zane Lowe interview suggests, interestingly, that "We didn't deserve to be that band"), that is, to rise from the ashes of (implicit) commercialism with a renewed image and refreshed mission. U2 were now at an unprecedented position in terms of their career. U2 wanted to change their sound and shake themselves from the creative comfort zone they occupied. The band truly did turn from their past sound, serving up distorted vocals and noise, a sound informed by the destruction of the Berlin Wall and its associated political ideology. This shake-up was catalysed by the choice of Berlin and the Hansa Studio as a place to shape their new musical expression. For Eno, Berlin was a nostalgic location, as was the Hansa Studio. It was there that Eno worked with Bowie to create *"Heroes"*; Hansa also reminded Eno of the 1930s, during which Berlin was a booming city that was yet to be thrown into the turmoil of World War II. It was also the centre of a tumultuous political change in the 1990s, optimistic and alive. At the intersection of these elements, all under the shadow of the falling Berlin Wall, the album was going to be made. The role of the producer on this project was slightly different than on previous U2 projects. For *Achtung Baby*, Eno was given the luxury to come and go as he pleased. His input was simply an instinctual one, while it was co-producer Daniel Lanois's job to make sure that the sound Eno suggested came through in the recording, or to put into place certain improvements that Eno felt were needed. Although Eno's role was thus somewhat limited, he seemed to make his presence felt nonetheless, by discovering the creative pulse of the artists involved and working with them for a successful result. The first thing apparent to a listener of this album is the introduction of noise to the music of U2. Eno suggests that there was a language that was developed as they worked on the album:

> a language starts to evolve. It's a language of praise and criticism, the first flagpoles marking out the landscape within which this new music is being made. Buzzwords on this record were *trashy, throwaway, dark, sexy* and *industrial* (all good) and *earnest, polite, sweet, righteous, rockist* and *linear* (all bad). It was good if a song took you on a journey or made you think your hifi was broken, bad if it reminded you of recording studios or U2.[2]

Berlin was a site of nostalgia for Eno in particular, and he calls the city the "conceptual backdrop" for *Achtung Baby*. He seems to suggest that 1930s Berlin has something in common with the version of the city in the early 1990s, as "reborn, chaotic and optimistic". Eno states, "the record came to be seen as a place where incongruous strands would be allowed to weave together and where a probably disunified (but definitely European) picture would be allowed to emerge".[3]

Eno had worked with David Bowie in the Hansa Studio. Bowie's track, "'Heroes'", is an example in which the spatiality of the room is important in terms of the recorded sound. Popular accounts of the recording process describe Bowie in a room with microphones that were each placed at a different distance from the singer. As he began to sing more loudly, his voice was registered by a microphone further away from his position. The further the microphone, the more reverb (or echo) was applied to the voice, as those microphones had effects applied to whatever sound they received. This arrangement of microphones and sound processing made Bowie's voice sound bigger as he sang louder. His voice took up more *space* as it became stronger, increasing in physical volume as it increased in amplitude. With U2 and the Hansa sessions, Eno was hoping, it seems, that the cultural context of being the site of Bowie's critically acclaimed *"Heroes"* album, and of a lost Berlin (Hansa had, at one time, contained a Nazi-era concert hall that was bombed by the Allied Forces in 1943), would inform the band's creative output. Eno was wanting the sound to evoke the space, and, in turn, he was counting on the space to bring to the sound all of the grittiness of the past of a divided Berlin, as well as the myriad opportunities of a fallen wall and reunified country.

Instead of rising from the ashes, so to speak, of commercialism, the band embraced the idea of rock stardom, and instead of moving away from the trappings of celebrity and the distance that is afforded celebrities, the band relished in that distance, constructing a yet greater gulf between the fans and the band. Bono began wearing dark oversized sunglasses and leather outfits (evoking Elvis Presley) and going by the moniker "The Fly". They were one of the biggest bands in the world, and now had to figure out how to navigate their way in a world in which all eyes were on them and their artistic output. The result was the *Zoo TV* tour, a massive two-year tour that involved a spectacular stage design and lots of electricity. *Achtung Baby*, the *Zoo TV* tour and a new album, *Zooropa*, were hugely important for U2, and highlight their creative strategies at this point in their career.

Elysa Gardner writes that *Rattle and Hum* was "the product of U2's self-conscious infatuation with American roots music [and] wasn't a full-out disaster, but it was misguided and bombastic enough to warrant concern". Gardner continues, "In the past, U2's frontman has turned out fiercely pointed social and political diatribes, but his more confessional and romantic songs, however felt, have been evasive. On *Achtung*, though, Bono deals more directly with his private feelings – not to mention his hormones".[4] Jon Pareles states, "The revamped U2 isn't trapped in sophomoric seriousness because it's no longer so sure of itself".[5]

It is no exaggeration to suggest that the album is the single most dramatic musical change of the band's career. There are many fans who would divide their fandom by this album: they were fans of U2 before *Achtung Baby*, and prefer the "older material", but passionately dislike the new U2. If pre-1990s U2 are arguably "authentic" or "political", the 1990s, as ushered in by *Achtung Baby*, present the band as completely and purposefully "inauthentic", though they remain political throughout. What is perhaps problematic for early fans is that U2 do not appear to be *themselves*: they betray the earlier concern for, say, peace in Ireland or environmental care. Rather, the band appears *complicit* in the machinery of stardom. If fans spend money, time and attention on the spectacle of a U2 concert, they cannot spend those resources on changing the world. Or, at least, that is the perception.

Stephen Catanzarite calls *Achtung Baby* "the antithesis, in many respects, of *Boy*, the band's virgin outing recorded a dozen years earlier, which brimmed with the excitement and irrational exuberance of youth. *Achtung Baby* is not your kid brother's U2; it is an album for adults – or for those at least aspiring to adulthood".[6]

"Aura of the 'sublime'"

Brian Eno felt that Berlin held an intrinsic allure, a quality that would act as a sort of muse, as a catalyst of the band's reinvention. Modern cities like Berlin can be embedded with a rich history of physical hardship, and are often characterized by a certain industrial character or aesthetic.[7] These buildings and monuments have historically acted as sites for artists in various disciplines who would feed from their history as inspiration for the production of their art, since hardship can be read as a catalyst for a compelling life, that is, one of hardship and, in turn, overcoming that hardship. Hardship might lead to what some would consider a more "vital" way of life. Sharon Zukin discusses what she calls the "aura of the 'sublime'", that is, this sense of vitality that emerges from such historic sites (buildings or monuments), or those urban features that hold strong associations to hardship, history or culture. It is easy to consider that the urban landscape, or the grit and pulse of a cityscape, might fit into this "aura of the 'sublime'" as well. To explain what she means, Zukin suggests that many city dwellers in the 1960s were dismayed by the destruction of urban historical sites. She explains: "For a long time, demolition signified improvement. But the destruction in the early 1960s of Pennsylvania Station, a railroad terminal of the grand era whose soaring glass dome was replaced by a mundane office building, dramatized the loss of a collective sense of time that many people felt".[8] This is reminiscent of Paul Virilio's stance regarding progress. He asks the question, "why did the positive aspect of progress get replaced by its propaganda?" He suggests that the prevailing thought regarding progress – that progress results only in good things – is replaced by the propagandist notion that all progress is good. Obviously, Virilio would understand the idea that something is lost in the destruction of urban sites.[9]

Zukin also suggests that there emerges a type of regional tourism based on what has happened in the past. This translates into such trinkets as, say, pieces of the Berlin Wall, whether they be fragments available for purchase as keepsakes, or whole sections of the wall that are transported to museums and monuments all over the world. These sites become extensions of the original; they become secular relics, objects imbued with some sort of nostalgic power, that the hardships represented by their decaying forms might inspire new creative expressions. This is different from a kind of draw from the nostalgic; rather, it is the call to experience something that no longer exists (what Zukin might call "a collective sense of time" that is lost). These sorts of places (or their relics) have "character" that can be difficult to define. Zukin states that "Once these old places are depopulated, decayed, and abstracted from the organization of production, they take on the appealing aura of the 'sublime'". She comments that tourists "can view an entire 'living panorama' of industrial history and contrast it with their own everyday environment".[10] In Berlin, the Berlin Wall had developed its own tourist industry, drawing those who wanted to view this monument of history, and perhaps experience what Zukin calls its "aura of the 'sublime'". As opposed to the Pennsylvania Station, the Wall has no link to a "grand era" but certainly does embody a rich and difficult history. It is powerfully linked to a long political conflict and remains a symbol of the oppressive power of communism as well as the victory of a united Germany.

U2's B-side from the *Achtung Baby* sessions, 'Oh Berlin', refers directly to the Hansa Studio (with Bono speaking/singing the address in German: *Köthener Strasse*). This city is a site of the unknown: the narrator seems to lament the fact that they are unable to know the spirit of the city. It is also a site of refuge. The narrator hides themselves in the city, which lends itself to such seekers of refuge. In a lyric from the chorus, the narrator laments that they cannot know Berlin "by name", but later in the song suggests the idea of a "single name", referring to the reunification of the city after the fall of the Berlin Wall. Beth Nabi writes, "Bono changes the final line slightly by inserting 'single', which is an acknowledgement of Berlin's (and the band's) reunification. It is no longer East Berlin and West Berlin. There are no longer two names; there is one".[11]

Tokyo and *flânerie*

In Bill Flanagan's excellent *U2 at the End of the World*, there are a number of photographs of the band from during their time in Japan during the *Zoo TV* tour. The photos are all in black and white, and taken by the band's familiar photographer Anton Corbijn. Because of this, the photos could be considered quasi-official, though they do not appear on any music releases to date. In these photos, the city of Tokyo becomes what Walter Benjamin calls the "properly sacred ground of flânerie".[12] Benjamin is referring to the *flâneur*, an urban figure who explores the city. The *flâneur* – originally a literary figure from Charles Baudelaire and Edgar Allan Poe – is a detached observer that is unhurried by the world that surrounds him, taking the pace of a tortoise in the covered streets – or arcades – of Paris (there is an illustration from Benjamin that a person that is walking a pet tortoise is moving at the correct pace of a *flâneur*). The *flâneur* is a particularly urban phenomenon: "the old Romantic sentiment for landscape dissolves and a new Romantic conception of landscape emerges – of landscape that seems, rather, to be a cityscape".[13]

Flanagan's book includes sixteen pages containing twenty black and white photos. The first few are of the band in Japan in December 1993. The first photo shows the band outside on the street, with Bono squeezing Clayton's cheeks and the other two members of the band leaning in from just outside of the frame of the photo. The group is photographed in front of a line of motorcycles. The next photo shows Clayton and Bono in a tea room: the two musicians are out of focus in the foreground while Tokyo at night is clearly in focus in the background. A third photo shows Mullen Jr and The Edge in an alley in Tokyo, the city lights reflecting off of the wet sheen of the street surface. Finally, there is a photo of Clayton eating at a sushi bar alone. All of these photos point to the band exploring the city, and doing things that might seem mundane and regular. They are doing these things at night, exploring a city that looks both labyrinthian and beautiful (even in the monochrome of black and white photography).

Benjamin seems to describe the band involved in the various mundanities of the city. Benjamin quotes Georg Simmel (and his *Mélanges de philosophie rélativiste: Contribution à la culture philosophique*): "Social life in the large city ... shows a great preponderance of occasions to *see* rather than to hear people ... they could or must look at one other without talking to one another".[14]

Anke Gleber points out that Siegfried Kracauer describes something that can be thought of as a kind of ethics of *flânerie*: "this reporting job [that is, the observations of a *flâneur*] is done with unconcealed compassion for the people depicted". Gleber quotes Kracauer's comments regarding a short documentary film from 1948 called *In the Street*, which focuses on life in 1940s Spanish Harlem. Kracauer notes that the short sixteen-minute film is "a reportage pure and simple". He continues, "the camera dwells on them tenderly; they are not meant to stand for anything but themselves".[15] The "reporting job" to which Kracauer refers is the act of the camera in documenting the world, in being the observer's eyes on the world. For Kracauer, the *flâneur* is a kind of camera, registering the world, which explains his use of the notion of reporting. Is the band engaging in an ethical *flânerie*? What does it mean for the band to present themselves in mundane situations, engaging in normal tasks? Consider the photo of Clayton eating noodles from a bowl, seemingly alone save the presence of Corbijn the photographer. Can this be considered part of an ethical reporting of the city? Corbijn could be considered the *flâneur* in this situation, reporting on people that he encounters, who, in this case, happen to be the members of the band. But, of course, the streets of Tokyo are not the band's territory, per se. One can imagine the band leaving a restaurant post-performance in order to wander and explore the city "unfettered" (though within the constraints and frameworks that being world celebrities demand). Corbijn is the *flâneur* who records the *flânerie* of the band as they, in turn, report the city of Tokyo.

The city and the *Zoo TV* tour

It was out of the recording sessions in Berlin, and the "aura of the 'sublime'" that Berlin provided, that the next stage of U2's development would emerge, in the form of the *Zoo TV* tour. Launched in 1992 and running for two years, the *Zoo TV* tour was, of course, in support of the *Achtung Baby* album, but it was also an opportunity for the band to employ new (at that time) technologies, and to work on the cultivation of spectacle in live performance. The tour included: "4 mega video screens, 4 Philips Vidiwalls [large video displays], 36 video monitors, 18 projectors, 12 laser disk players ... 11 Trabant cars used as spotlights ... 176 speaker cabinets and the sound system used over a million watts of power and weighed over 30 tonnes".[16] David Fricke describes the scene and atmosphere of the *Zoo TV* tour:

> Zoo TV's agitated splash of appropriated video images and glib buzz phrases triggers eye-popping juxtapositions of cliché and truth: EVERYTHING YOU KNOW IS WRONG; GUILT IS NEXT TO GOD; ... EVERYBODY IS A RACIST ... George Bush calls the congregation to order in hilariously doctored footage, chanting Queen's "We will, we will rock you!" in that irritating read-my-lips whine. Two East German Trabant cars attached to huge mechanical arms and outfitted with spotlights scan the crowd like alien prison sentries while a patchwork video quilt of Gargantuan screens, multi-image Vidiwalls and TV monitors spews words and pictures with exhausting velocity – Rock & Roll Mission Control running on amphetamine fast forward.[17]

Flanagan suggests that the space created by the *Zoo TV* tour stage is a place "where there is supposed to be no moralizing, where symbols are held up to raise questions and examine contradictions".[18] The notion of examining contradictions may remind one of Eno's *Oblique Strategies*, a deck of cards, each inscribed with an interesting phrase for the purpose of inspiration in a recording situation, and rightly so; Brian Eno was one of the creators and contributors to the whole *Zoo TV* tour experience. In a television interview with Canada's MuchMusic in 1998, Eno claims that the idea for a stage covered in televisions was his: the concept was to use a number of different video sources in order to create a sort of *melée* of information. The video sources would hinder rather than help the audience to see the band more clearly.[19] Eno was hoping to create visual chaos on the stage in order to go against the idea that video should help the audience to see the band more easily from the distance of seats at the back of the arena or stadium. Instead, video becomes a way to *obscure* the band, making them a single element in a wall of seemingly disparate visual information. McLaughlin adds to this that the *Zoo TV* tour – and U2's "reinvention" during this time – could be regarded as "'delayed' post-punk", an embracing of performance practice that was not afforded in the Irish cultural context. Furthermore, this was a move that sated "the desire to explore self-consciously mediation itself", rather than the creation of what McLaughlin calls "a psychedelic backdrop".[20]

The *Zoo TV* tour was a great success and was very interesting in its political implications as well. The tour was unique in featuring live satellite feeds from Sarajevo during the civil war in the former Yugoslavia, and for giving controversial figures such as Salman Rushdie a voice in the middle of a rock concert. Rushdie was under the condemnation of a *fatwa*, a non-binding but authoritative opinion decreed by the Ayatollah Khomeini of Iran in 1989, which subjected Rushdie to a death sentence because of the content of his novel, *The Satanic Verses*. It was from the energy and atmosphere of the *Zoo TV* tour that the album *Zooropa* emerged, released in July 1993. Rather than waiting for the end of the tour to record, the band decided to create a new collection of songs during the break in the tour. Some of the songs on the album were inspired by the science-fiction novels of Canadian author William Gibson. His novels *Neuromancer* (1984), *Count Zero* (1986) and *Mona Lisa Overdrive* (1988) take place in the Sprawl, an urban wasteland of computers, corporate espionage and cybernetic body enhancements. Gibson's "cyberpunk" world provided a fictional setting for the band to situate the songs. The sonic material for U2's songs seemed to originate from the cyberpunk world of Gibson's novels. For U2 and *Zooropa*, the musical atmosphere (the ambient sound) was of utmost importance. Bono states:

> We were opening this kind of Bladerunner-type world ... It starts with this neon winking and blinking and these two characters come out of it. There's this image of the "overground". It was a time when everyone was all indie and grey and dull – the "underground". The overground was like coming out into the bright light of the modern city. It's an amazing place to be, walking around these modern cities like Houston or Tokyo. And the idea was coming out into that, embracing it, going after it.[21]

The *Zoo TV: Live from Sydney* concert film was recorded after the release of *Zooropa* and presents the live manifestation of the general atmosphere of the album.

The album begins with the title track, which seems to describe a future world in which there is both an "underground" and an "overground". The atmospheric sound of the track does not betray that it is a song by U2: The Edge's delay-effect-laden guitars do not emerge until two minutes into the track. And the song changes sonic directions around four minutes into the six-and-a-half minute song. The song picks up tempo, evoking a visual image akin to floodlights turning towards a futuristic city. About *Zooropa*, Anthony DeCurtis writes, "the chilling emotional atmosphere of *Zooropa* – one of grim, determined fun, a fever-dream last waltz on the deck of the *Titanic* – is well suited to contemporary times in the Old World". DeCurtis ends his review with a startling phrase: "The album's true strength lies in capturing the sound of verities shattering, of things falling apart, that moment when exhilaration and fear are indistinguishable as the slide into the abyss begins".[22] Is the album a sort of nihilistic anthem? Not necessarily. Rather, it seems a vehicle for an even more enigmatic project for the band.

Consider a performance of 'Zooropa' by the band in Turin in September 2015, for the opening concert of the European leg of the *iNNOCENCE + eXPERIENCE* tour. Around this time, European countries were struggling to deal with an influx of refugees crossing the Mediterranean, originating primarily in Syria. In *Rolling Stone*, Andy Greene writes that "Bono used his platform to beg for mercy on their behalf. 'I'm not dangerous!' he said at the conclusion of 'Bullet the Blue Sky'. 'I'm in danger!'" Answering the repeated question that a heavily-processed Bono asks during the introduction of the studio version of 'Zooropa', Greene quotes Bono in Turin as saying, "'What do you want?' he asked the crowd. 'A Europe with its heart and its borders closed to mercy? Or a Europe with its heart open? What do you want? A place called home'".[23]

If this is the answer to the question of "what do you want?" in 2015, what was the answer to the question in 1993? Perhaps U2 were being prescient to the tensions in the European Union that would transpire in the late 2010s: the answer to "what do you want?" was illustrated by the falling stars of the European Union flag at the entrance of The Fly at the start of *Zoo TV: Live from Sydney* and the opening sounds of 'Zoo Station' (as described earlier). Perhaps the answer is a kind of freedom, a sort of break from oppression, the call to go "overground". Whatever the answer might be, it is not explicitly about immigration. But it might be about movement, a movement from "underground" to "overground", a movement from the margins to the centre. If looked at in this way, 'Zooropa' is a site, then, of revelation, of bringing to light those things that need to be revealed, addressed and repaired. The tempo changes of the song treat the listener not only to sonic difference and novelty but demonstrate this sense of movement: things do not stay the same, and there are urgent affairs that need to be addressed. In that way, 'Zooropa' is again prescient to contemporary concerns. The movement in 'Zooropa', the underground to the overground, is not so far removed from the movement of oppressed people from sites of conflict and personal danger to places of safety and opportunity. The movement in 'Zooropa' is not unlike the movement on the part of the band to highlight the struggle of migrants on their journey from the Middle East to an overwhelmed Europe that is not altogether equipped – in terms of resources and, perhaps, willingness – to deal with them. Another track, 'Daddy's Gonna Pay for Your Crashed Car', relies on a similarly new sonic landscape to bring an even more strange and alien U2 to the world. Here, the band wrap themselves in a further disguise, whether it be Bono as Mr MacPhisto (one of his many on-stage personae) or the other band members ironically dressed as paramilitary members.[24]

The unified vision of *Zooropa* was created in a curious manner, however, which may account for the range of styles present on the album. Stokes explains that the band would fly from concert performance back to the studio in order to record, and then back out to perform. The band would sometimes record in the middle of the night, and Eno and co-producer Flood (Mark Ellis) would divide the work between them and tinker with the recorded material, creating rough mixes as they were able.[25] The result of mere weeks of work in the studio was one of the most interesting albums of the 1990s, released in the middle of a world-wide tour of epic proportions. At the end of the tour, they began working on new material.

Before the band began work on a new album in earnest in early 1995, the band spent a couple of weeks with Eno working on improvisations that they thought might work as film soundtrack material. This was the beginning of what is now known as *Passengers: Original Soundtracks 1* (released in November 1995), not an official U2 album, but rather one featuring Brian Eno as a full collaborator rather than simply a producer. Essentially, Eno became the "fifth member" of the band, working with them over a seven-week period. Songs like 'United Colours' (an attempt to capture the sense of speed on the bullet train), and 'Slug' (which describes the lights coming on in a city like Tokyo) seem to valorize the idea of the city and modern technological progress.[26] *Passengers: Original Soundtracks 1* was also an opportunity for Eno to work with Howie B, a remixer who met Bono in the late 1980s. Howie B is credited as a key contributor to the creation of the idea of space in the music. Rather than fill in all the gaps (Eno suggests this is something that tends to happen in a studio environment, where sound continues to be added to the mix), Howie B decided to leave out elements of the mix that Eno and the others had thought were very important. The space left turned out to be rather satisfying.[27] Although U2, Howie B and others make themselves known on *Original Soundtracks 1*, U2 maintain that the album was a show of gratitude to Eno, and as such, Eno was given the final word on almost every element of the recording.

In *Hot Press*, Bill Graham writes, "Let's not argue whether or not this is U2's best album but instead agree that it is certainly their most relaxed, and their most playful".[28] The album includes liner notes that recount and describe the films that feature the various musical pieces (which do not all feature vocals); the notes describe films that do not exist (except for a few). Even David Browne, writing for *Entertainment Weekly*, gets fooled by the premise, stating that "the record is a collection of songs written ... for various independently released international films".[29] Jon Pareles writes, "Among true recording-studio obsessives, songs are just a framework for sonic hanky-panky, and sometimes songs are just too confining". Pareles continues that "Throughout the album, what matters is texture".[30]

The songs continue to use some of the sonic language that was introduced in *Zooropa*: the album paints pictures through sound, whether it be speed (a recurring theme during and after the *Zoo TV* era) or whether it be colour. The song 'Your Blue Room' seems to sound like the colour *blue* and features Adam Clayton on a rare recorded spoken-word vocal. This track was one that *was* actually used in the soundtrack for the independently released international film, *Beyond the Clouds* (1994), directed by Wim Wenders and Michelangelo Antonioni.

Varèse, Rosenfeld and "skyscraper mysticism"

By looking at the work of early-twentieth-century music critic and journalist Paul Rosenfeld, as well as the idea of Marxist cultural critic Frederic Jameson's "double hermeneutic" and the idea of the "neutral" term, the city in U2 can be seen as a site of utopia, a promise of vitality, life and progress, as well as a site of an ethical engagement with others.

The attitude of Bono concerning the city is reflected in Paul Rosenfeld's definition of "skyscraper mysticism", which the critic applied to electro-acoustic composer Edgard Varèse. It was through Varèse's portrayal of the inhumanity of his surroundings that Rosenfeld felt the composer was able to transcend them.[31]

There are similarities between the approach taken by Eno and U2 and the music of twentieth-century electro-acoustic composer Edgard Varèse. Varèse's world is much different than that of U2: he existed within the avant-garde of the electro-acoustic music scene in the middle of the twentieth century. The whole concept of the *Zoo TV* tour, though, is reminiscent of the Philips Pavilion at the Brussels World's Fair in 1958. Varèse created the "Poème électronique" especially for the pavilion designed by the Swiss-French architect Le Corbusier. The pavilion was outfitted with over 400 loudspeakers and the musical piece was accompanied by images of masks, skeletons, cities, human bodies, and beasts projected on every surface. Varèse was trying to accomplish, wanting to develop, a sort of "poetics of space": "the superior capacity of all kinds of music to capture emergence in complex phenomena; transient, non-articulated feelings; or what Gaston Bachelard called the Poetics of Space, whether the ambience of a room, the ribbon of a road or the boundless envelopment of oceanic space".[32] This seems to evoke Howie B's work with the U2-Eno collaboration *Passengers*.

Paul Rosenfeld, who died in 1946, conceived of the notion of "skyscraper mysticism", which the critic applied to Varèse:

> this is a feeling of the unity of life through the forms and expressions of industrial civilization, its fierce lights, piercing noises, compact and synthetic textures: a feeling of its immense tension, dynamism, ferocity, and also its fabulous delicacy and precision, that impels artists to communicate it through the portions of their mediums [sic] most sympathetic to it, and through forms partly imitative of those which excite their intuitions.[33]

It was through Varèse's portrayal of the inhumanity of his surroundings that Rosenfeld felt the composer was able to transcend those surroundings.[34] The *Zoo TV* tour does something similar: it allows the viewer to transcend the inhumanity of their urban surroundings through the very spectacle of the concert experience.

Although Rosenfeld experienced much solitude and great tension in the 1930s, resistance was one of his major themes. The tension was sparked by the social consciousness movement, to which many of his one-time associates and colleagues were subscribing. It was commonly thought that the fostering of individual wealth was something to be sought for, and it was promoted even among the American intelligentsia. Social consciousness was supported also by those in American politics in the early 1900s. Rosenfeld did not feel that political figures promoted either the right to proper and fulfilling employment or the need for what Sherman Paul cites as "the social necessity of a living use of material", which might refer to environmental sustainability and creation care.[35] Rather, there was only the idea of distributed wealth, not in order to improve an individual's quality of life, but in order to provide frivolous commodities for all.[36]

In an essay published in 1928, Rosenfeld gives an explanation as to why he writes the journalistic criticism that he does:

> I write "because" of a sympathetic relationship existing between myself and something invisible and unknown to me, enveloping me like a living atmosphere and moving within me like my blood. This curious oceanic substance fascinates and solicits me incessantly; and might, as a steady object of interest, be called the cause of the activity directed toward it. Always ranging somewhere upon its borders, I feel it close behind things that are known to me, man-made as well as natural things, buildings and streets and works of art as well as faces and bodies, land- and cloud-scapes.[37]

He later mentions possible hereditary factors that have contributed to his love for writing and the arts, namely the aestheticism and intellectuality from both of his parents, his mother's love of music and his father's love of literature.[38] One cannot help but think that Rosenfeld is channelling both Benjamin and Kracauer, evoking the ethical *flâneur* and the wonder of the city evoked by the music of Passengers.

Rosenfeld was not only a champion for the idea that music can somehow express something of the human condition *in relation* to the city, but he considers the idea of humanity itself as paramount. He considers the humanity expressed in Western European art music as being almost more important than the quality of musical performance. For Rosenfeld, the idea of expressing the heights as well as the depths of human experience are particularly essential in the creation and performance of music.

In a review published in Rosenfeld's *Discoveries of a Music Critic* (1936), he discusses a performance of Monteverdi's *L'Incoronazione di Poppea* by the operatic pupils of the Juilliard School in the winter of late 1932 and early 1933. In Rosenfeld's opening statement, he is already saying something of the state of the art music tradition, where the beauty of those works shines only through heavy disguise; as for the actual review of the performance, the critic reserves this to three words: "It was clumsy".[39] He concedes that what had been presented were simply fragments of the grandeur of the work, but extols the praises of the expression in the performance:

> [These expressions were] deeply articulative of the human heart and its passions in all their nobility and misery, their incandescence in moments of intense desire, ambition, moral elevation, despair, cruelty, and endurance of anguish. Each expressed a human essence and communicated the actual forces of the human creature, almost the force of nature in him.[40]

Rosenfeld wrote that Monteverdi was "one of the superior genus of men and of men of art: an uncoverer of god-nature with the means of music; the seeker and the finder of the truth".[41] About the "clumsy" performance, Rosenfeld takes a rather sympathetic stance: "And they fortified the revelation, the gift of the little performance on Claremont Avenue – the revelation of the figure of a great artistic representative of the spirit of the naturalistic Renaissance added to humanity's rank of heroic inspiring ones".[42] Finally, he praises the composer with the label,

> the prince of all those who have held the mirror of realistic music up to god-nature as it burns in man: such by virtue of what I at last had to recognize as one of the freest, broadest, noblest contacts

> with it ever achieved by a composer – a deep, mature, entirely certain and undeluded feeling of Creative Nature, and a proud glory in her actuality.[43]

What is clear in these writings is Rosenfeld's sympathy towards the performers of this work. Suggested in passing, he finds the essence of all humanity expressed in the performance of this flawed group. Although he applies genius only to the composer of the work, he also seems to be sympathetic to the plight of humanity of the present. Perhaps Rosenfeld is again concerned with social consciousness, and the unbridled individualism and stress on commodity consumption that was being promoted in politics and the academy. Rosenfeld would be sympathetic to the underlying thread of U2's multi-decade project, of outward focus, but the form and format of U2 would perhaps prove more challenging to Rosenfeld. After all, the band are, if nothing else, in the novelty business, relying on consumer consumption for their living. This is a problem: Rosenfeld's utopia in the reflection of "god-nature as it burns in man", as expressed in music, is tempered by the dystopia of U2's quasi-social consciousness, the novelty-driven individual consumption of the contemporary fan of U2's music. New music must be released for U2 to remain both relevant and successful.

Douglas Kellner suggests that Marxist cultural critic Frederic Jameson engages in "analysis of ideology and utopia in a 'double hermeneutic' which will criticize the ideological elements of popular culture while analyzing their utopian projections of a better world whereby they attract an audience".[44] Jameson's "double hermeneutic" refers to the discovery of both the negative aspect, pertaining to the reflection of a societal ideology, and the positive aspect, or the underlying cry for a utopia, in a work. In his criticism, Rosenfeld is primarily concerned with the new and unrecognized in music, which was not the music of the people. Neither was the music of Monteverdi afforded that distinction. Rather, he is looking at the essence of this music, finding in it a vitality that is lost in the "disguise" of the classical bourgeois tradition. The new music, and, in this case, a performance of the old, is a kind of reaction against and criticism of that tradition. But instead of a liberation of an art, resulting in it becoming the property of the proletariat, there is a conflict within the same arena as the bourgeois tradition. It is within the very classical bourgeois structure (its concert halls, scholarly circles, etc.) where this reaction is taking place. Here, the utopia is revealed in Rosenfeld's discussion of new music and the essence of the old, while, upon closer examination, the ideology is present in the societal structure which the music inhabits.

Rosenfeld's concept of new music finds its meaning in the music of Varèse, and it is no secret that the two were close friends. There is an account written by Varèse of his last conversation with Rosenfeld, a mere two days before the critic's death. Rosenfeld had wanted to set up a meeting with the composer over *un bon pot de vin* to discuss the centres of force and Varèse's concept of rhythm as an element of stability.[45] It was also in this conversation that Rosenfeld referred to a quotation from Ernest Renan, "Happy the man who carries a god within him, a living source, an ideal of beauty that he obeys".[46] Varèse recounts a rather tragic portion of the conversation:

> He then spoke to me of certain painful spiritual deceptions he had suffered, as well as demoralizing financial losses. "I feel that all these unpleasant experiences of the last decade have made it necessary for me to revise my scale of values and, moreover, in spite of the emotional anguish I went through during the war, I am almost grateful to it, for it acted as a very much needed filter.[47]

Varèse felt that Rosenfeld was entering into a new phase of his existence, finding a new lease on life and new ambition to continue living. Unfortunately, there would not be that meeting over wine to discuss the matters further. This account of the final conversation between the composer and the critic not only reveals the friendship between the two, but also reinforces the beliefs of Rosenfeld: that there is an inner god that only some have access to, that is a source of creativity beyond the banal and temporal.

Rosenfeld often wrote about Varèse, and often praised the work with such emotion rarely seen in critical writing. Speaking of Varèse and fellow composer Schoenberg, he described their work as, "the thinking introverted solitary against mass-movement in which the individual goes lost".[48] About Varèse's *Intégrales* (1926), Rosenfeld writes:

> [The elements of the music] were the tremendous masses of American life, crowds, city piles, colossal organizations; suddenly set moving, swinging, throbbing by the poet's dream; and glowing with a clean, daring, audacious and majestic life. Human power exulted anew in them. Majestic skyscraper chords, grandly resisting and moving volumes, ruddy sonorities and mastered ferocious outbursts cried it forth. For the first time in modern music ... it had something to do not with the hegemony of romantic Germany, but with the vast forms of the democratic, communistic New World.[49]

About *Arcana* (also by Varèse), Rosenfeld states: "For its impulse is not only ... desire to control and dominate an environment as it is found in scientists, technicians, and engineers [but] ... one of unity, or perfection, borne of a wholeness in the psyche and moving towards a condition satisfactory to the entire man".[50] In his writing on Varèse's *Ionization* (1931), Rosenfeld begins by discussing the increasing importance of percussion from the time of Mozart. He suggests that this increase is due to factors that include "skyscraper mysticism" and the astringent quality of modern life. The concept of "skyscraper mysticism" is one that Rosenfeld ascribes to Varèse. Through the barrage and the noise, akin to an alchemist, "[Varèse] is moved by the desire to unveil god-nature and its divine or diabolic springs".[51] And within an environment of concrete and immovable material, Varèse is still able to transcend his surroundings:

> The old antithesis between mind and matter has been proving more and more illusory; and Varèse ... would seem to have been standing before this new reality; finding it charged with emotion and generative of feelings of the relation between the forces known to physics and chemistry and those of the human psyche, and of ideas in the form of complexes and relations of the sounds and timbres of the instruments related to the whole realm of the semi-material.[52]

It is through the inhumanity of the music that one feels life, and that very inhumanity "somehow suggests the life of the inanimate universe".[53] And this article also contains a rare example of the passion of the critic, almost to the point of anger:

> It is a little work of genius, born of the evolving life of music and its means, and the spirit of an individual and an epoch, a credit to its mother and its father. And it is both an individual and an epoch that are being denied in the stupid, extreme, entirely undeserved neglect – the most stupid, extreme, and entirely undeserved of all that are being inflicted by the musical world upon any living composer – that is still the part of the brilliant composer of *Ionization*, of *Hyperprism* and *Intégrales* and *Arcana* and all the rest of his powerful music.[54]

For Rosenfeld, Varèse's music is a force against the hegemony of Romanticism, and is also a revelation of individual expression. The composer is trying to control and dominate an environment, but, through doing so, he taps into the spiritual. This transcendence of the surrounding is Varèse's utopian vision.

While Paul Rosenfeld is obviously not working on the side of the masses, as he seems to express elitism in his writings and surroundings (that is, of course, the context of classical music, an arena of the elite and, often, the wealthy), it can be argued that he is sympathetic to them. Rosenfeld's agenda is neither a political one nor an economic one, but a *human* one. In Kellner's description of Jameson's hermeneutic, the ideology is at the surface with the utopia beneath, whereas with the writings of Rosenfeld, the utopian vision is at the forefront with the ideology in the background. Rosenfeld might be synthesizing positive and negative aspects of the hermeneutic, creating a "complex" term (using Jameson's language).

Rudolphus Teeuwen provides a useful and concise overview of what Roland Barthes considers utopic that ties into Jameson's framework. He writes, "to Barthes, utopia becomes a private retreat in which the world cannot exercise its designs upon one, and the Neutral is the arsenal of strategies that allows one to absent oneself from the world's designs".[55] Though not clearly defined by Barthes, the "Neutral" designates "an escape from meaning". Teeuwen uses an example from Louis Hébert (who is, in turn, explaining Algirdas Greimas and Francis Rastier) to indicate this neutral: consider the terms "life" and "death" as two options; add to those options "life and death" (which is here called the "complex term", perhaps what Rosenfeld is doing by melding both ideology and utopia in the music of Edgard Varèse); finally, add the two negatives together as "neither life nor death", which is here called the "neutral term".[56] Teeuwen then draws from Frederic Jameson in explaining the idea of opposites (he uses the terms "for" and "against") and their relationship to their own opposites ("for" and "not against" as well as "against" and "not for"). Like the example of life and death, holding the terms "neither for nor against" means holding the neutral term. Jameson states that these two negatives:

> must neither be combined in some humanist organic synthesis [Varèse, perhaps], nor effaced and abandoned altogether: but retained and sharpened, made more virulent, their incompatibility and indeed their incommensurability *a scandal for the mind*, but a scandal that remains vivid and alive, and that cannot be thought away, either by resolving it or eliminating it: the biblical stumbling block, which gives Utopia its savor and its bitter freshness, when the thought of Utopias is still possible.[57]

Furthermore, about historical utopias, Jameson states, "all of our images of Utopia, all possible images of Utopia, will always be ideological and distorted by a point of view which cannot be corrected or even accounted for".[58] For Jameson, the question is whether there is the possibility of a "zero-degree utopia", something that is utopic for all.[59] And so, Jameson concludes,

> We must therefore conclude that the search for a minimal Utopian demand, a universally acknowledged zero degree of Utopian realization – even so seemingly obvious one as "that no one shall go hungry any more" – cannot escape the force field of ideology and class-situatedness. The fallback position, then, confronted with the multiplicity of Utopian concerns which we have discovered to be in violent opposition to each other, is evidently the pluralist one,

> in which we acknowledge the authenticity of the Utopian impulse invested in each option, no matter how distorted it may be, while at the same time seeking to identify its "moment of truth" and to isolate and appropriate its specific Utopian energy.[60]

Jameson's ideas emerge from his categorizations of postmodernity, which might be useful when considering U2's presentation in live performance in the early 1990s in particular. For Jameson, postmodernity is characterized by four elements: depthlessness or superficiality; lacking in affect and emotion; a loss of the sense of one's place in history; and technologies that are implosive, flattening or reproductive (rather than modernism's productive technologies).[61]

What, then, is U2's "moment of truth", if one agrees that there is no such thing as a "zero-degree utopia" in U2, or, at least, that such a thing is impossible? U2 cannot escape their own subject position. So, do U2 hold to the two negative positions? Do U2 act as a sort of neutral, a "scandal of the mind"? Jameson explains, "This neutral position does not seek to hold two substantive features, two positivities, together in the mind at once, but rather attempts to retain two negative or privative ones, along with their mutual negation of each other".[62]

Jameson suggests something helpful, to get U2 out of the mire of their own complicity:

> In postmodernity representation is not conceived as a dilemma but an impossibility, and what can be termed a kind of cynical reason in the realm of art displaces it by way of a multiplicity of images, none of which corresponds to "truth". I have argued elsewhere that such alleged relativism offers new and productive paths to history and to praxis; and there is no reason to fear that postmodern Utopias will not be as energizing in their new historical context as the older ones were in previous centuries.[63]

Thus, U2 are not bound to "truth", but one might still be able to locate a relative "moment of truth" in them.

Roland Barthes also defines the moment of truth in the novel: "Moment of truth = when the Thing itself is affected by the Affect; not imitation (realism) but affective coalescence".[64] In *Camera Lucida*, he explains what he means by the notion of "not imitation (realism)" in another medium:

> the realists do not take the photograph for a "copy" of reality, but for an emanation of past reality: a magic, not an art. To ask whether a photograph is analogical or coded is not a good means of analysis. The important thing is that the photograph possesses an *evidential force*, and that its testimony bears not on the object but on time.[65]

This is the "moment of truth" for Barthes in the photograph. U2's evidential force, what U2 are able to do "on time", is what is most important. One example of U2's "scandal for the mind" is the Product (RED) campaign, launched in 2006. The purpose of (RED) is to create awareness of the African AIDS epidemic, and to help to fight the disease and other ailments that affect the continent of Africa. Nathan Farrell describes the campaign as "a 'business model' and, moreover, as 'a simple idea that transforms our collective power as shoppers into a financial force that helps those affected by AIDS in Africa'".[66] (RED) works with partner companies, including such high-profile brands as Apple (Beats), Nike and Starbucks, to create products specially branded (and coloured) as Product (RED). A portion of the proceeds from those specially branded products (though small) goes towards the campaign to fight AIDS. Farrell, in discussing Bono's ability to advocate for this kind of "philanthrocapitalism", discusses two apparent opposing aspects of Bono's public persona, Bono-as-activist and Bono-as-rock-star, making Bono himself a "complex term".[67]

Teeuwen adds, "For Jameson, the Neutral is a call to utopian arms, a refusal of the compromise, humanism, transcendence, and irony (irony being a form of the 'both/and' of the complex term) that makes utopia a caricature of Hegelian synthesis". So, the Neutral is utopia for both Barthes and Jameson. He then concludes,

> Jameson wrote of the "biblical stumbling block" that the double negative of neither-nor threw in the way of the mind's efficient falling back upon known categories so as to keep the possibility of utopia in play; Barthes's Neutral is designed to be such a biblical stumbling block: a passage so contradictory and puzzling that it invites a prolonged, meditative attentiveness.[68]

This is where U2 shine, then: they are the contradiction and the puzzle. As neutral, U2 forbid the experience of transcendence. Teeuwen describes what it might have been like to listen to Barthes deliver his lectures on the Neutral, that there would have been a sense that one understood more than one actually understood. Barthes' lectures, Teeuwen suggests, were not all nonsense, nor were they completely understandable (at least to those listening). But they did invite "a prolonged, meditative attentiveness". Certainly during the *Zoo TV* tour, though not at all times during that tour, the band forebode transcendence. They wished the audience to be with them where they were and to linger there, or to *wallow* there. Consider Bono's invitation (as The Fly) to photographers in the front of the stage to take his picture: he poses for them specifically, cocking his head in a certain direction and moving his legs in another.

The audience is invited to accept the band as they are (as rock musicians and celebrities, rather than activists or as "authentic" or accessible people), and to participate in the band's complicity. Is this utopian? Certainly in the context of Jameson's utopia, what appears dystopian (the *Zoo TV* tour televisions, the stage as a science-fiction *Blade Runner*-esque landscape) can be read as neutral, and moving *towards* a zero-degree utopia.

It is useful to look at similarities between the approach taken by Eno and U2 in relation to concepts in the realm of the musical avant-garde, particularly in the music of Edgard Varèse. But in the music of Varèse, the question of oppression of the audience through sheer sound could be raised. Rosenfeld suggests that the noise is somewhat liberating, tapping into the realm of the immaterial within humanity. Well prior to the recording sessions for *Achtung Baby*, Eno was already disenfranchised with the recording studio as the "standardization of space", to use McLaughlin's term. The recording process had become particularly uninteresting for Eno, so he turned to the space of the recording for inspiration. McLaughlin writes, "he was interested in 'capturing' the peculiar 'quality' of rooms, and hence of emphasizing the specificity of space, place and sound often read as a symptom of postmodern culture".[69]

Similarly, the *Zoo TV* tour can be thought of as an assaultive barrage of the senses, seemingly oppressing the audience. U2's presentation can also be seen as an emancipating force, even if only an optimistic response to the pessimism of society towards the future and technological progress, and even if this optimism is veiled by sheer sensory overload. The *Zoo TV* tour, with its questioning of symbols and apparent contradictions, may seem like a reaction against the institutionalized industry of music, much like Varèse's music. Where Varèse is fighting the bourgeois tradition from within that infrastructure, U2 may be doing the same thing from within the arena of rock music and the concert spectacle.

In U2, the utopia is in the presentation, with its "skyscraper mysticism" pointing to an optimistic future. The contradictions are evident again with the appearance of the stage during the *Zoo TV* tour, seeming dystopian while conveying utopian ideas. The ideology may be the whole rock aesthetic, prompting the lead singer, Bono, to make fun of it by becoming the largest rock star possible, in his appropriation of the "Fly" persona. The problem lies in the *Zoo TV* tour's goal to obscure rather than reveal. But this may only provide the audience to question things further, reminiscent of Brechtian drama (again, perhaps influenced by the proximity of East Germany in the conception of the album). Perhaps the impulse of the *Zoo TV* tour is not only the desire to control and dominate an environment, but also one of unity or perfection, moving towards a condition satisfactory to the entire human race.

Pop

In March 1997, the band released *Pop*, an album that seemed to move the irony – and also the artifice – of the previous two albums to a new, higher degree. The album again showcases the band's politics (with tracks like 'Please') and their religion (songs like 'Mofo', 'If God Will Send His Angels', 'The Playboy Mansion' and 'Wake Up, Dead Man'). Richard S. Briggs notes that critics at the time recognized the high number of religious references in *Pop* as compared to many of the explicitly Christian recordings released in the so-called contemporary Christian music industry, "but since it did so in the tone of relentless despair, with a psalmist's harangue …, many Christians were rather nervous of embracing it".[70]

Pop reveals an interesting U2, both very honest and still veiled in mystery, featuring the largest television in history on their *PopMart* tour, but still assumedly trying to establish a personal connection with their audience. Andy Greene suggests that the "electronica-influenced disc" was either loved or hated by fans and critics, and that "it forced them to retreat back to a more traditional U2 sound for 2000's *All That You Can't Leave Behind*".[71] But Greene ignores Barney Hoskyns's review of the album in *Rolling Stone*, in which it was rated four out of five stars. Hoskyns writes, "What we can say immediately is that *Pop* sounds absolutely magnificent … the group has pieced together a record whose rhythms, textures and visceral guitar mayhem make for a thrilling roller-coaster ride".[72]

Sean Sennett suggests that *Pop* and, in particular, the *PopMart* tour that accompanied it, relied on the music, "albeit against the pure spectacle that is the world's largest TV screen" at the time.[73] The Edge states, "People talk about how U2 reinvented themselves and evolved beyond recognition, but the core of what we do, the essence of our beliefs and the driving force behind the band, is exactly the same as it was when we started out. If there has been an evolution, it's been because of experience and openness".[74] Clayton adds that the band does not see themselves as a "university", which is at odds with how many people think the band functions.[75] Clayton is referring to the various visual artists with whom U2 collaborate from time to time. During the *PopMart* tour, the band use animated versions of "pop art" by artists such as Roy Lichtenstein and Keith Haring, and the band's promotional music videos feature writers Allen Ginsberg and William Burroughs.

It is unclear if *Pop* forced the band to "retreat back to a more traditional U2 sound", as Greene suggests. It could be argued that the three albums released in the 1990s did much to create a new U2 aesthetic; the band at that point in its history could be as easily identified with the mass mediation of the 1990s as it could with the Americana and "authenticity" in activism of the earlier work in the 1980s. If anything, *All That You Can't Leave Behind* could be considered a synthesis of what came before: it was a new brand of U2, "activist" perhaps, religious, certainly, but not necessarily more "authentic". They just appear that way.

Notes

1. Beats 1 on Apple Music, "U2 and Zane Lowe on Beats 1", *YouTube* (20 July 2017); available from https://www.youtube.com/watch?v=vsKZ3YrF_3Q (accessed 30 July 2018).
2. Brian Eno, "Bringing Up Baby: A Behind-the-Scenes Look at the Making of U2's New Album", *Rolling Stone* 618 (28 November 1991), 48.
3. Ibid.
4. Elysa Gardner, "U2: Achtung, Baby", *Rolling Stone* (9 January 1992); available from https://www.rollingstone.com/music/albumreviews/achtung-baby-19920109 (accessed 1 February 2018).
5. Jon Pareles, "RECORDINGS VIEW; U2 Takes a Turn from the Universal to the Domestic", *New York Times* (17 November 1991); available from https://tinyurl.com/NYT-1991-11-17-arts (accessed 1 February 2018).
6. Stephen Catanzarite, *U2's Achtung Baby: Meditations on Love in the Shadow of the Fall* (New York: Bloomsbury, 2007), xiv.
7. These ideas first appear in Nicholas Greco, "The Berlin Wall: Bowie, U2 and the 'Urban Real'", in *Culture of Cities: ...Under Construction*, edited by P. Moore and M. Risk (Oakville, ON: Mosaic Press, 2001), 92–94.
8. Sharon Zukin, *Landscapes of Power: From Detroit to Disneyland* (Berkeley: University of California Press, 1991), 191.
9. Caroline Dumoucel, "The Catastrophes Issue: Paul Virilio", *Vice* (1 September 2010), translated by Pauline Eiferman; available from https://www.vice.com/en_ca/article/qbzbn5/paul-virilio-506-v17n9 (accessed 1 September 2018).
10. Zukin, *Landscapes of Power*, 204–205.
11. Beth Nabi, "Every Poet is a Thief: Bono Channels Rilke in 'Oh Berlin'", *BethandBono.com* (1 November 2011); available from http://bethandbono.com/2011/11/01/every-angel-is-terror-every-poet-is-a-thief/ (accessed 27 June 2018).
12. Walter Benjamin, "M", in *The Arcades Project*, edited by Howard Eiland and Kevin McLaughlin (Cambridge: The Belknap Press of Harvard University Press, 1999), 420–21.
13. Ibid., 422. The *flâneur* is a male figure in Benjamin. The female equivalent would be the *flâneuse*.
14. Ibid., 433.
15. Anke Gleber, "Flanerie, or The Redemption of Visual Reality", in *The Art of Taking a Walk: Flanerie, Literature, and Film in Weimar Culture* (Princeton, NJ: Princeton University Press, 1999), 152.
16. Bill Flanagan, *U2 at the End of the World* (New York: Delta, 1995), 149.
17. David Fricke, "U2 Finds What It's Looking For", *Rolling Stone* 640 (1 October 1992), 42.
18. Flanagan, *U2 at the End of the World*, 266.
19. Brian Clark, "U2 – Egos and Icons '97 – Part 4 of 7". *YouTube* (9 February 2008); available from https://www.youtube.com/watch?v=a7FHPlw1JK8 (accessed 31 July 2018).

20. Noel McLaughlin, "Bono! Do You Ever Take Those Wretched Sunglasses Off?: U2 and the Performance of Irishness", *Popular Music History* 4.3 (2009): 320–23. McLaughlin also suggests that a postcolonial approach would be more useful in analysing this period of U2's history, rather than a more attractive postmodern approach.

21. Niall Stokes, *Into the Heart* (London: Carlton Books, 1996), 111.

22. Anthony DeCurtis, "U2: Zooropa", *Rolling Stone* (5 July 1993); available from https://www.rollingstone.com/music/albumreviews/zooropa-19930705 (accessed 9 February 2018).

23. Andy Greene, "Watch U2 Play 'Zooropa' for Syrian Refugees at European Tour Launch", *Rolling Stone* (5 September 2015); available from https://tinyurl.com/U2-2015 0905 (accessed 9 February 2018).

24. Perhaps U2 were trying to relive the days when they were unwittingly associated with Republican forces in Northern Ireland.

25. Stokes, *Into the Heart*, 116.

26. Ibid., 134.

27. Ibid., 138.

28. Bill Graham, "PASSENGERS: ORIGINAL SOUNDTRACKS 1", *Hot Press* (15 November 1995); available from https://www.atu2.com/news/passengers-original-soundtracks-1.html (accessed 11 February 2018).

29. David Browne, "Original Soundtracks 1", *Entertainment Weekly* (10 November 1995); available from http://ew.com/article/1995/11/10/original-soundtracks-1/ (accessed 11 February 2018).

30. Jon Pareles, "Pop Briefs: PASSENGERS: 'ORIGINAL SOUNDTRACKS 1' Island", *New York Times* (19 November 1995); available from http://www.nytimes.com/1995/11/19/arts/pop-briefs-048070.html (accessed 11 February 2018).

31. Paul Rosenfeld, *Musical Impressions: Selections from Paul Rosenfeld's Criticism*, edited by Herbert A. Leibowitz (London: George Allen & Unwin, 1969), 283.

32. David Toop, *Ocean of Sound: Aether Talk, Ambient Sound and Imaginary Worlds* (London: Serpent's Tail, 1995), 82–84.

33. Rosenfeld, *Musical Impressions*, 278.

34. Ibid., 283.

35. Paul Rosenfeld, *Port of New York: Essays on Fourteen American Moderns* (Urbana, IL: University of Illinois Press, 1961), xxxviii.

36. Ibid., xxxviii–xxxix.

37. Paul Rosenfeld, *By Way of Art* (Freeport: Books for Libraries Press Inc., 1967), 304.

38. Ibid., 307.

39. Paul Rosenfeld, "Monteverde", in *Discoveries of a Music Critic* (New York: Harcourt Brace, 1936), 21.

40. Ibid., 22.

41. Ibid., 22–23.

42. Ibid., 23.

43. Ibid., 28.

44. Douglas Kellner, "Marxist Criticism", in *Encyclopedia of Contemporary Literary Theory: Approaches, Scholars, Terms*, edited by Irena R. Makaryk (Toronto: University of Toronto Press, 1993), 97.

45. Edgard Varèse, "Wine of Good Omen", in *Paul Rosenfeld: Voyager in the Arts* (New York: Creative Age Press Inc., 1948), 237.
46. Ibid., 238.
47. Ibid.
48. Rosenfeld, *By Way of Art*, 58.
49. Ibid., 64.
50. Rosenfeld, *Musical Impressions*, 278.
51. Ibid., 283.
52. Ibid.
53. Ibid., 284.
54. Ibid., 285.
55. Rudolphus Teeuwen, "An Epoch of Rest: Roland Barthes's 'Neutral' and the Utopia of Weariness", *Cultural Critique* 80 (Winter 2012): 1–2.
56. Ibid., 2.
57. Frederic Jameson, *Archaeologies of the Future: The Desire Called Utopia and Other Science Fictions* (London: Verso, 2005), 180. Emphasis added.
58. Ibid., 171.
59. Ibid., 172.
60. Ibid., 175.
61. George Ritzer and Jeffrey Stepnisky, *Sociological Theory*, 9th ed. (New York: McGraw Hill, 2014), 629–33.
62. Jameson, *Archaeologies of the Future*, 180.
63. Ibid., 212.
64. Roland Barthes, *The Preparation of the Novel: Lecture Courses and Seminars at the Collège de France (1978–1979 and 1979–1980)*, translated by Kate Briggs (New York: Columbia University Press, 2011), 107.
65. Roland Barthes, *Camera Lucida: Reflections on Photography*, translated by Richard Howard (New York: Hill and Wang, 1981), 88–89. Emphasis added.
66. Nathan Farrell, "Celebrity Politics: Bono, Product (RED) and the Legitimising of Philanthrocapitalism", *British Journal of Politics and International Relations* 14 (2012): 396.
67. Ibid., 397. It should be noted that even (RED) seems to be at least a complex term, though the way it is presented by Farrell would point towards (RED) as being neutral: "As a relatively new form of corporate philanthropy (RED) occupies a grey area between charity initiative and business venture, between philanthropy and cause-related marketing" (398). (RED) is not a charity.
68. Teeuwen, "An Epoch of Rest", 8.
69. Noel McLaughlin, "Another Green World?": Eno, Ireland and U2", *Popular Music History* 9.2 (2014): 181.
70. Richard S. Briggs, "Sarajevo and the Popmart Lemon: The Fractured Form and Function of U2's Walk through the Valley of the Shadow of Death", in *U2 and the Religious Impulse: Take Me Higher*, edited by Scott Calhoun (London: Bloomsbury, 2018), 76.
71. Andy Greene, "U2's 'Pop': A Reimagining of the Album 20 Years Later", *Rolling Stone* (14 March 2017); available from https://tinyurl.com/w471642 (accessed 11 February 2018).
72. Barney Hoskyns, "U2: Pop", *Rolling Stone* (20 March 1997); available from https://www.rollingstone.com/music/albumreviews/pop-19970320 (accessed 11 February 2018).

73. Sean Sennett, "U2: Making Music to Blow their Minds", in *Off the Record: 25 Years of Music Street Press*, edited by Sean Sennett and Simon Groth (St Lucia: University of Queensland Press, 2010), 246.
74. Ibid., 252.
75. Ibid., 249.

3 Beautiful Day: Technological Optimism, Gesture and Intimacy

U2's first album, *Boy*, includes the song 'Into the Heart', an exploration of nostalgia and memory. In the song, the narrator expresses the desire of going 'Into the Heart' of a child, and how this might be possible. For the tour in support of the album *All That You Can't Leave Behind*, released in 2000, the band constructed a walkway that extended out into the crowd and surrounded the stage. The band sold tickets for purchase that allowed fans to be *in* the perimeter of the heart, literally 'Into the Heart'. Other promotional imagery during this period used a heart in a suitcase, evoking ideas of movement (again) and travel.

These ideas are reinforced in the cover art of *All That You Can't Leave Behind*, which features the band standing in an airport with guitar cases and bags surrounding them. It appears that they are waiting to travel. Above the band on a sign (presumably used to inform travellers of delays or similar) is the figure "J33-3". Michael J. Gilmour states that this is a biblical reference:

> One biographer observes that during the 1970s "some members of charismatic prayer groups used those figures as a code for prayer, based on Jeremiah 33:3 [which states, "Call to me and I will answer you, and will tell you great and hidden things that you have not known"] ... Confronted with this discovery by a journalist, Bono responded sheepishly, "Yeah. It's, like, God's phone number".[1]

So the religious impulse is clearly informing the work, even if the impulse is in the form of a puzzle on the cover. But the band also reveal this religious impulse more explicitly in concert: at the end of 'Walk On', which would close the live show during the *Elevation* tour, the band would add the refrain of "hallelujah", repeating the word until the conclusion of the song and their exit.

The album provides many recognizable singles that have become a part of the band's "hit" canon: 'Beautiful Day', in particular, has become an anthem of sorts for sports teams and politicians. The song won three Grammy Awards in 2001, including "Record of the Year" and "Song of the Year". Robert Hilburn writes of the album, "U2 reinvents itself yet again, but this time the band has jettisoned experiments in electronica and irony, and rediscovered its own identity".[2] It seemed a return to form for the band, a return from some sort of self-induced exile into irony and electronica that seemed to confuse its audience. The album provided accessible radio singles – 'Beautiful Day' and 'Walk On', in particular – after many years of arguably challenging material. James Hunter writes, "*All That You Can't Leave Behind* gets serious about simplicity. The songs aren't obscured by excessive production, but the band doesn't commit the common sin of boring people silly in the name of scaling back ... U2 are no longer idealistic kids".[3] This points to one of the transformations of the band at the start of this third period of their career: the band return to what might be perceived as a more "authentic" sound and presentation, scaling down their production, including the look and content of their live performances. But, as Hunter suggests, the band are no longer idealists: rather, the band are more experienced. *All That You Can't Leave Behind* becomes the first album of a new transformed – and newly transformative – U2. This is a band that again recognize their potential as agents of change, and a band that have a renewed moral impulse. Songs like 'Peace on Earth' and 'When I Look at the World' seem to convey an agenda for the band that perhaps was always attributed to those early idealists, but never to a group of people that wield real power (even if this is only in the form of influence or cultural capital). In the former song, Bono sings about the abilities of a higher power to bring peace to conflict. Fundamentally, the band are different than they were before this point because of their position and power as celebrities.

In 'When I Look at the World', the narrator asks the listener how they might look at the world, and how they see the world around them. The narrator then attempts to be empathetic, though they ultimately fail. This might be the admission of someone who experiences first-hand the challenges of relativity or perspective. But then the narrator describes how the world looks through their own U2-coloured glasses, so to speak. They contrast how the world is (or how others see it) with how they (and, perhaps, by extension, the band) see the world: affected by the power of individuals who are full of empathy. But, as the narrator realizes early on, empathy is not enough; there needs to be the formation of true community as well, not just the empathy of individuals. In the place of the narrator, Bono's world is one of a community that strives to see the world through each other's eyes. In describing this view, he seems to be inviting his listeners to share this view as well, to see the world through *his* eyes. He stresses the importance of this idea, suggesting that he is unable to wait for all to adopt this view of the world. This project is urgent.

Through the lyrics of 'When I Look at the World', Bono suggests that the song is written from the point of view of someone who is struggling with faith; it is unclear if Bono is speaking about faith in some generic sense of God, or faith in Jesus Christ, or a faith in some other higher power, or perhaps faith in the goodness of humanity. The narrator of the song looks to a person who is, in fact, not struggling in their faith. Rather, their faith is unmovable even in the face of violence. Bono suggests that *he* can be the figure that the person is looking to for support. Elsewhere, Bono states, "I'm amazed at people's ability to sacrifice for each other. I'm amazed at how people can show love where it's not expected and how love can conjoin disparate groups".[4] Bono suggests that, while he was shaken by violence in his upbringing – and the continued violence of "The Troubles" – his faith was never shaken because he recognized that evil exists. Bono believes that, in the face of that evil, humanity has the potential to act in extraordinary ways. The narrator of the song, though, has some trouble with this, and the fact that the person to whom the narrator is speaking is somehow unshaken in their faith is a source of *annoyance*.

The narrator (Bono?) seems to approach institutional religion in a less than positive manner. It might be that he is pointing specifically to the rush to judgement that many religious people display. For instance, he might be calling attention to behaviours such as the reluctance of some evangelical Christians or Christian groups to commit resources to those suffering with AIDS, with the justification that the disease is a result of some error or "sin" on the part of the sufferer. Bono refers to "bread" and "wine" and "smoke", three markers of institutionalized Christianity, specifically Roman Catholicism: he makes a blatant reference to the Eucharist. In fact, it would have only been more explicit if Bono had referred to the body and blood of Christ rather than the bread and wine, the pre-consecrated species that are not yet the holy substance of the real presence of Jesus. Bono's "smoke" might be the incense burned during Roman Catholic Mass, a symbol of the prayers of the people going up to Heaven. It can also evoke a sort of cleansing ritual. When Bono mentions it, though, the smoke does not result in prayers or purity; rather, the people are unable to breathe.[5]

About the smoke that the lyrics describe, Bono clarifies that he intends it not to come from a church at all.

> I don't know why it is set in a hospital waiting-room in the days when people could smoke in such places. It is so heavy, I can hardly think about it. It could almost be the voice of my father, looking at me. The glower. The put-down. But that is the thing that runs through that album, that gives it its cohesiveness, the ring of truth, connecting with what was going on in my life, connecting to my father and to my mother, which is probably what it all really comes back to, because I haven't been in a waiting room filled with smoke since I was fourteen years old.[6]

Of course, the waiting room of the lyrics could refer to the world and one's life in it. Generally, in Christian belief, one is not meant to live primarily for the things of the present world. Rather, one should be looking forward to the world to come after death: "Do not store up for yourselves treasures on earth, where moth and rust consume and where thieves break in and steal; but store up for yourselves treasures in heaven, where neither moth nor rust consumes and where thieves do not break in and steal. For where your treasure is, there your heart will be also" (Matthew 6:19-21). Bono uses the song not *only* as an instruction for his listeners to look at the world through his own eyes, but as a sort of mirror in order to critique his own position in the world. It is not that Bono is somehow struggling with his faith *here*, but rather, he understands the plight of those whose faith has been shaken. 'When I Look at the World' is a study of empathy for Bono *and* for his listeners even while it acknowledges that one is unable to be empathetic. And Bono seems to want for humanity to join together in this empathy, though they might be disparate; he wants humanity to be empathetic in the face of forces that want them to avoid being empathetic, even if that force is from within. It is an interesting contradiction. Blogger Beth Nabi, recounting her meeting with Bono in 2014, makes the following profound statement: "It's not megalomania steering Bono through the room from fan to fan; it's empathy. It was obvious how important it was for him that every fan get his or her moment".[7]

Before the band released their next album in 2004, they released two concert films, *Elevation 2001: Live from Boston* (in November 2001) and *U2 Go Home: Live from Slane Castle, Ireland* (in November 2003). U2 also released the second comprehensive compilation of their music, *The Best of 1990–2000*, in November 2002. The first major compilation was *The Best of 1980–1990*, released in November 1998.

'Beautiful Day'

The video for 'Beautiful Day' begins with an image of a beautiful blue sky, with passing clouds and a bright sun. The viewer then sees Bono singing, with an extreme close-up of his face. Intercut are images of Bono wandering around the grounds of what appears to be a major airport, in one instance throwing what appears to be money to a passing car. He is also shown entering the airport through a revolving door. As the song reaches the chorus, Bono is joined by the rest of the band. They are all featured performing in a darker environment (most probably, a section of the airport terminal at night). It is notable here that Bono uses what can be read as sexual gestures, in the form of pelvic thrusts, while continuing to sing directly into the camera, as if directly to the viewer. As the song continues, Bono is shown singing in the darker environment (with the band), interspersed with shots of him being mischievous with various airport travellers. Importantly, there are many images of the airport structure itself; the terminal's design evokes the various elements of an aeroplane, such as the wings, the tail, and so on. All four members of the band are shown entering the airport through the revolving door, the same one that Bono had entered earlier in the video. Members of the band are even depicted carrying their luggage through an airport security checkpoint, during which their luggage is screened and inspected through an x-ray machine.

During the segment of the song that would be called the "bridge", three distinct images are cycled through: a young couple is shown in a close-up, passionately kissing; the beautiful sky is featured; and Bono is shown wandering the airport, stealing a woman's apple and lying on a luggage conveyor belt. During what might be called the video's "third act", the band are shown performing on the runway in full daylight, apparently in the direct path of arriving and departing planes. There are also images of the band simply walking on the runway, culminating with Bono himself running towards the camera while on the runway. Finally, the young couple (first shown in the bridge section) continues to kiss, and Bono is shown jumping into the air on the runway, as if he, himself, is taking flight.

There are some interesting formal distinctions which can be made when observing this video. Bono is featured in what can be considered various guises or personae. There is the "roaming" Bono, wandering the airport and its environs. There is the "mischievous" Bono, stealing a departing passenger's bag and apple. Finally, there is the "performing" Bono, who interacts directly with the camera. These various versions of Bono also correlate to specific musical sections of the song: "roaming" and "mischievous" Bono are active during the verses and bridge of the song. In the chorus of the song, "performing" Bono is featured, as are the other members of the band (although they are also featured briefly in other parts of the video).[8]

There are three ways to read the 'Beautiful Day' video by U2. It can be read as a kind of encouragement to see the beautiful in an increasingly technological and "cold" society. If one takes into account U2's history of appreciation of technology (consider the band's use of televisions and video technology in the tours of the 1990s), then a slightly different second reading emerges. U2 seem to encourage an optimistic reception of technology and modern architecture. Finally, when analysing the video from the viewpoint of gesture and intimacy, there are certain familiar gestures, such as Bono's physical interaction with the camera (holding it with his hands or gazing into it in extreme close-up), which contribute to the general "structure of feeling" of the video.

For the release of the first single from *All That You Can't Leave Behind*, U2 filmed a promotional video, directed by Jonas Åkerlund, in Airport Terminal 2F of Charles de Gaulle airport in Paris. In this environment of steel and glass, with much of the structure resembling an aeroplane, the band are shown playing the song and wandering on the runway. The lyrics of the song convey optimism while also recognizing failure: in the lyrics, the narrator sings that he hopes that he is not perceived as being hopeless, incapable of improvement. The lyrics also address the attraction of industry and the urban condition: the lyrics refer to the colours and wonderful sights of nature, the beauty of other foreign countries (the narrator mentions China), the devastating effects of over-fishing, and a contrast between oil fields and nomadic Bedouin people. Finally, the lyrics speak of the biblical flood that eliminated most of humanity (except for the righteous Noah and his family), but as the water receded, the beauty of the rainbow was revealed.

These lyrics are suggestive of a critique of the contemporary state of the world, with specific reference to the destruction of dolphins which has accompanied the harvest of tuna fish, while also making reference to non-technological images such as the Bedouin people's fires, and canyons. Among these references to nature, Bono includes the oil fields at sunrise. In a way, these elements of the material world become performers in the video, including the sun, clouds and blue sky featured during the bridge section of the song. As Carol Vernallis states, "With music video we track the play of light and shadow against sound".[9] In a musical sense, the accompanying tonal structure (mostly in a major key, in a rather upbeat song) would support the reading of these lyrics as being positive. The lyrics seem to suggest a tenuous relationship between nature and technology. After all, in a contemporary world in which creation care is a popular discourse, oil fields can signify the unbridled harvesting of the planet's resources with the result of further polluting it through carbon emissions. Oil fields also point to so-called "big oil", the faceless corporations that control gasoline production and distribution, which seem to have a relationship to governments that hope to secure oil reserves by the use of military force, if necessary (even if this relationship is completely false). The images in the music video, though, counter such a reading: the modernist architecture of the airport – a stand-in for technology (and, perhaps, the oil fields) – is embraced by the band. The sun shining during the beautiful day of the video shines on the glass and steel of the airport.

The Airport Terminal 2F at Charles de Gaulle airport was completed in 1996 and was one of many additions to Paris's major airport. The task of designing the airport was given to architect Paul Andreu, who is the head of the ADP, the group in charge of France's airport development. When the Charles de Gaulle airport was first conceived (to be built in the early 1970s), the team of architects working under Andreu would have needed to think of the airport as a sort of arriving and departing machine, being one of the busiest airports in the world. Andreu states, "In a good airport, you get to your plane without being lost and exhausted. Also the airport should not be a disturbing experience. An airport is a place where you follow signs. But at the same time my goal is to give you freedom ... A good airport is beyond a building; it is a landscape".[10] An airport can be seen as a model of efficiency and speed, and perhaps this notion is reflected in the building materials of the terminal. The steel and glass are "pure" and "clean" materials, antiseptic and, perhaps, cold. Why did U2 choose this architectural site for their video? Why is this somewhat positive song set in what can be read as a cold and unfeeling environment?

Bono's playful actions and gestures serve to transform the cold space into an intimate one. Michael Saenz, in his article "Television Viewing as a Cultural Practice", suggests that the television viewer gains a general sense of cultural reality and experience from the medium. He explains,

> In the "generalized culture" promoted by television ... narrative events and meanings are likewise changed from particulars into signs – signs for moral speculation, signs of motivation, signs of how to represent. These signs are thought of as "capable of coding all behavior", hence the medium's apparent scope and inclusiveness.[11]

In other words, television suggests to the viewer how to act and how to feel. U2 choose this particular architectural site for their promotional video, presumably because they enjoy the design. Perhaps they also wish to counteract the reading of the environment as being cold and sterile. The clean, perhaps antiseptic, nature of the airport might be read in a more positive fashion: the airport is an example of the pinnacle of efficiency, as a "machine" for receiving travellers and quickly sending them on their way. U2 may be drawing from an older tradition of a kind of "grand era" of architecture (Zukin's railway stations and factories which are imbued with rich histories, and an "aura of the 'sublime'"). Arguably, the modernist wonder of transport – the sheer power of moving people through a transportation hub – has been lost. This is not only due to the destruction of many of these older urban sites, but also due to the opinion of many that the processing of travellers through transportation hubs is more akin to the herding of cattle: transportation is inhumane. Though it might be necessary to travel in an increasingly globalized world, it is something to be avoided unless absolutely necessary. There is nothing *human* about it. U2 might be suggesting that the modern monument of efficiency in the form of the glass and steel terminal of the airport, either evokes the historical past or establishes anew the "grand era" of optimism in human progress (a particularly modernist ideal in a postmodern world). And this new "grand era" could also be a "human" (humane) one.

Towards the end of the video, the band are featured performing on the runway, seemingly in the path of arriving and departing planes. The repetition of their arrivals and departures creates an interesting effect. Sean Cubitt suggests that (televisual) repetition can act in two ways: as a "mechanism for diffusing excitation in the system"; and as "an aesthetic device [that] can become extremely anxiety inducing as well".[12] Therefore, the constant images of the planes arriving and departing over the heads of the band members causes excitement in the viewer, by feeding off the beginning of the aggressive chorus immediately following a mellow bridge. But the repetition of the coming and going of the planes also signals a potential danger to these beloved celebrities (even if the band are not actually in any danger, or, in fact, in the path of planes at all). This repetition also creates a sense of anxiety. How can they perform like this? Can they hear themselves, and are they not afraid of the planes? Like the performance space in a darkened airport lounge, or the idea of a runway as a stage, Vernallis identifies these as "hybrid spaces" in Åkerlund's *oeuvre*.[13] These questions, and ultimately, this anxiety, is resolved with the final scenes of the roaming Bono running along the runway and jumping in the air, perhaps as a human plane departing the airport. This final resolution also gives a sense of peaceful closure, and yet another element contributing to the optimistic character of the video.

U2 have had a history of conveying a sense of optimism towards technological development, a history that supports a reading of the video as an optimistic view of the urban condition. If one takes into account this rich history of U2's acceptance and embracing of modern technology (particularly in live performance), and a positive view of the modern city and urban condition, perhaps the reading of the 'Beautiful Day' video as an optimistic view of supposed cold and sterile modern architecture (and the greater technological advances to which the particular airport design points) is a viable one. Nevertheless, the band, though mediated, move beyond the technology to connect with the audience.

Gesture

Keith Thomas explores the notion of gesture, which is defined as "a significant movement of limb or body" or "use of such movements as expression of feeling or rhetorical device". Of course, Thomas points out that the body can transmit messages through its lack of gesture as well. He states that "The human body, in short, is as much a historical document as a charter or a diary or a parish register ... and it deserves to be studied accordingly".[14]

Thomas continues by suggesting that historically, gesture referred to the general carriage of the body, and that the study of gesture is nothing new. Most modern writing on gesture, however, assumes that it does not constitute a universal language, but rather that gesture is largely a product of social and cultural differences. Recent writing on gesture concerns itself with the study of communicative body movements, or kinesics. Linguists have suggested that gesture can be a language of its own, or is actually pre-lingual, and have tried to "document" gesture with corresponding meaning, resulting in sorts of "dictionaries". Gesture also delineates such characteristics as moral conviction: bodily feature was a symptom of the inner life of the soul. In studying the past, much may be gleaned in order to understand the present. Thomas sums the worth of the study of gesture in this sentence: "To interpret and account for a gesture is to unlock the whole social and cultural system of which it is a part".[15]

If gesture has been historically perceived as the marker of an internal character, it follows that Bono's use of gesture in order to cultivate intimacy reflects an inner desire for the creation of an "arms-length" community (appropriately labelled because of the use of gesture in its cultivation). Bono's inner morality – his belief in what phenomenologist Edith Stein calls "fellow-feeling" – is directly evoked in his cultivation of intimacy.[16] Viewers who recognize U2 in various videos because of common gestures become part of an imagined community of U2 fans. Conceivably, the viewers are now *with* others in spirit, and perhaps then open to sharing in the same moral character of the band, open to empathy *with* others, empathy in community. Of course, Bono can also be read as a foil to all of this.

One way in which U2's gestures have been decoded is by considering Bono as a dandy. Lynn Ramert calls Bono a dandy in the vein of the Irish writer Oscar Wilde. Bono shares some traits with Wilde, who was "artificial, effeminate, arrogant, classless, self-centered, hedonistic, aesthetic, performative, and paradoxical" as a dandy.[17] Drawing from Glick, Lane and Halberstam, Lynn Ramert states that the dandy "actually serves as a sort of foil for his time, pointing out hypocrisies and the social climate by testing boundaries".[18]

While Ramert suggests that Bono's use of gesture serves as a foil, Bono seems to act as a foil *for himself*. Bono often uses gesture to both connect with his audience (through the various ways in which he interacts with cameras in live performance) and to distance himself from them (an example would be his use of various personae, including The Fly). During U2 concerts, notably since the *Zoo TV* tour, the band have had to utilize large television screens to aid the audience in seeing them (or, cleverly, to *conceal* them). This move was due to the fact that they were now performing in larger venues to larger audiences, with the stage being a great distance away from fans in cheaper seats, not to mention the need (and desire) for a more spectacular visual manifestation for the band. Their tours have incorporated the theme of television (especially in the case of the *Zoo TV* tour, where an explicit theme was "Watch More TV", and which featured Bono flipping through local television channels on the stage screens during concert stops on tour), while the *PopMart* tour featured a stage backdrop consisting of the world's largest television (at the time). Since the band's performances were always subject to (their own) cameras, Bono would often approach and "play" with them. For instance, a camera would be placed at the end of a large crane, or "boom" (which allows the camera operator to swing it up and over the crowd for a more dynamic shot). Bono would often grab the sides of the camera apparatus and sing while looking directly into the lens, causing his entire face to fill the receiving television screens. In other words, Bono would become intimate with the audience, and though mediated, would get as "close" to the audience as he could.

In contrast, Bono has also used gesture to alienate himself from the audience. This is most prevalent in Bono's appropriation of The Fly persona during the *Zoo TV* tour. Bono, clad in shiny black leather trousers and jacket wearing large "bug-eye" sunglasses, would pose for press photographers congregating at the front of the stage. His gestures embody (and mock) the stereotypes of *machismo*, as he would pose, run his hands through his greased hair, and sweat profusely, aided by his black leather jacket and pants. The Fly is an egomaniac; his posing for the cameras makes him the ultimate rock star, posing not for the audience but for the press near the stage. Presumably, his attention is not always on his performance to the paying audience, but on his performance to the cameras; The Fly is primarily concerned with his image to be photographed.

Some of these gestures have continued through the years. Bono has continued to play with cameras, actually placing his sunglasses over a camera lens during the *PopMart* tour. These gestures continue in the video for 'Beautiful Day' and contribute to the video's sense of playfulness. When the band are featured on the runway, the first shot is a pull-back upwards from Bono's face, a shot probably achieved by the use of a crane as described above, with the singer grabbing the apparatus around the lens of the camera and pushing it upwards. As for other bodily gestures in the music video, his repeated pelvic thrusts towards the camera could be thought of as an inherent part of the rock aesthetic. The preponderance of sexual gestures in rock is a grand tradition, with performers such as Elvis Presley, Robert Plant from Led Zeppelin and even Michael Jackson (a far from exhaustive list) contributing to this aesthetic by their gestures. Plus, it seems something that The Fly would do.

On the other hand, Bono's gestures can be thought of as melodramatic because of their exaggerated nature, but not pejorative or selfish (if one may read The Fly as such from his narcissistic gestures). Lynn Joyrich would suggest that such gestures are far from alienating: "Melodrama allows us both closeness and certainty through its appeal to a prelinguistic system of gesture and tableaux that aims beyond language to immediate understanding. In its attempt to render meaning visible and recapture the ineffable, melodrama emphasizes gestures, postures, frozen moments and expressions".[19] If Joyrich's definition of melodrama can be applied to these playful gestures, then Bono's movements can be thought of as creating a kind of direct prelinguistic link with the audience. Instead of the audience being alienated, they become linked, or intimate.

To further problematize Bono's gestures, McLaughlin states that through his transformation into The Fly persona, "Bono was able to perform the explicitly (hetero)sexual and authentic male rock star as a necessary masquerade, overtly sexualizing the apparently sexless paradigm of Irish rock stars".[20]

Television

The music video is a form of media programming that found its first exposure on television as a way to further promote the music being released (thus the moniker of "promotional music video"). Vernallis, though, suggests that this definition of music video, as "a product of the record company in which images are put to a recorded pop song in order to sell the song", is no longer an accurate description of the medium. On the one hand, she suggests that a possible (if too broad) definition might be "a relation of sound and image that we recognize as such". On the other hand, music videos might share a number of features while being quite different: Vernallis uses the phrase "made up of family resemblances". She continues by suggesting that there is a *relationship* between the music and images, resulting in the video as a "new hyper-being".[21] At the time of the release of 'Beautiful Day', the format of the music video was still featured on networks (MuchMusic in Canada and MTV in the United States, for instance). These channels based their programming on the free promotional material. Television and the ways that images on television work, then, are of fundamental importance in the discussion of this video. It functions, at least in part, as an advertisement for the band.

Robert Shayon suggests that "The mass media are phenomena that transcend even the broad worlds of literature. They call for the discovery of new laws, new relationships, new insights into drama, ritual and mythology".[22] Television is important because of its ability to bring a mass audience in relationship with a specific set of values. These attitudes and values are engrained in the dramatic presentations on television, and therefore, Horace Newcomb suggests "an aesthetic understanding of television is crucial". He presents three elements which "process and unite ... other aspects of the television aesthetic".[23] These elements are intimacy, continuity and history. Much of this discussion of television seems to be of its time, that is, when televisual content was of particular cultural import because of its central position as an appliance in the home. But it is not difficult to transplant the ideas that Newcomb and others explore in television theory to more recent television-like media. For instance, the online site YouTube is currently the most common place for a viewer to engage with promotional music videos. Streaming services like Apple Music also act as a portal for consumers to access musicians' artistic output, including video.

By intimacy, Newcomb is both referring to the size of television itself, allowing the placement of the device in any room of the house and often in any location, and also to the notion that the acted dramas presented on television become very much the viewer's own. In a post-television world, this idea is even more pronounced. For the most part, the screens upon which the material appears are small, accessible and ubiquitous. These screens are not only available in the home but in the pocket! The contemporary fan has access to their favourite music (both audio and video) literally at their fingertips. Newcomb states, "its presence brings people into the viewer's home to act our dramas".[24] Newcomb suggests that, in television, importance is not placed on action but rather on reaction to that action, or, in other words, a human response. Newcomb gives the example of Alistair Cooke who, during an episode of the documentary television series *America: A Personal History* (BBC, 1972), provides the television viewer with his personal history, by demonstrating the splendour of autumn in New England. Cooke describes his own journey of change and development, analogous with the changing colour of the leaves. In other television genres, personal drama takes centre stage, often because, unlike cinema, budget constraints limit the ability to convey a sense of physical drama. For instance, in the quintessential Western movie, the grand storyline would consist of some conflict between the good cowboys and some bandits coming into town, and the conflict would find its resolution in a grand gunfight and fist-fight on horseback somewhere in the wilderness. Because these grand physical conflicts cannot be properly conveyed by television (due to both screen size constraints and, often, budget limits), human conflict has become the main focus of the narrative.[25] The viewer becomes intimately involved with the personal dramas presented on television, unlike a kind of amused observer of a Western movie. Although a moviegoer might also be concerned that the cowboys win against the bandits, it is not an *intimate* concern. If the television cowboy can become the sheriff to get some extra money to support his family, then the viewer is sated. Newcomb suggests that "what has emerged in place of the 'sense' of the physical West is the adult Western. In this form, perfected by television, we concentrate on crucial human problems of individuals".[26] This can be thought of in a physical sense: the viewer is brought into the confines of characters' lives, their houses, and so on. The viewer has the opportunity to spend time with these characters and their spaces.

Of course, while television-like screens are widely available (at least in the North American context), Newcomb's idea of the size of televisual devices, and their ability to be placed in any location in the home, is problematized by the increasing size of home televisions and home theatre set-ups. Televisions have become more shallow (that is, televisions are no longer large boxes with heavy internal elements and with glass screens) and have evolved into "picture frames" that can hang on a wall. Televisions have, at the same time, become much larger in terms of screen area or screen "real estate". But what has accompanied the increasing size of home televisions (and the sound systems that are often installed alongside them) is the proliferation of *smaller* screens upon which televisual material can be accessed. Laptop computers, tablet computers (like Apple's iPad) or cellular phones seem nearly ubiquitous. With media content being able to be streamed (only limited by Internet access), televisual devices have become even more intimate than Newcomb suggests.

Consider, then, the amount of live material that U2 have released. The concert films make the space that the band inhabits intersect with the space that the viewer inhabits. The performance space becomes conflated with the viewer's personal space, and the viewer, then, has the opportunity to literally spend time with the band in their work space, the stage in live performance. U2 fans have access to the band's performance space almost anywhere and at any time. Viewers also experience a proximity to the band that they might not have ever experienced. Even in live concert contexts, the audience will experience being *with* the artists, or at least in close proximity to them. On these new television screens, one can have the artists both in their pockets (for instance, in the case of cell phones), but can have the artists in their pockets *close up*. It is not only that U2 accompany the audience in their daily life – on tablets or phones – but that the audience can see U2 closely, with an intimacy that even concert experiences fail to deliver.

Newcomb suggests that importance is not placed on action but rather on reaction to that action, or in other words, human response. Bono's actions are intimate with the viewer's own because, unlike a concert experience, the singer is not simply on a video screen for a crowd to view, but rather on one's own home television screen on a music video television station or programme. Bono is communicating with this specific audience, and the television viewer is intimately involved in this communication.

With this intimacy, the viewer experiences U2's concerns as their own. The global dramas that U2 present include the plight of refugees from Syria and the failure of the European Union to intervene in order to alleviate some of that plight in terms of immigrant flow from the Middle East to its borders. These global dramas then become the dramas of the viewer to experience: it is *theirs* as well. Of course, there can be a problem with this. In the same way that fans engage with the celebrities in U2 as people that they know *even though they do not* (a kind of suspension of disbelief), an audience might be tempted to think that, by simply engaging with a U2 concert on television, they are engaging with these global dramas and are resolving these dramas. In fact, an audience is simply engaging in a sort of "slacktivism", an impotent activism that is rooted in inaction.

Consider a part of that intimate communication: although sexual in nature, Bono's gestures also suggest a sort of freedom. In one scene, his legs, bent at the knees, are spread wide apart while he thrusts his hips. Perhaps Bono's sexual gestures evoke the sense of transcendence often attributed to sexual intimacy. This gesture could be read as analogous to an aeroplane taking off. This suggestion is not as radical as it seems, if one takes into account the many references to flying in the video: the design of the airport is reminiscent of a plane; there are planes taking off and landing constantly in the last section of the video of 'Beautiful Day'; and in one of the final scenes, Bono runs along the tarmac, jumping into the air as he runs, much like an aeroplane attempting to take off. Also, there are images of a young couple kissing, apparently transcending (or "taking off" from) their surroundings. These images suggest a kind of optimism towards or transcendence from the everyday.

Structure of feeling

In Raymond Williams's book, *Television: Technology and Cultural Form*, the author describes what he calls the "structure of feeling". This notion can be clarified by Williams's comments regarding televisual drama:

> It was possible [with the coming of television] to transmit performances of an orthodox theatrical kind, and it could be argued that the television play was the ultimate realisation of the original naturalist convention ... Since a major structure of feeling, in the art of the period, was in any case of this time, it is not surprising that many television plays reproduced this assumption of the nature of representative reality.[27]

Williams refrains from explicitly defining what he means by "structure of feeling". As he discusses televisual drama, he mentions the successful transition of stage plays to television, because they convey the same "structure of feeling", or perhaps atmosphere, on television as they do on the live stage: "the enclosed internal atmosphere; the local interpersonal conflicts; the close-up on private feeling".[28] In a similar vein, U2 also convey a certain "structure of feeling" through the music video. The video contains images of sleek and clean architecture, obviously modern and "progressive". Throughout these images, Bono is featured as a playful and mischievous character within this architectural context, along with the band in a role as performers. The "structure of feeling" that is conveyed works in a similar way to Saenz's idea of television as a conveyor of proper cultural behaviour. With the various gestures that are common to a history of U2 performance, the viewer immediately experiences a kind of U2 "structure of feeling" (no other band could produce it), which, when combined with the other elements of the video as discussed previously, conveys a generally optimistic "structure of feeling". This notion also supports the various readings of the video: as being a force for positive acceptance of modern technology and the urban condition, and also as an encouraging example of one living and enjoying life within a cold and increasingly alienating environment, due to the progress of technology.

Newcomb discusses the notion of continuity, a concept manifest in a television series as a continuing exploration of a set of characters' situations. The continuity of a series is also enhanced by the crossover of characters from other programmes, which expands the universe of the particular show into an interesting web of relationships for the viewer to explore. It is in this way that television is most like the novel. Newcomb states: "Details take on importance slowly, and within repeated patterns of action, rather than with the immediacy of other visual forms. It is this sense of density, built over a continuing period of time, that offers us a fuller sense of a world fully created by the artist".[29] This is an interesting idea in terms of U2, especially when one considers the transformations that the band have experienced. The band were, at first, relatively simple in their live concert presentation and in their public appearance. They do not generally wear any sort of explicit costuming, but instead present themselves as rock musicians emerging out of the punk tradition, hoping perhaps to appear to break down the artifice of rock music rather than contribute to it. Thus, one part of the "set of characters' situations", as Newcomb would put it, is the authenticity that comes from early U2. In their early career, the band are trying to break into the mainstream of the music industry while exploring a flavour of evangelical Christianity and even participating in some of the "squeaky-cleanness" that the lifestyle brings with it. Even so, they stop short from discarding popular music altogether. As the band's popularity grows, they are thrust into performance spaces that demand that they *fill* them. Bono's charisma, then, is what shines here: his physical gestures and his voice in live performance take centre stage (literally) in compelling large audiences in large venues to be fully engaged with what is happening there.

This is why the video for 'One Tree Hill' that appears on *The Best of 1980–1990* music video compilation is interesting, in that it seems to *reach back* to make the embracing of technology that is seen in the *Zoo TV* tour happen earlier, during *The Joshua Tree* tour. Because the video is from a portion of the *Rattle and Hum* film that was removed in the process of editing the final theatrical release, the video has time stamps, or running time indicators, along the bottom of the frame. This adds a sense of rawness to the video (it is literally raw in that it has not been processed for final release, assumedly since it is cut footage). The numbers make the viewer aware of both the passage of time and which camera is capturing the footage (each recording camera is numbered). These are all technical aspects of the recording and performance, but these on-screen elements also foreshadow (or, actually, the footage is made to *appear* that it foreshadows) what happens during the *Zoo TV* tour. The footage that appears on the *Zoo TV* tour screens on stage always looks raw and not properly processed. With the 'One Tree Hill' footage, the viewer is made to think that the band were already experimenting with this sort of "situation" earlier than the 1990s and the live tours.

In terms of the "crossover of characters", the band seem to have this covered as well. The televised broadcast of a performance at the Abbey Road Studios in London in December 2017 includes a sequence in which the host, Cat Deeley, joins the band on tour in São Paulo, Brazil. After seeing their accommodation in the stadium (in the form of "green rooms" and catering areas), and experiencing the concert, Deeley joins them in a small restaurant. There, the band and Deeley meet up with a cadre of influential musicians and celebrities, including Noel Gallagher (from the English band Oasis), actor Matthew McConaughey and producer/performer Daniel Lanois. While Gallagher and McConaughey are not usual members of the U2 "crossover of characters", Lanois was a producer of U2's albums. One might expect to see someone like Brian Eno in U2's entourage, or figures like writer Salman Rushdie, who was featured during the *Zoo TV* tour. As mentioned, the author was in hiding due to a *fatwa* that was placed on his life for his book, *The Satanic Verses*.[30] Other figures in U2's "crossover of characters" might include, say, Gavin Friday (Bono's childhood friend), Bono's wife Ali (who appears at the very beginning of the music video for 'The Sweetest Thing') or Bono's daughter Eve Hewson, who appears on stage at the very end of 'Mysterious Ways' in the live concert film, *U2 Go Home: Live from Slane Castle, Ireland*.

Advertisements

U2 are in the advertising business. They produce content in order to promote their brand, and thus sell more product. Popular music is, surely, commodified: it is the product of an industry that relies on the continued production of novel commodities for consumption. So, U2 are advertising their own brand. And that branding includes the various causes that the band wish to promote: gender equality; the eradication of poverty; the plight of refugees; environmental concerns; and so on. It is not so far-fetched to consider U2 as advertising. The *Zoo TV* and *PopMart* tours seem to make this clear. The band announced the *PopMart* tour from a Kmart department store, literally becoming a commodity, announcing a new product – the world tour – for purchase and consumption.

Without placing Newcomb's elements of a television aesthetic into the context of advertising, one may notice a problem with the concept of intimacy at this point in history. Newcomb states: "The smallness of the television screen has always been its most noticeable feature. It means something that the art created for television appears on an object that can be part of one's living room, exist as furniture. It is significant that one can walk around the entire apparatus".[31] While it is true that the television has pervaded much of Western life, and that many households do in fact own multiple televisions placed in various rooms, television screens have also become extremely large. While Newcomb also attempts to separate television from the art of cinema, the contemporary television has become a substitute for the cinematic experience with the advent of wide-screen televisions, which mimic the shape of a movie theatre screen, and high definition televisions equipped with "home theatre" sound systems and other features. Televisions are no longer intimate objects in the home; rather, viewers become intimate with the content displayed on the television, becoming physically engaged (engulfed) in it during its presentation of programming. As Marshall McLuhan suggests, "TV will not work as a background. It engages you. You have to be *with* it".[32] While Keith Negus suggests that television can act as "wallpaper" (as ubiquitous background without being a focus of attention), it is indisputable that television has become empowered to fully engage the observer. In his discussion, Negus suggests that "music video can become an element of audio-visual furniture. In a domestic environment it can be used as a mute moving picture or as a soundtrack to accompany other activities".[33]

Have viewers become intimate with television, in terms of advertising programming? If the historical popularity of many commercial "jingles" is any indication, then this television content has become intimate. While some may feel that ads waste time and are an intrusion, viewers generally want to watch music videos. Some viewers might actually reaffirm their self-image with new releases, which provide for them new ways of expression, or new styles of clothing to purchase, or lifestyles to emulate. For example, in the case of advertisements for, say, clothing stores, a viewer might wait for a new commercial, and desire to approve and further view it so as to show some kind of loyalty to the company, which serves to reinforce the identity of that viewer. With a new music video release, a viewer will consume it with glee, exercising their fan loyalty by adding to its view count on YouTube or Vevo. The viewer will in turn reinforce their "brand loyalty" to the band whose video they repeatedly view. On the other hand, it is difficult for a viewer to get involved in any "personal drama" except in a very cursory way, simply because there is little time to develop any character or situation in a thirty-second advertisement (or, for that matter, a four-minute music video). A popular music fan, though, looks at a band along a string of releases: over time and across various media. Perhaps in the case of advertisements for clothing stores, the "personal drama" with which the viewer becomes involved is a grand narrative of a particular company as one's clothing provider. Viewers of music video invest in the band's grand narrative, even if the videos are only "made up of family resemblances" (as per Vernallis).

Intimacy becomes a hallmark of U2's visual output. But also, U2 are an advertising entity: their causes, for the various disenfranchised people groups with whom they concern themselves, implicitly and explicitly come to the foreground in these videos. They would probably hope that the intimacy overshadows the commodity nature of these videos, and the "slacktivist" potential that comes from simply learning about the lives of others without action. These are the sites, then, of the tension between an "authenticity" (welcomed by fans in the form of intimacy) and a complicity with commercial interests. In addition to everything else, videos are still promotional material, in order to sell a song.

'City of Blinding Lights'

The official video for 'City of Blinding Lights' (from *How to Dismantle an Atomic Bomb*) has U2 performing in concert during the *Vertigo* tour. In fact, the video was shot at the very start of the tour, in Vancouver. The filming of the video was announced on the band's website, and between three and five thousand fans came to be a part of the audience. In addition to playing the song a number of times for filming, the band played a few other songs as a sort of impromptu concert.[34]

The stage is bathed in darkness and as the first strains of The Edge's guitar are heard, the lights flood the crowd from the stage: the lights are not above the stage, but rather originate from behind the band. These lights do nothing to reveal the musicians, but actually work to conceal them. Then a number of large curtains or banners consisting of coloured balls – these can be thought of as pixels on a display – fall to the stage. The curtains are both surfaces for the display of images and are opaque: the balls are on strings, not unlike a kind of beaded curtain. But the band remains bathed in darkness lit only from behind, which is unusual. This was deliberate, though; the directors Alex Courtes and Martin Fougerole explain, "We wanted to reflect the mood we've seen at the concerts, so we played with that lighting knowing that you are more blinded from a light if it was darker before".[35] So, the directors are trying to demonstrate what the blinding lights of the city might look like for the audience.

Later in the song, Bono and The Edge are momentarily lit by purple lights at the foot of the stage, but these moments of illumination only happen sporadically. The screens behind the band are most probably the focus of much of the audience since the band are obscured by darkness, and those screens display various bright colours passing quickly as if these are the colours of a city at night from the vantage point of a speeding car. As the band begin the chorus, during which the narrator exclaims how beautiful the subject looks, streamers fall from the arena ceiling. Even the shape of the curtains contributes to the idea of a city: the curtains are rectangular and reminiscent of the tall rectangular faces of city skyscrapers lit up in the night.

In *U2 by U2*, Bono describes the song in the following way:

> The first verse is in London and the chorus is in New York. The thing I had in mind was my first trip to London with Ali when we were teenagers, on the ferry and the train, walking into Piccadilly Circus and up Wardour Street and just discovering what a big city could offer you and what it could take away. And then, of course, New York, the scene in Madison Square Garden during the Elevation tour, where the lights came on [during a performance of 'Where the Streets Have No Name'] and eighteen thousand New Yorkers were in tears, jumping up and down, and I shouted out to them, "Oh, you look so beautiful tonight". It is such a naive and innocent line. That's what this song is about, remembering those times. *I miss you when you're not around.* It's not necessarily a curse, it's that part of us that is missing. It's about recapturing a sense of wonder, being in a city, and reminding yourself that you don't have to lose your soul to gain the world.[36]

The song, then, is not only about the cities of London and New York, or about the resilience of the residents of New York and their abilities to overcome the difficulties and pressures of the terrorist attacks of 11 September 2001. The song is greater than that, showing a sort of amazement at the development of human creativity. Certainly, this is a humanist view, but it is also a view that suggests a certain embracing with the modernist notion of progress, of technology and the human spirit to create and maintain, even when things are being torn down. It is not only the emotional audience in New York after 9/11 that looks beautiful. The city itself looks beautiful. The city – what it can offer and what it can take away – is what looks beautiful to Bono.

But there is more than simply the idea of the city as a wonderful monument to the engineering and creative skills of humanity. Bono states, "The song ends with the line 'blessings are not just for the ones who kneel, luckily'. I thank God on a daily basis for endless amounts of grace and covering the cracks that I would have fallen through".[37] The wonder of the city is not the end: its wonder is not what is really the focus of the song, but rather the *humanity* upon which the city is built, and from where the city springs. The video is so unusual because it does not showcase the band, even though U2 in performance are the central element of the video. Here is an example of *subtle deflection*: one expects to see the band, but instead considers the screens, the city and (perhaps) themselves, and (perhaps) God's role in blessing them.

'Song for Someone'

The video for 'Song for Someone' (from *Songs of Innocence*) is about the release of a prison inmate, played by Woody Harrelson, and the reunion with his daughter (played by Harrelson's actual daughter, Zoe Harrelson). The video can be considered a seven-minute film rather than a simple promotional music video.

The first scenes in the film feature various locations in the prison compound, such as the recreation yard, the space where inmates meet visitors (with visitors separated from the inmates by glass, able to speak through closed-circuit phones), and the prisoner's cell. He gathers up some of his possessions, including some loose photographs, books and a small Irish flag. After the prisoner shaves, a guard enters to escort him out of the cell.

The prisoner is brought to an open room where he removes his prison uniform and is given his civilian clothes. In a striking moment, on his way out, the prisoner passes by someone that is being escorted *into* the prison. The prisoner recognizes himself in this new inmate (the prisoner was in the same situation a number of years earlier), and the prisoner looks back at the new inmate as he passes by. As the prisoner is escorted to the outside gate through a pathway surrounded on both sides by tall fencing, he begins to cry. At the end of the pathway, his restraints are removed from his wrists, the gate is opened and he is set free. He looks back to his guard with a nod and walks through the gate to the open parking lot.

As the song ends, the man (no longer a prisoner) walks towards a parked car. The man's daughter is waiting for him. The two of them shake hands awkwardly; a moment prior to this gesture, he reaches out towards her shoulder and she seems to awkwardly recoil from his touch. She offers him a paper bag containing "fast food" as they drive off. As they begin travelling, he thanks her for picking him up and comments on her driving: "You drive better than your mother", he says. He mentions that she is beautiful, and she responds with an awkward "thank you". The video for 'Song for Someone' is about reconciliation. The director Vincent Haycock states, "Listening to the track, I was just thinking about stories that potentially haven't been told". The director further suggests that the video fits in with the "language" of the album and all that it is about.[38]

There is a moment during the music video that resonates with other themes in U2's arsenal. Woody Harrelson's character, called Aaron in the script, walks through the pathway with his guard escort on the way to the outer gate of the compound, and this pathway is lined on both sides by a high fence topped with barbed wire. As he walks, he begins to weep, and he needs to pause against the fence. A moment after this, Bono sings a lyric about being distant from Jesus' crucifixion on Calvary (distant in terms of time, presumably). The pause at the fence mimics the conventional image of Christ pausing in the midst of his suffering during his Passion. In the traditional Roman Catholic devotion of the Stations of the Cross, Jesus falls while he is carrying the cross, the device on which he will die, three times (Stations Three, Seven and Nine refer to the extrabiblical events of Jesus falling on his way to the site of his crucifixion on Calvary, also called Golgotha). At first thought, it might seem far-fetched to make this connection considering that Aaron is not being led to a torturous death but rather to freedom, and that his tears are probably tears of happiness, rather than a sign of any sort of physical suffering or humiliation. But Aaron is also being led to his daughter who, in the context of the narrative of the video, he has not seen for a number of years (he comments that she has grown up). The tears are, of course, tears of happiness upon his release, but they might also be tears of regret: he is overcome with what could have been. Aaron's Passion is that walk away from the place of his incarceration to the car. His place of "crucifixion" is where his daughter turns her face from him. The relationship he will have with her – the reconciliation (a sort of resurrection of some sort of relationship) – will take a few days to come to fruition.

The image of Aaron pausing in grief, as Christ might have done on his way to his death, works on two levels. First, Aaron might be a type of Christ. That is, Aaron is the prisoner that was Jesus: Matthew 25:36 states, "I was in prison and you visited me". And verse 40 states, "Truly I tell you, just as you did it to one of the least of these who are members of my family, you did it to me".

Like Jesus, Aaron suffers. Like Jesus, Aaron needs to be served; prisoners are also made in the image of God, and serving them is equal to serving the Son of God himself.

Linked to this idea, U2 often suggest that, in human experience, a kind of suffering takes place at first, with "glory" to follow. In the song 'Yahweh' (from *How to Dismantle an Atomic Bomb*), Bono sings about the pain of childbirth that must occur before a child comes into the world: suffering happens first before the miracle of new life. Psalm 30:5b states, "Weeping may linger for the night, but joy comes with the morning". Perhaps what Aaron is experiencing, then, is a sort of purgatory in the "real" world, a passage of purification and cleansing before the glory of being properly reconciled to his family.

'You're the Best Thing About Me'

The video for 'Song for Someone' is about reconciliation. The video for 'You're the Best Thing About Me' (from *Songs of Experience*), directed by Georgian filmmaker Tatia Pilieva, is about separation. There are two versions of the music video: one version features the band in New York, visiting various tourist sites and exploring the city at night. The second video focuses on four real-life couples who are being separated for various reasons. One American same-sex couple, Ciara and Alicia, have been married for three weeks and Ciara is leaving to serve in the military. A Syrian couple, Maha and Abed, are on the Greek island of Tilos, and Abed leaves his wife and five children in search of work in the city of Athens. India and Matthew, an American couple, are separated as one of them goes off to university in another state (Matthew remains in Chicago while his partner moves out of state to attend the University of California at Berkeley). Finally, the video features Natalia and Gonzalo from Mexico City. They are both chefs and live with their respective parents. Natalia gets a job offer in Paris and Gonzalo is simply unable to follow her. The video follows the last twenty-four hours of the couples being together before they are separated. Detailing how the idea for the film came about, Pilieva says,

> I was trying to figure out an interesting way to highlight love by bringing people together, and I was not coming up with any good ideas. Then my grandmother passed away. So I flew to the Republic of Georgia ... and spent 24 hours there, saying goodbye to my grandmother and all these people that I love, because all of my family is back there.
>
> I hadn't slept for two days and I'm sitting on the plane and it just hit me: what's interesting is not the bringing people together; it's the separation.[39]

Even Bono's own description of the inspiration behind the song seems to resonate in these stories that are all about separation:

> It's a song ... Written about a dream I had – a nightmare, really – where I woke up in a strange house and ... that my wife and my kids had left me. And then I realised I was in this strange house. I thought: No, I've left them. I don't know where this came from ... but I told my darling wife Ali and she just laughed at me and she said: "It's OK. I'm not going anywhere. You're not going anywhere. And if you wanted to find the door, you wouldn't even know where it was, would you?"

The difference with the couples in the music video, though, is that they *do* separate: one member of each couple needs to find that door and needs to leave. Pilieva explains that, in choosing the couples that would appear in the film, she was looking for a "bigger picture", so to speak, a diverse group from various contexts. As a part of the narrative of the film, Pilieva was hoping to explore immigration but from a different viewpoint. She shows immigration from a more conventional viewpoint in the case of Natalia moving to Paris for work, but the other separations are much more localized (though the distance – and the pain of separation – are not erased, certainly). Furthermore, Pilieva wanted to expand the definition of a refugee, at least in the eyes of the viewer: "The way we approached the film was let's make sure the audience understands the people as people – as human beings ... They're people and they happen to be refugees". Central to the video was the idea that viewers need to feel *something* for the couples and their plights: the call for empathy is the central impulse behind the video and the account of separation therein.

Besides the pedantic or political sides to the video, there is also a real sense of intimacy, not only because the viewer would presumably know the song by U2 and want to experience it again in a new context (say, once they have viewed the original music video of the band in New York), but also because of the cultivation of empathy. Pilieva explains that she had access to Ciara and Alicia's home so that she could take video footage of the couple waking up, trying to document their last moments together with as little interference on her part as possible. Pilieva remembers being with the couple and finding the moments prior to their separation as terrible: she experiences the pain first-hand in that she is *with* the couple as they are being separated from each other, and she hopes that the viewer will feel a similar empathy and pain when watching all of these separations occur, even in the not quite five minutes of the video. But there is more than empathy here; Pilieva states,

"I personally drove Ciara to the base and to the airport and I was the one who gave her the last hug. We couldn't film [on the military airbase] but I was there". Ciara and her wife said their goodbyes in the parking lot. "They were crying the whole time. I mean, I was a mess and the two grown men with me – my husband [her frequent collaborator, cinematographer Andre Lascaris] and our sound man, Chris, who could hear better than any of us – he was in tears.

"It was heartbreaking. To some degree I think it's important to fall in love with the people you work with, whom you portray, and there was so much love all around", she said.[40]

The question is whether Pilieva would think that it is important for the viewer to fall in love with the people featured in the video. Is it enough for the viewer only to empathize with Gonzalo and Natalia when she hugs him and asks him if he'll visit? Should the viewer be required to fall in love with them? Pilieva makes the point in the interview that the couple did not break up, nor did they get married, before the separation, but they did not have any sense as to what the future held for them as a couple. This particular separation has less of the personal drama so required for televisual intimacy. Nevertheless, the radical idea would be for the video to foster not just empathy but *love*.

Notes

1. Gilmour is quoting from Mark Allan Powell, "U2", in *Encyclopedia of Contemporary Christian Music* (Peabody, MA: Hendrickson, 2002), 983. For more, see Michael J. Gilmour, "The Prophet Jeremiah, Aung San Suu Kyi, and U2's *All That You Can't Leave Behind*: On Listening to Bono's Jeremiad", in *Call Me the Seeker: Listening to Religion in Popular Music*, edited by Michael J. Gilmour (New York: Continuum, 2005), 35. See also Deane Galbraith, "Meeting God in the Sound: The Seductive Dimension of U2's Future Hymns", in *The Counter-Narratives of Radical Theology and Popular Music: Songs of Fear and Trembling*, edited by Mike Grimshaw (New York: Palgrave Macmillan, 2014), 128–29.

2. Robert Hilburn, "Far Down the Road, a Sudden U-Turn", *Los Angeles Times* (29 October 2000); available from http://articles.latimes.com/2000/oct/29/entertainment/ca-43738 (accessed 14 February 2018).

3. James Hunter, "U2: All That You Can't Leave Behind", *Rolling Stone* (26 October 2000); available from https://www.rollingstone.com/music/albumreviews/all-that-you-cant-leave-behind-20001026 (accessed 14 February 2018).

4. Neil McCormick, *U2 by U2* (London: HarperCollins, 2006), 373.

5. A colleague comments, "Not what the writer was thinking (I assume he refers to incense) but I like that trilogy of terms in relation to Bono: bread, wine (Christianity), and the smoke of a strutting rock star's expensive cigar" (conversation with author, 15 February 2018).

6. McCormick, *U2 by U2*, 373.

7. Beth Nabi, "Dream Out Loud: The Day Beth Met Bono", *BethandBono.com* (31 Octo-

ber 2014); available from http://bethandbono.com/2014/10/31/dream-out-loud-the-day-beth-met-bono/ (accessed 27 June 2018).

8. Another interesting formal distinction can be made: when the band are performing together during the chorus, they are apparently in a section of the airport at night; the environment surrounding them is dark. It is only towards the end of the song that the band are seen performing in bright daylight and on a runway, seemingly in the path of arriving and departing planes.

9. Carol Vernallis, "Music Video's Second Aesthetic", in *The Oxford Handbook of New Audiovisual Aesthetics*, edited by John Richardson, Claudia Gorbman and Carol Vernallis (Oxford: Oxford University Press, 2013), 447.

10. Vladimir Belogolovsky, "Paul Andreu: 'I would only take on a project if the ideas were mine. Otherwise, I am not interested'", *ArchDaily* (7 March 2017); available from https://tinyurl.com/DAILY-806698 (accessed 13 July 2018).

11. Michael Saenz, "Television Viewing as a Cultural Practice", in *Television: The Critical View*, 4th ed., edited by Horace Newcomb (New York: Oxford University Press, 1987), 579.

12. Sean Cubitt, "How to Watch Video Art: My Father Will Heal You with Love", in *Timeshift: On Video Culture* (London and New York: Routledge, 1991), 93.

13. Vernallis, "Music Video's Second Aesthetic", 454.

14. Keith Thomas, "Introduction", in *A Cultural History of Gestures*, edited by Jan Bremmer and Herman Roodenburg (Ithaca, NY: Cornell University Press, 1993), 2.

15. Ibid., 11.

16. Edith Stein, *On the Problem of Empathy*, translated by Waltraut Stein (Washington, DC: ICS Publications, 1989), 14–15.

17. Lynn Ramert, "A Century Apart: The Personality Performances of Oscar Wilde in the 1890s and U2's Bono in the 1990s", *Popular Music and Society* 32.4 (October 2009): 447–48.

18. Ibid., 448.

19. Lynn Joyrich, "All that Television Allows: TV Melodrama, Postmodernism and Consumer Culture", *Camera Obscura* 16 (1988): 147.

20. Noel McLaughlin, "Bono! Do You Ever Take Those Wretched Sunglasses Off?: U2 and the Performance of Irishness", *Popular Music History* 4.3 (2009): 324.

21. Vernallis, "Music Video's Second Aesthetic", 438–40.

22. Horace Newcomb, "Towards a Television Aesthetic", in *Television: The Critical View*, 4th ed., edited by Horace Newcomb (Oxford: Oxford University Press, 1987), 613.

23. Ibid., 613–14.

24. Ibid., 615.

25. This has been problematized by recent television series, such as Netflix's *The Crown*, having single-episode budgets that match or surpass that of many theatrical films.

26. Newcomb, "Towards a Television Aesthetic", 617.

27. Raymond Williams, "The Forms of Television", in *Television: Technology and Cultural Form* (Glasgow: Fontana/Collins, 1974), 56.

28. Ibid.

29. Newcomb, "Towards a Television Aesthetic", 622.

30. Rushdie does appear in the video for the song, 'The Ground Beneath Her Feet', from the soundtrack for *The Million Dollar Hotel*.

31. Newcomb, "Towards a Television Aesthetic", 614–15.

32. Marshall McLuhan, "Television: The Timid Giant", in *Understanding Media: The Extensions of Man* (New York: McGraw-Hill, 1964), 271.

33. Keith Negus, *Popular Music in Theory: An Introduction* (Hanover: Wesleyan University Press, 1996), 94.

34. "U2 Perform for Fans at Video Shoot", *RTÉ* (10 January 2007); available from https://www.rte.ie/entertainment/2005/0429/404017-u2/ (accessed 23 March 2018).

35. Matt McGee, "Directing U2: From Vertigo to Vancouver with Alex & Martin", *@U2* (26 July 2005); available from https://www.atu2.com/news/directing-u2-from-vertigo-to-vancouver-with-alex--martin.html (accessed 23 March 2018).

36. McCormick, *U2 by U2*, 408.

37. Ibid.

38. U2, "U2 – Song for Someone (Behind the Scenes)", *YouTube* (12 July 2015); available from https://www.youtube.com/watch?v=w6jrEtTznYQ (accessed 4 August 2018).

39. Cathleen Falsani, "Why am I Walking Away", *U2.com* (5 October 2017); available from http://www.u2.com/news/title/why-am-i-walking-away (accessed 15 March 2018).

40. Ibid.

4 The Irish in America: Nationalism and Politics on Tour

On 6 June 2001, U2 performed at the Fleet Center in Boston, Massachusetts, for the second time in as many nights. Their first concert served as a dress rehearsal for the recording of their concert film (to be released for home video viewing), while the actual recording took place the following night. To add to the pressure of this undertaking, the band were also scheduled to simulcast two songs from the concert live to the NBA basketball finals broadcast on NBC, to an estimated audience of some fifty million viewers from the United States and elsewhere.

Throughout their career, the members of U2 have often presented themselves as part of a particularly Irish band, and they have been constructed as such by the media as well. As well as the fact that the band are based in Ireland, and that the members grew up in the Irish context, U2 have also engaged with Irish issues in their music and outside of it. While doing so, the band have become associated with a kind of global "sense" by referring to non-Irish cities in their music, such as London, Paris, Munich, Berlin and New York. Bono's involvement with international concerns, and his lobbying of politicians, along with global philanthropic work, has no doubt contributed to this cosmopolitan image. However, not all of U2's coverage has made a positive contribution to Ireland and Irish culture. Noel McLaughlin and Martin McLoone suggest that the amount of academic writing on U2 has had the effect of "disguising the wider musical context in Ireland, and of marginalizing discussion of other acts and other musical strategies".[1] McLaughlin and McLoone consider U2's Irish status as somewhat problematic; Irish music is not all like U2. In other words, "authentic" Irish music has become overshadowed by U2, due to the band's broad popularity. Nevertheless, U2 have maintained their Irish image. But Bono himself has thrust the "Irishness" of the band into flux with his use of national icons in concert. This chapter explores the relationship between U2, Ireland and America, keeping in mind U2's approach to cities like Boston and New York as sites of Irish-Americanism.

In U2's *Elevation 2001: Live in Boston* DVD, there are various examples of nationalism evoked through national symbols, particularly in the form of flags. For instance, fans of presumably Irish descent are often the subject of the cameras as they wield Irish flags. In one instance, Bono motions to one of these fans to throw the flag to the stage. Bono then makes the flag the object of his focus. This concert takes place in Boston, a city identified as a centre of Irish immigration in America. Thus, the concert could be seen as a venue in which Americans of Irish descent are able to celebrate their heritage on the occasion of a visit of one of the most famous groups of Irish musicians.

The Fleet Center performance, though, is not only a celebration of common ancestry. With the inclusion of a simulcast to the NBA Finals Halftime Show, the concert is open to be experienced by a wider American audience. This is further reinforced by the concert film's later release on home video for a much wider American and international audience. This concert, then, is no longer just for Irish Americans, but for all Americans, symbolized by Bono throwing a basketball into the crowd.

'Bullet the Blue Sky'

In a particularly interesting moment, Bono opens his leather jacket to reveal an American flag stitched into the lining. 'Bullet the Blue Sky', the song during which this display takes place, has often been the accompaniment to Bono's use of the American flag. In the album version of the song (from *The Joshua Tree*), the narrator explores the role of the American government in arming government forces in the civil war in El Salvador in the 1970s and 1980s, "the worst side of the American dream".[2] The narrator embarks on poetic spoken-word interludes describing details like approaching fighter planes and greedy, powerful men. The song has been a staple in U2's live show, usually read as critical of the United States' role in global politics as "world police", which acts only to serve its own interests rather than a greater global good.

During the performance of 'Bullet the Blue Sky' during the *Zoo TV* tour, as documented in the *Zoo TV: Live from Sydney* concert film, Bono comes on stage wearing a costume that evokes a fighter pilot. At the start of the performance, Bono is wearing black, including the shiny leather pants that he was wearing earlier in the concert as The Fly, though he is no longer wearing his Fly sunglasses. Thus, he is (more like) "himself". The television screens on the stage display the outline of a cross filled with the image of burning flames, coinciding with Bono's description of burning crosses, a hallmark of the American white-supremacist group Klu Klux Klan. These crosses then transform into swastikas, while Bono exclaims, "Don't let it happen again!" He proceeds to leave the stage at the beginning of The Edge's guitar solo.

He returns to the stage wearing a fighter pilot costume. He is wearing a tactical vest (which has the "ZOO TV" logo painted on the back in white lettering), dark aviator-style sunglasses and a black baseball cap, emblazoned with a red five-pointed star in outline. He is also wearing a head-worn microphone, which leaves his hands free. Some of the camera footage of this segment of the concert film is superimposed by what appears to be a head-up-display (or HUD) for a fighter plane in combat, complete with faux targeting information and the like. He also seems to speak with a southern States drawl. During this segment, the cameras focus on the stage screens which show American flags, though their orientation is not clear due to the unknown position of the cameras. The flags are rotating in the viewing frame, and are certainly not conventionally displayed; the flags themselves are in flux.

In the introduction segment (a sequence of footage that acts as an interstitial between live concert performances) for 'Bullet the Blue Sky' in the *Outside Broadcast* concert film from November 1992 (a full year prior to *Zoo TV: Live from Sydney*), The Edge is in front of a screen that appears to be a display for a video-game-based combat simulator involving battle tanks. He comments on the conflation between the reality of war and the experience of the combat simulator, and the American combat experience in Iraq during the first Gulf War (which took place from 1990 to 1991). The crosses that appear in the later concert film are featured in this performance as well. Here, Bono wears a black sleeveless shirt reminiscent of scenes from the *Rattle and Hum* concert film. Like in the later film from Sydney, he leaves the stage at the start of the guitar solo.

He comes out wearing the same outfit as in the later concert film, but the subsequent footage is not superimposed by the HUD graphics. Bono also speaks with a southern drawl here. As in the *Zoo TV* performance, Bono ends by stopping at the end of the walkway connecting to a smaller stage that extends into the audience with his arms upraised in a posture of religious ecstasy or prayer. The cameras only linger on the American flags on the stage screens for a few moments.

During the *Popmart* tour, Bono appears during 'Bullet the Blue Sky' wearing a green cap and green army jacket. He is also wearing a head-worn microphone, which allows him to play with an umbrella as an on-stage prop. During the guitar solo, the huge *PopMart* screen features what appears to be an animated version of Roy Lichtenstein's famous pop-art diptych "Whaam!", which depicts a fighter plane in combat stylized as a comic book illustration. During the guitar solo, Bono opens the umbrella, which has the appearance of an American flag, with red and white stripes emanating from the central hub, and white stars on a blue background around the umbrella edge. Bono opens the umbrella and overextends it, breaking the dome of the umbrella, as one might experience in a windstorm. Bono pretends to use the overextended umbrella as a golf club, teeing off an imaginary golf ball as he sings about dollar bills being counted off by those in political and social power. Earlier in the performance, Bono shoves the closed umbrella between his legs, transforming a symbol of American patriotism into a symbol of phallic power.

Towards the end of the song, Bono removes his cap, with the broken umbrella leaning over his shoulder, and holds the cap in front of him as he walks towards the camera. It is as if he is a less fortunate member of the Irish immigrant community that came to the United States in search of prosperity and sustenance. In past performances of the song, he identifies the Irish who run into the open arms of a welcoming America before the end of the song. This is a charged reenactment of the immigrant experience, especially as the *PopMart* concert takes place in Mexico City, the capital city of the country that is often the focal point for discussion regarding migrant movement.

During the *Elevation* tour, the dynamic of the criticism in 'Bullet the Blue Sky' changes. In the concert film, the song is introduced by a video (shown on screens surrounding the stage) of actor and then-chairman of the National Rifle Association, Charlton Heston, speaking in opposition to gun control legislation: "There are no good guns, there are no bad guns. A gun in the hands of a bad man is a bad thing. Any gun in the hands of a good man is no threat to anyone, except bad people". The video then shows a child finding a gun in a bag, perhaps making the unbelievable suggestion that children are among the "bad people" that Heston mentions. This image shockingly reinforces the message of the song, which can be argued as expressing the paradox of America: it is both the "land of the free" and the land of guns; America is a global peacemaker while also acting as a supporter of what can be characterized as a domestic war. U2 criticize American domestic policy in terms of its lax gun control, and while doing so, Bono opens his omnipresent leather jacket to reveal an American flag stitched upside down into the lining within it. This is an ironic gesture; it is a playful and improper display of the American flag, not unlike Bono's use of the broken umbrella as a golf club during the *PopMart* tour.

During the guitar solo, Bono strolls around the walkway that extends out into the crowd, with his arm raised to cover his eyes. It appears that he is walking blindly on the raised walkway. In his hand, he is holding a battery-powered spotlight similar in shape to a megaphone; he points the spotlight into the crowd, pointing it towards various sections (similar to what he does during the song in the *Rattle and Hum* and *Vertigo 2005: Live from Chicago* concert films). While he does this, Bono begins speaking about the death of John Lennon, one of the former members of the English band The Beatles. Lennon was shot and killed outside his apartment building in New York in December 1980. For Bono, Lennon is a single casualty in an ongoing problem of gun violence in America. Bono comments that the country is waging war on itself. Towards the end of the song, Bono calls himself "Mark Chapman", taking the name of Lennon's shooter, and points the hand-held spotlight at his head; the song ends with a bass drum "gunshot" and the extinguishing of Bono's spotlight as the singer suddenly moves his head as if he has suffered from a self-inflicted wound. Bono not only represents "Mark Chapman", but also America: America is at war with itself, and will end up killing itself if there is no intervention.

After the *Elevation* tour, U2 were asked to perform at Super Bowl XXXVI in February 2002. During the performance of 'Where the Streets Have No Name', Bono again opens his leather jacket to show the American flag. This time, the flag is stitched into the lining of the jacket in a correct orientation, with the stars at the top of the flag. He did so not as a gesture of criticism, but as a gesture of support for the victims of the American tragedy in New York, Washington, and Pennsylvania on 11 September 2001. In a short article in the *Ottawa Citizen* just after the Super Bowl, Juan Rodriquez states, "Relentlessly touring with something called *Elevation* – post-irony earnestness, or cynical put-on? – the Irishmen became America's band". Criticizing the Super Bowl performance, Rodriquez continues,

> There's Bono wailing 'Where the Streets Have No Name', backed by a list of U.S. September 11 victims' names scrolling upward in alphabetical order. Then the cathartic moment: Bono, lump in throat, opened his black jacket to reveal a Stars and Stripes lining. (Did he buy the thing off the Internet?) This gesture cemented his status as Honorary American, free, free at last to join the nauseatingly long list of 9/11 profiteers.[3]

In a response to Rodriquez's opinion column, reader Chuck O'Donnell suggests that U2 provide what America needs at this moment: "It wants songs about emotions, perhaps with a hint of uplift. Since Sept. 11, America wants to sit down and think for a minute and consider something more than Britney Spears bemoaning her choice of eye shadows".[4] O'Donnell reclaims the notion of Bono as an "Honorary American", agreeing with Rodriquez without accepting his cynicism and negativity. This notion of U2 as ambassadors of hope is also reflected in the booklet which accompanies the home video of the Boston concert film. In it, Danny Eccleston, the editor for the British music magazine *Q*, states, "U2's music lifts you up. It's big enough to do that. And in this turbulent year – where Hate has hit the headlines and Hope is in the small print – we've really needed it". Bono later appears on the cover of *Time* magazine performing the same gesture with his jacket (with a correctly oriented flag stitched into the lining), with the caption, "Can Bono Change the World?"

Suddenly, Bono is an honorary American, a title recognized by his supporters and his critics. He becomes a global figure as well, ready to sway world leaders towards the path of peace, hope, debt reduction and AIDS awareness in Africa, far from his Irish roots. His sudden American-ness affects the whole band; the members of U2 become associated with America as well as greater global issues. Their interests cover not only American politics and global economics, but also the Irish in America. There is a discourse which runs through the documentary portion of the home video which suggests that U2 had "won over America" on this tour. And though they had played Boston, the city of New York – "where the Irish had been coming for years" – was yet to come. For U2, New York is a city worthy of its own song, a city that is a source of magic and inspiration, and a subject that is presented heavily during this tour. Of course, U2's engagement with the city is nothing new; from as far back as 1984's *The Unforgettable Fire*, U2 have tried to evoke a sense of the urban landscape in their music. *Achtung Baby*, with its use of noise and technology, seems to move the idea of aural urbanity into the foreground. And, of course, New York is the city described in the song, 'City of Blinding Lights'.

In the *Vertigo 2005: Live from Chicago* concert film, Bono is wearing a leather jacket that has both white stars and prominent red stripes, as well as a headband that has "COEXIST" written on it. The "C" is a crescent, symbolizing Islam; the "X" is a Star of David, symbolizing Judaism; the "T" is a cross, symbolizing Christianity. The stage is bathed in red and blue light. During The Edge's guitar solo, Bono falls to his knees and raises and crosses his hands above his head, as if he is a prisoner or a protestor. He is, in this posture, one who has lost his voice, or his ability to speak about situations or to effect change. Once the solo is over, Bono stands with his headband now covering his eyes. He feels his way to the microphone and begins to sing a line from the band's song 'The Hands that Built America', a song that describes the contribution of various immigrant communities in the development of the eastern urban landscape in America, in cities like New York.

In September 2017, the band performed 'Bullet the Blue Sky' on the late-night network television programme, *The Tonight Show starring Jimmy Fallon*. Black and white stars and stripes appear intermittently on a screen behind the band. After singing the verse and chorus twice, Bono begins to sing (in a mocking tone) the beginning notes of 'The Star-Spangled Banner' in the place of the European Union anthem, 'Ode to Joy'. Before he begins the monologue portion of the song, he quotes the Temptations/Edwin Starr lyric, "War, what is it good for?", and then begins to make reference to President Trump. Bono refers to the social network Twitter, and mentions how much power the President holds when he composes a single Tweet (Twitter was Trump's medium of choice for quick takes on various issues). During the guitar solo, the screen behind the band features footage of North Korean military parades: U2's concerns now include the potential of global conflict including the threat of the use of nuclear warfare. This is in addition to the idea of the United States as adverse to immigration, closing its doors if not in terms of policy, but certainly in terms of climate, at the very top of its government administration. It is a sort of "perfect storm" of issues for late U2.

The band released the promotional video for the first single from *Songs of Experience* in late September 2017. 'You're the Best Thing About Me' does not seem to be a song about American foreign or domestic policy, immigration or the threat of nuclear annihilation. Rather, it seems to be a sort of love song to a lover: if that person constitutes the best part of the narrator's life, why would the narrator leave that person behind? The music video features the band strolling around New York at night, as if they are tourists, taking in the sights of the city.

The video begins with images of the American flag and the Statue of Liberty. At the start, a voice-over describes the Statue of Liberty as "the mother of exiles". The band are then shown wandering around New York, visiting landmarks, signing autographs, eating pizza (procured from a small, street-side restaurant) and taking a double-decker bus tour of the city at night. They even appear to be taking a ferry ride on the Hudson River; they are also featured performing on the ferry.

Many of the scenes in the video show that it is raining. Instead of having any random or nondescript umbrellas, the band opens umbrellas that are *all* decorated with the stars and stripes of the American flag (these are perhaps the easiest umbrellas to procure from tourist shops in New York). There is an obvious connection – at least for viewers who have seen the *PopMart* tour live concert film – between these umbrellas and Bono's earlier *broken* one: these umbrellas are *not yet* broken. It is almost impossible for the scenes with the umbrellas in the New York rain not to evoke the earlier broken umbrella of 'Bullet the Blue Sky'.

The lyrics that suggest that the narrator is leaving the best thing about him (that is, his lover) are now matched with images of the Statue of Liberty. What was previously a song about lovers becomes a song about America and the best thing about it. The best thing about America, according to U2 here, is the ideal that is represented by the statue: the voice-over at the very end of the video quotes "The New Colossus", the poem that appears on the pedestal of the statue: "Send these, the homeless, tempest-tossed to me, I lift my lamp beside the golden door".

The Statue of Liberty becomes a central figure for U2's performance during the Grammy Awards at the end of January 2018. The band perform the song 'Get Out of Your Own Way', also from *Songs of Experience*, live but outside the awards ceremony venue, on a platform that appears to be floating almost in the shadow of the Statue of Liberty, on the Hudson River. In the performance, Bono lifts his arm in a defiant, close-fisted salute that was used by activists in the civil rights movement of the 1960s, and, more recently, in the "Black Lives Matter" movement against police brutality and for racial equality in America. At the end of the performance, Bono grabs a megaphone – now decorated with the stars and stripes, red, white and blue of the American flag. Careful viewers will notice a small outline of the animated version of one of Bono's previous personae, Mr MacPhisto, on the flat part of the centre post of the megaphone. Bono yells into the horn, "Blessed are the shithole countries, for they gave us the American dream". This is a direct reference to President Trump's alleged remarks earlier that month in a private meeting that seemingly lamented the fact that there were few immigrants coming to America from more affluent European countries like Norway, and an abundance of immigrants coming from less affluent, so-called "shithole" countries.[5]

Space and place

In his book, *Space and the Irish Cultural Imagination*, Gerry Smyth analyses the music of U2 in terms of "certain special practices and motifs that recur throughout their music".[6] Smyth points out that ethnicity and nationality are not necessarily "resident 'in' the music, but are 'achieved' or 'constructed' by the subject through musical performance and consumption".[7] Part of this "imagined geography" of U2 consists of their relationship to Ireland as a base of operations and as a point of origin. Smyth points to the band's early dissatisfaction with traditional Irishness, and their recognition of America as an ambivalent site of Irish culture, as a site of emigration which Smyth calls both a "promised land" and "land of exile". Furthermore, U2 recognize Ireland's liminal position between Europe and America. Smyth explains:

> The band exploited Ireland's traditional imaginative location – marginal from Europe, residual to America – to produce deeply compelling engagements with both those large cultural entities. Ireland was nominally and aspirationally European, yet problematically so given the peculiarities of its history and geography. At the same time, given the history of emigration, there were strong cultural and

political links with America, yet these also were uncertain, productive of an intense trans-Atlantic cultural traffic in which images of "home" were exchanged and distorted.[8]

This homelessness is what Smyth focuses on in discussing U2's music in the 1980s and their fascination with the United States and its deserts in particular, most evident on *The Joshua Tree*. And the notion of an exchanged and distorted view of "home" is reflected in the band's song 'Stateless', which was released on the soundtrack to the Bono-penned film, *The Million Dollar Hotel*, directed by Wim Wenders and released in 2000. Bono's first words in the song make clear that he (perhaps embodying fully the voice of the narrator) has no home in this world.

While the desert is no longer evident as an image in U2's most recent work, homelessness continues as an important theme, manifesting itself in images in the album artwork and tour merchandise. For instance, the cover of U2's *All That You Can't Leave Behind*, the album that was supported by the *Elevation* tour, features the four members of the band in a French airport terminal, complete with luggage and belongings. A persistent image used during the tour was that of a heart shape within a suitcase, connoting travel and movement. The notion of leaving something behind or being unable to do so, and bringing along one's heart, suggests movement without return, perhaps mirroring the emigration of previous generations from the hardships of Ireland. In fact, U2 inhabit a further liminal space, sympathetic to the plight of the Irish in the United States, those who left behind a *home* that was already challenged, due to its geographic location and circumstance in the region. Therefore, U2's supposed embracing of America and its icons, such as the American flag, as well as being in visible support of American efforts in the so-called "War on Terror", may be simply a move in sympathy and recognition of their own "American-ness" at this point in their career.[9] Just as other Irish emigrants became American, so U2 become American for at least a short time, to support the notion of their continued homelessness. In a sense, cities like New York and Boston can be read as a type of "home" for Irishness, as a place of their own. U2 can come "home" for a short time before reclaiming their liminal space or statelessness between Ireland and the United States.

U2 make an interesting case to study because of their constant tangible links to Ireland, as a place where the members of the group have chosen to live, raise their children and record their music. Ireland, with its hardships and sectarian conflict, have been important elements in the music of U2. Noel McLaughlin states it more forcefully: "U2 is the only globe-straddling rock band that is not straightforwardly Anglo-American".[10] But their fascination with the United States is nothing new; Smyth bases an entire chapter on U2's expression of America from *The Joshua Tree* and traces the band's fascination with the country back to *The Unforgettable Fire*. In the context of *The Joshua Tree*, Smyth suggests that their interests focus upon the deserts of America. Later, though, U2 seem fascinated with an urban America. It is an America built by the Irish and an American urbanity in danger of terrorist attack. Bono and his fellow band members choose to reinforce this version of America and thus find for themselves a place to rest. They count themselves among the "Irish in America", able to relish in the glory of the great American city and to remind their fellow migrants that they can rebuild, both physically and spiritually.

Lynn Ramert points out that Bono has never identified himself as English, nor has he left Ireland, but rather has lived in Ireland and established a business base there. She continues, "U2's music even contributed positively to Ireland's balance of trade in the 1980s, before the Celtic Tiger gained strength".[11] Ramert suggests that the band needed to explore the United States – that is, its people, culture and music – in *Rattle and Hum* in order to understand their own Irishness.[12] But, in reality, U2 are not Irish *or* American. Rather, "U2 is best understood as a transnational phenomenon: global recording artists signed to a multi-national conglomerate, hailing from and residing in a small, post-colonial nation with off-shore monies that largely bypass its by now fragile post-Celtic Tiger economy", that is, the growing but unsustainable Irish economy of the mid-1990s to mid-2000s.[13]

For all intents and purposes, U2 become "American" in the early 2000s. At the time, they had seemingly been given the task of providing hope, and they were successful in providing it. Because of their massive global success, how particularly "homeless" are they, and what does it matter when each member of the group is worth millions upon millions of dollars? What does it say about fans when they look to a celebrity or a group of popular musicians for hope?

Transformations

In the concert video in support of the *iNNOCENCE & eXPERIENCE* tour, the band change their object of criticism yet again: during 'Bullet the Blue Sky', the criticism moves away from American foreign policy, or the commonly perceived propensity of gun support in the United States resulting in rampant gun violence. It also moves away from support for the United States in the face of terrorism. Rather, 'Bullet the Blue Sky' becomes an opportunity for the band to criticize the European Union, and its immigration policies. In a testimony to a Congressional subcommittee in April 2016 (which occurred after the *iNNOCENCE & eXPERIENCE* tour ended in December 2015), Bono states, "As a European, I'm here to tell you that in Europe the problem has moved from practical to existential. In 1989, the wall that divided Europe came down. In

2016, barbed wire fences that divide Europe are going up. The integration of Europe – the very idea of a Europe 'whole and free' – is now under threat".[14] The European Union is being criticized not because of its policies per se, but because of the potential of ultra-nationalism impeding the flow of refugees through Europe and to a better life. After all, Bono says in a 1992 MTV television interview (included in the deluxe release of *Achtung Baby* in 2011, in celebration of the twentieth anniversary of the album), "I love this satellite thing. I love watching it beaming *across borders*. That's what U2 is all about".

This might be the reason why the members of U2 have moved from the local to the global, or from the idea of Ireland-as-home and America-as-new-home to the greater idea of the world-as-home. They are pushing against nationalism and nationalist movements – including their own – because they feel that these categories do more harm than good. Borders serve to contain and protect from infiltration, whereas the band seem to increasingly desire fluidity in terms of movement on a global scale.

On 20 June 2016, Bono posted on the official U2 account on the photo-sharing service, Instagram. Accompanying a photo of a pair of women in black *hijabs* smiling towards the camera and embracing each other, Bono writes, "Millions of refugees forced to flee their homes. They deserve our support, not our suspicion. Proud to stand #WithRefugees and to sign @UNRefugees petition". The petition that Bono mentions is one promoted by the UN Refugee Agency for World Refugee Day. The petition reads, in part, "To escape the violence, they leave everything behind – everything except their hopes and dreams for a safer future. UNHCR, the UN Refugee Agency believes that all refugees deserve to live in safety". The petition is addressed to a United Nations General Assembly summit on refugees and migrants and encourages governments to ensure that refugee children have access to education, to safe living conditions and access to work or education to learn new skills in order to contribute to their community.[15]

In the presentation of 'Bullet the Blue Sky' during the *iNNOCENCE & eXPERIENCE* tour, Bono sings through a megaphone, painted the blue of the European Union flag, with the twelve yellow stars of the flag circling its horn of the megaphone. He also intones the beginning verse of the anthem of the European Union and the Council of Europe, 'Ode to Joy'. All of this is reminiscent of the *Zoo TV* tour, which also featured the European Union flag, though disintegrating: the stars begin to wobble and fall away from the circle, perhaps a symbolic representation and foretelling of the future fragmentation of the European Union precipitated by the proposed exit of the United Kingdom from a united Europe (after the UK referendum to do so in June 2016). Furthermore, stars falling from the sky-like blue field of the flag evokes Christian apocalyptic imagery, that of stars falling from the sky (as happens at the start of the *Zoo TV: Live from Sydney* concert film). The lyric from the song 'Zoo Station' also alludes to this: "and the stars of the sky fell to the earth as the fig tree drops its winter fruit when shaken by a gale" (Revelation 6:13). This is an example of how U2 use religious imagery and its accompanying associations, such as "the end of the age", the control of the world by a "spirit of Antichrist", or an evil "spirit" at work in the world, what Marcus Moberg calls "the perceived 'reality of evil in the world'".[16] The apocalyptic is linked to what Moberg calls "chaotic themes such as war, chaos and madness", and impending doom.[17]

Ahead of the national referendum in the United Kingdom on the question of whether it should remain part of the European Union or leave, the band posted a video by a group called "Irish4Europe" on the official U2 Facebook page, and commented that "For Irish voters in Britain, don't go we'd miss you ... Europe without Britain seems unimaginable to us". Their sentiment is based on the idea of an open Europe. Posting to the same Facebook page, Irish actor Liam Neeson commented, "Border controls would be implemented to allegedly stop illegal immigrants coming into the UK through the back door ... It would be truly a shame to sacrifice all the progress that has been made by the peace process regarding border controls. There is strength in unity. A Brexit vote will make us weak".[18] Bono and the band – and other celebrities like Neeson – criticize the European Union because they believe it can do more for the refugee crisis in particular, and because of its potential for building fences. They do not think that Ireland would be served by a European Union without the United Kingdom.

There are a number of reasons why what has been colloquially referred to as "Brexit" was the popular choice. First, a "Brexit" vote was seen to keep the United Kingdom safe from the influx of immigrants from the Middle East. As Rebecca Omonira-Oyekanmi explains, though, "the UK is [still] a signatory to the refugee convention and is obliged to do its bit for people fleeing persecution". Second, the United Kingdom would be saved from immigrants who would invariably place pressure on the social system, leeching support programmes at the expense of the "domestic" taxpayers. Omonira-Oyekanmi explains, though, that many immigrants cannot access the very support programmes that they are accused of squandering.[19]

What is truly fascinating is how Bono takes the words originally meant as criticism of American foreign policy, or American "meddling" in non-American matters, and applies them to his own subject-position. During 'Bullet the Blue Sky' in the *U2 iNNOCENCE & eXPERIENCE: Live in Paris* concert film, Bono is singing through a blue megaphone decorated with the yellow stars of the

European Union around its horn. On the screens above him are images of stock market traders on one side, and protestors and the ruined streets of Syria on the other, placing them in opposition to each other. Bono speaks to *himself*: in the spoken-word segments, Bono describes a man who comes up to him, using a familiar description of events as in all live performances of the song ("A man comes up to me ...", Bono states). Bono says that the man looks very much like himself, and it is revealed that the person is actually a younger version of Bono. The younger Paul Hewson confronts Bono regarding his origins and nationality, and his current affluence and position of power and privilege: the younger version of Bono asks, "Can you hear those fighter jets in your private jet?" Because of this, the younger version of the singer accuses Bono of being a "part of the problem" rather than an agent for positive change in the world, working towards socioeconomic equality and the safety and access to sustenance that accompanies such a position. In fact, the nineteen-year-old Hewson is described as being on one side of a police barricade, assumedly protesting, while the present Bono is standing on the side with the police, obviously not a part of the protest or "revolution". The suggestion is that Bono cannot rightly speak using the words of the group on one side of the police barricade, if his position is now on the other side of the barricade. The position of being oppressed or suppressed cannot be taken by one who is on the side of oppression or suppression. One cannot be part of the solution if one is part of the problem. Bono engages with the accusations of complicity that many of U2's (and Bono's) critics employ. To play into the idea that Bono is working against – rather than helping – the cause that he purports to support, he puts his microphone stand over his shoulder as if it is a rocket launcher. He "fires" it towards the audience a number of times before he continues the dialogue with his younger self. Towards the end of his monologue, he concludes that everyone needs everyone else in order to enact change. Bono even calls on "the living and the dead and the unseen", a call to the "community of saints" and perhaps even the Christian trinity of God the Father, God the Son Jesus Christ and God the Holy Spirit. All need to be involved, including the millionaire rock band with their private jets. Of course, this is a convenient conclusion for Bono and the band.

This is, in fact, what many critics have posited about the band's involvement in political affairs: as unelected players, rock musicians are simply amassing "conscience capital", to use McLaughlin's term, by being involved in doing good. Are they performing authenticity, or put another way, are they *being real*? Even Bono seems to recognize here that his "campaigning has always been safely inside the dominant neoliberal consensus and in no sense has the singer offered a radical critique of existing geo-politics".[20]

Bono's response to the criticisms of his younger self is that it takes all people to effect change, and presumably, that he is in a good position to fill a role in encouraging such positive societal transformations. Even while trying to justify his role, Bono does acknowledge that he is spending much of his energy making sure that he does not make mistakes, or prove to be an embarrassment to himself. At the end of the song, instead of running into the protective arms of America, he runs into the arms of the Paris audience, an audience that represents, for him, a welcoming Europe, a Europe that can be a safe home for those fleeing conflict and injustice. Bono goes so far as to suggest that those refugees are searching for the French notions of liberty, equality and fraternity, ideas with which the Paris audience would be familiar.

Bono is being critical of his own subject position in the world in which he finds himself. About this kind of self-criticism, Adorno states,

> it is clear that something like the good life is not conceivable unless you hold fast to both conscience and responsibility ... we need to hold fast to moral norms, to self-criticism, to the question of right and wrong, and at the same time to a sense of the fallibility of the authority that has the conscience to undertake such self-criticism.[21]

Judith Butler puts it this way: "Do I establish myself in the terms that would make my life valuable, or do I offer a critique of the reigning order of values?"[22]

The band's discomfort with the European Union is a complex thing: U2 both want the European Union and make it the subject of criticism. But it seems that the band want the European Union to remain strong (and for the United Kingdom to remain a part of it) because the band want the European Union to work *better*: Bono and the band want it to accept more immigrants, and to be more accepting and open to those in need. The European Union is a site of potential for the open movement of migrants who need to be accepted into safety; the European Union is a site of potential or penchant for creating fences or walls in order to stop the movement of those in need. Leaving the European Union means a sloughing off of its influence in terms of immigration policy, or so some believe.

Perhaps this is the very apocalyptic vision that Bono portrays during the *Zoo TV* tour, with his goose step, his Nazi salute and the yellow stars falling from the sky-blue of the European Union flag: the European Union will fragment into hyper-nationalism, ushering the age of "Antichrist", or chaos – a reality of evil. Like the biblical apocalyptic writers, U2 are prophetically proclaiming this potential evil.

A new political imaginary in 2017's U2

In early 2017, U2 announced that they would be embarking on a tour to mark the thirtieth anniversary of the release of *The Joshua Tree*. *The Joshua Tree* was an international "break-out" album for the band, cultivating a widespread fan base. Some thirty years later, fans of the band anticipated a tour in support not of *The Joshua Tree*, but of a new release called *Songs of Experience*, a follow-up to 2014's *Songs of Innocence*. In an early 2017 interview with *Rolling Stone*, The Edge mentions that, after the iNNOCENCE + eXPERIENCE tour, the band went into the studio to finish work on the follow-up album: "when we came off the last tour, the Innocence and Experience indoor tour, we headed straight into finishing the second album of that set, *Songs of Experience*, which we were pretty much complete with … leading up to the end of the year. And then the election [happened] and suddenly the world changed".[23] The U.S. presidential victory of businessman, television celebrity and Republican candidate Donald Trump marked 2017 as somehow different for the band. Much of the follow-up album was written (and completed) in 2016, which was, for The Edge, a "different time" than 2017, and caused the band to pause, to rethink the album.

In response, the band decided to tour to celebrate the thirtieth anniversary of *The Joshua Tree*, an album that The Edge says is "really born again in this context". The new tour must be read in the context of Bono's own continued work for global social justice. In late 2016, Bono appeared in Montréal, discussing Canada's role in fostering The Global Fund, an initiative to help fight AIDS and other diseases in the developing world. Importantly, the band also released videos criticizing Trump as the Republican candidate in the American election. Bono – and, by extension, the band U2 – have rekindled a political imaginary that finds, at its core, a concern for the outsider and a dismay with power that is unchecked. This political imaginary is also problematic as it functions in a context which evokes Paul Virilio's notions of the "dromocracy" and "dromosphere", as examined in his books *Pure War* and *The Administration of Fear*.

In the 2017 interview with *Rolling Stone*, The Edge states that, at the time of *The Joshua Tree* in 1987, the band were exploring the roots of the musical styles with which they had previously engaged. Along with musical explorations came further cultural explorations into American literature and American ideals. The Edge states, "for someone from Ireland it [America] is a vast source of ideas and aspirations and inspirations and generations, America being the Promised Land … And this time was a Reagan moment where, in some ways, the vision of what America would be seemed under threat". Referring to historical figures such as Thomas Jefferson and John F. Kennedy, while evoking poet Emma Lazarus, known for the sonnet that is engraved at the base of the

Statue of Liberty in New York, The Edge states, "these were visionaries talking about the ideals of what America can be. We were grappling with those big ideas and now here we are again. It's crazy".[24]

Bono confirms these sentiments in comments made to Charlie Rose in an interview in September 2016: "America is like the best idea that the world came up with. Donald Trump is potentially the worst idea that ever happened to America, *potentially*". He continues by suggesting that America is not a *place* but an *idea*, representing, for instance, equality and justice for all, and, again, with a reference to Emma Lazarus and her sonnet, "The New Colossus", "Give me your tired, your poor, your huddled masses yearning to breathe free", that is, a haven for immigrants who are weary of travel.[25]

At the iHeartRadio Music Festival in Las Vegas in late September 2016, the band performed a politically charged version of 'Desire'. Katie Atkinson, writing for *Billboard*, describes the scene:

> We then got to hear from Trump himself: "The American Dream is dead", he asserted from the jumbotron, with Bono countering, "Are you ready to gamble the American Dream?" Then there was [a clip of] Trump's appeal to a predominantly black crowd in Michigan last month: "What do you have to lose?" That sound bite repeated throughout the song's finale before Bono shouted, "'What do you have to lose'? *Everything*!" to roaring applause and video of a fiery explosion taking over the big screens.[26]

In a concert performance, this time for the software company Salesforce, called "Dreamfest", live from San Francisco in October 2016, Bono questions then-candidate Donald Trump on the large screen behind the band: "What is your vision for this great nation?" Interspersed with clips of Trump's campaign speeches played over the band's forceful rendition of 'Bullet the Blue Sky', Bono continues to question the candidate, wondering if the well-publicized wall between the southern border of the United States and Mexico (which, as the clips make plain, the government and people of Mexico will pay for) will be "like the Berlin Wall", a wall that divided the city of Berlin from 1961 until the beginning of its dismantling – and, ultimately, fall of East German communism – in 1989. He continues and states, forcefully, "Good people are not going to stay silent while you run off with the American dream!" Bono continues to yell, "Inside it's America – Fortress America!" as barking dogs fill the screen, and The Edge begins the song's guitar solo.[27]

Virilio and dromocracy

Urban theorist Paul Virilio describes the state of the contemporary globalized world as one that threatens – and follows through with – what he calls an "informational bomb", brought about by the almost instantaneous communication of local catastrophic events to a global audience. He writes, "the same feeling of terror can be felt in all corners of the world at the same time".[28] This is due to the separation of communication from transport, a movement begun by the telegraph but intensified by current communications technologies.[29] Further to the idea of the information bomb, Virilio identifies the (potential) resultant society as one organized by the speed of its transport, weapons and communication: he calls this a "dromocracy", from dromology, Virilio's own conception of the science of movement and speed (taken from the Greek noun "dromos", referring to race or racetrack).[30] A dromocratic society suffers from the effects of an "information bomb", with what Virilio deems an excess of "dromospheric pressure, the tension created by speed in our daily lives and work".[31] Virilio states also, "As you know, I think about speed, about speed that becomes increasingly faster through technological progress, with which it combines to form what I call a 'dromosphere'".[32]

When asked about the song 'In God's Country', and the suggestion that long-suffering fans might be happy to hear that song live, The Edge responds, "That's the thing about *The Joshua Tree*. It's a very broad, CinemaScope kind of record. At the time we were thinking about it in cinematic terms ... the scope was cinematic. We were thinking of songs from that standpoint".[33] Using similar terms, Virilio writes,

> The world becomes a cinema. It's this effect of speed on the landscape that I called a *dromoscopy*, in the strict sense. We speak of stroboscopy, in other words the effects induced by an energy and a relation of observation on an object. But this stroboscopy is also a dromoscopy. What happens in the train window, in the car wind shield, in the television screen, is the same kind of cinematism. We have gone from the aesthetics of appearance, stable forms, to the aesthetics of disappearance, unstable forms.[34]

This is the world in which U2 had – and have – their being.

Virilio explores the world as dromoscopy "in the train window, in the car wind shield, in the television screen". For Virilio, the "focus" of the viewer through this screen is *distorted*. Away from the mediating screen, things are present and fixed (he describes these things as conforming to the "aesthetics of appearance, stable forms"), but through the mediating screen, the world – subject to dromocracy – is absent, or in a state of constant change. The "truth" of the world is subject to new forces that problematize it, that move it towards "post-truth", a time when perceived truth is in flux. For an idealistic band like U2, this can be a challenge, and it is no surprise that the group decided to shelve the release of an album and accompanying tour (if the band's explanation is the truth) and embark on a completely new tour with all of its monetary and temporal challenges.

Consider The Edge's words at the conclusion of the *Rolling Stone* interview: "I'm interested to see if in this new post-truth world, music sort of reconnects with the activist-protest thread that it had for so many years and seems to have lost recently ... I think it's time to get back to some of that".[35] Could the "cinematism" of Virilio's "dromoscopy", with its aesthetics of disappearance, unstable forms, be translated to what is being experienced in the early twenty-first century and a "post-truth" world, as The Edge puts it? Furthermore, The Edge seems to describe a world that seems to be living in a sort of "dromoscopic" drugged sleep, a world that has lost the "activist-protest thread" of vitality. This links to Virilio's notion of the dromocracy: Virilio suggests that the aim of the way of the world is "unconsciousness", that is, to be "taken by speed".[36] It is from this "unconsciousness" that U2 hopes to wake the world.

But what of the "cinematism" of a contemporary U2 concert performance? Does this not contribute to the "dromoscopy" of the world? Do the Trump clips and barking dogs constitute an aesthetic of unstable forms? From a certain perspective, U2 both contribute and push against the "dromocratic" nature of the contemporary world. Virilio's ideas regarding a "dromocracy" present themselves in U2's music: 'United Colours' from *Original Soundtracks 1* in 1994 refers to the city and speed trains; the distribution system for *Songs of Innocence* in 2014 (for many users, downloaded automatically through Apple's iTunes computer desktop application) does nothing to dispel a feeling of unchecked power. The band contribute to the immediacy and instantaneity of the contemporary global communications context: Virilio calls this a "dictatorship of speed at the limit", a culture of instant gratification and instant obsolescence.[37]

In his groundbreaking article on performance, Philip Auslander explores how the actor's performance works against the grounding principle of *logos*, or truth. The performing actor points away from themselves: the *logos* of a performance is the actor's self, or, more accurately, the actor in other roles and the knowledge that a viewer has of the actor in terms of private life and the general discourse that surrounds them.[38] Still, the viewer engages with the actor in the role of a persona. Auslander quotes Barthes stating that "The actor must prove ... that he guides meaning towards its ideality".[39]

Criticism towards U2 and their complicity is not new. But questions of complicity have come up more recently with revelations of Bono's investments in low-tax jurisdictions, in order to escape from paying taxes, as revealed in the Paradise Papers in late 2017. For instance, it was revealed that Bono had invested money in a company based in Malta. That company had, in turn, invested in a Lithuanian shopping mall.[40] Such labyrinthian financial dealings have cast a shadow on Bono's image as a supporter for the disenfranchised and marginal. In response to the Paradise Papers, Bono commented, "I didn't then, and I don't now, want to be complicit in a system that's got way out of control in terms of its opacity … I think you can be an investor as well as an activist – there's nothing wrong with being a thorn in your own side".[41] Steven Quinn suggests that criticism in terms of U2's complicity has occurred before, particularly in the context of the *Zoo TV* tour in the early 1990s. Quinn (following the work of Auslander) suggests that resistant performance can sometimes occur in the collusion between what he calls "the complicity of presence with the operations of power".[42] Auslander draws from Derrida in stating that "deconstruction cannot exist independently from the thing it deconstructs".[43] For Quinn, though, U2 are not resisting, but rather, transgressing: the band are "occupying the terrain that is being contested".[44] Quinn explains how Bono would answer interview questions as The Fly, who was, in turn, pretending he was Bono. There was no longer any distance between the two figures. Quinn quotes an interview in which the interviewer asks Bono the following: "The last time we saw you, you were a normal guy with normal clothes. Now you've got the fly boots, the fly suits, the fly goggles, what's going on?" In response, Bono (as The Fly mimicking Bono) states, "You didn't like me when I was me, so I've found somebody new, and you love him". Quinn concludes, "The critique of the rock star myth, then, is conducted through the very means that are used to construct it".[45] Auslander designates what might be going on as "post-Derridean acting", what Quinn calls "the practice that emerges when the activity of performing becomes an interrogation of those means through which it is constructed".[46] Auslander adds that "these tactics … produce polysemy, multiple meanings which imply the presence of an 'horizon' of meaning not the open, underground play of signification".[47]

Noel McLaughlin offers another possibility, though: one that is more simple and linked more closely to the *musical* journey of the band:

> this was not mere reversal – sincerity to irony; organic to electronic; authentic to inauthentic and so on. Rather, *Achtung*-era U2 offered a complex synthesis of authentic and inauthentic elements: of blues-country narratives – failed healing, partial redemption and the like – but set these in an unexpected sonic frame of dirty and distorted electronic timbres and "industrial" rhythms … This hybridity informed the approach to sound, with "expressive" or "warm" instruments, such as the Edge's guitar, being routed through vintage analogue synthesizers; and, in turn, synthesizers and keyboards were fed through guitar amplifiers and effects pedals, all of which created a bespoke sonic palette.[48]

Finally, Auslander adds: "Perhaps the actor can deconstruct her own work only to a limited extent within that work and it is the audience which makes the fundamental decision of whether to search for presence and determined meaning in a performance or to revel in the play of ungrounded significations".[49] It should be noted that U2 have always been aware of the roles that they play on stage. In an interview from 1979, Bono states, "There's [sic] two types of character being portrayed on stage: the Child – or the Boy – and the Fool, the clown. These are the two sides of what we want to project. If we always come across as serious, then we're not succeeding. We have no intention of playing the hero. We are *acting out* the role of hero".[50]

This might be what is happening with these examples of U2 criticizing Donald Trump. Referring to the band's subject position in the early 1990s, Quinn states, "They are inhabiting the very terrain of that contestation, their strategy not being determined by any sense of critical distance".[51] In other words, U2 are entering into the dromosphere, criticizing it while contributing to its construction. Perhaps the more accurate way of describing what U2 are doing is that they are *using* the dromosphere – and the context of a dromocracy – to *criticize* the dromosphere. This is what makes the band's strategy so interesting: the band are both the problem and the solution. Following in their own tradition, the members of the band construct contradictions, namely authenticity versus complicity, all within the context of commodity, that is, the band in live performance.

The dichotomy of authenticity and complicity in U2's late 2016 performances – performances that certainly inform the band's decision to embark on the shows commemorating *The Joshua Tree* in 2017 – puts U2 in a strange position, though not a new posture or attitude. The concerts demonstrate a problematic presentation of an often-constructed political imaginary, one that both transgresses against and contributes to the current cultural and political "dromospheric" context. The sleep that comes like a drug is not only a result of the dromocracy within which U2 operate, but a result of U2's own commodity construction.

"Herstory"

During *The Joshua Tree 2017* tour, the band made a point to change the narrative that has accompanied the song, 'Mothers of the Disappeared'. The song's title refers to a group of women from Argentina, Chile and El Salvador whose children had been secretly abducted by their governments (the term in international human rights law is "forced disappearance"). In the 2017 tour, the song is only a herald of an encore that Willie Williams, the band's artistic director, has called a third act that is an "ode to women".[52] Williams states,

"The thought was that we are currently living in a time when we could really use a more feminine spirit in our leadership and a way to illustrate this might be to celebrate some of the great female pioneers of the past".[53] This is obviously a thinly veiled critique of American politics in 2017: during the 2016 Presidential election, the Republican party candidate was Hilary Clinton, a woman who lost to Donald Trump. Thus, Williams and the band sought out Alice Wroe, whose project strives to "engage people of all genders in celebrating women's history – particularly women who have been left out (systematically or otherwise) of the traditional, historical canon".[54]

In the "herstory" portion of the show, the band dedicate the song 'Ultraviolet (Light my Way)' to the women in their lives, both personal (wives, mothers, daughters) and professional (such as the members of the U2 crew). Bono dedicates the song to the women who have "stood up or sat down for their rights. Women who insisted, resisted, persisted. You light our way". As Bono and the band begin the song, the giant *Joshua Tree 2017* screen above them displays the word "HISTORY" which transforms into "HERSTORY". On the screen come images of women including postcolonial scholar bell hooks, nurse and protestor Ieshia Evans (who is the subject of an iconic image from 2016 that has been called "Taking a Stand in Baton Rouge"), activist and author Angela Davis and eighteenth-century women's rights activist Mary Wollstonecraft. The song is transformed into a statement declaring male dependence on women, or, at least, the band's dependence on the women that are in their lives, including the women who are part of their audience. It is through the strength of these women that the band derive their strength. It is through the strength of women that the project of the band – and the idea of compassion and the future of leadership in the world – can continue.

Wroe suggests that the "herstory" portion of the show is of global importance in 2017: "If we don't look back and dig around for these women who were there and celebrate them in a serious way, how can we look forward and expect people like me and people like you to become the women we can be and change the world the way we can?" She taps into the sympathies of the band by stating that "practicing women's history is a political act".[55]

Speaking to Andy Greene about *The Joshua Tree 2017* tour, Bono suggests that he was attempting to ask the question, "Can we go into the future and what would the future sound like and feel like?" The answer, according to U2, is that the future is about women (Bono states, "[the] feminine spirit is crucial at times when the male hegemony is causing mayhem", which might be a veiled comment to counter Trump and his personal style). He continues to explain that the inspiration for the segment came from trying to determine the kind of person that those in power do not want to admit into the

United States (Bono mentions Trump specifically), and thus working directly against the tenets of Emma Lazarus and the sonnet on the Statue of Liberty. The band commissioned an artist to find one such person, a girl in a refugee camp named Omaima. Bono continues,

> She closes her eyes and J.R. asks her in another segment of the film we don't broadcast, "What do you see when you think of America?" She goes, "Oh, it is a civilized country and they are a good people". It was just heartbreaking ... Sometimes when we're playing it I have to turn away from the film. I can't sing when we're looking at it. It's very touching. She's so dignified and so authoritative. There's something of a future leader in her.[56]

The future, for Bono and the band, happens to be in the hands of women, which seems to be a direct counter to what the band perceives to be the spirit of America in the late 2010s. In the video, Omaima, a fifteen-year-old Syrian girl, says that she dreams of becoming a lawyer so that she could protect the rights of *all* people. In Omaima, U2 have identified a young woman, a refugee, a Muslim (as indicated by her *hijab*) who embodies much of what U2 are trying to accomplish: respect for women, and the opportunity for women to lead in a world full of patriarchy and misogyny; freedom of movement and freedom to succeed and flourish for refugees; and coexistence for Muslims in a sometimes Muslim-resistant West. Omaima is literally a spokesperson for U2's project in the late 2010s. The band are working for her, and are advocating for her, so that she could fulfil her dreams and advocate for others.

Chris Richards, writing for *The Washington Post*, describes a concert in Washington in June 2017 as one stop on a "tour across our damaged nation", supported by Bono's own declaration, "We will find common ground reaching for higher ground".[57] Richards echoes the sentiments of Quinn (and many others) of U2's intrinsic complicity: "Strangely, U2 won the night the same way that Donald Trump won the presidency: by promising to improve tomorrow by making it feel more like yesterday". Of course, it is not clear that *The Joshua Tree* itself emerged from a cultural and political context of "global optimism" (that is, the "yesterday" to which Richards refers). Rather, the album functioned for the band as a sort of defence of the American ideal, as Bono has made clear in interviews (including with Zane Lowe in July 2017). While the late 1980s might have been a "moment of global optimism", as Richards suggests, it was also the era of the conservative politics of Margaret Thatcher in the United Kingdom and Ronald Reagan in the United States, the former known for market deregulation and government privatization, the latter known for foreign policy that was, to some, meddling. And in stark opposition to the comments above, "The music certainly wasn't telling us to wake up", Richards writes, "Bono seems to believe that our planet's busted systems can and will be repaired, which makes it hard to decide whether he's a visionary, a saint, a power-groupie or a fool. His vague, bipartisan, ambiently patriotic rah-rah onstage Tuesday didn't help clarify any of that".[58]

Notes

1. Noel McLaughlin and Martin McLoone, "Hybridity and National Musics: The Case of Irish Rock Music", *Popular Music* 19.2 (2000): 184.
2. Bill Flanagan, *U2 at the End of the World* (New York: Delta, 1995), 52.
3. Juan Rodriquez, "Has Bono Sold Out?", *Ottawa Citizen* (11 February 2002), B2.
4. Chuck O'Donnell, "Bono's Music Fits American Mood", *Ottawa Citizen* (15 February 2002), A13.
5. Julie Hirschfeld David, Sheryl Gay Stolberg and Thomas Kaplan, "Trump Alarms Lawmakers with Disparaging Words for Haiti and Africa", *New York Times* (11 January 2018); available from https://www.nytimes.com/2018/01/11/us/politics/trump-shithole-countries.html (accessed 9 March 2018).
6. Gerry Smyth, "'Show Me the Way to Go Home': Space and Place in the Music of U2", in *Space and the Irish Cultural Imagination* (New York: Palgrave, 2001), 159.
7. Ibid., 163–64.
8. Ibid., 170.
9. There is little indication that the band are in support of American military intervention in the Middle East as a part of this "War on Terror". Their use of the flag does indicate a level of support for American's patriotic project, of which the "War on Terror" is a part.
10. Noel McLaughlin, "Bono! Do You Ever Take Those Wretched Sunglasses Off?: U2 and the Performance of Irishness", *Popular Music History* 4.3 (2009): 314.
11. Lynn Ramert, "A Century Apart: The Personality Performances of Oscar Wilde in the 1890s and U2's Bono in the 1990s", *Popular Music and Society* 32.4 (October 2009): 447–48.
12. Ibid., 450.
13. McLaughlin, "Bono! Do you Ever Take Those Wretched Sunglasses Off?", 319.
14. Bono, Testimony to the Senate Appropriations Subcommittee on State, Foreign Operations, and Related Programs, "The Causes and Consequences of Violent Extremism and the Role of Foreign Assistance" (12 April 2016); available from http://www.appropriations.senate.gov/imo/media/doc/041216%20-%20Bono%20-%20Testimony.pdf (accessed 5 July 2016).
15. United Nations Refugee Agency, "Will You Stand #WithRefugees?", *UNHCR.org*; available from http://www.unhcr.org/refugeeday/petition/ (accessed 11 July 2016).
16. Marcus Moberg, *Christian Metal: History, Ideology, Scene* (London: Bloomsbury, 2015), 28.
17. Ibid., 14, 16.
18. "With or without EU: U2 Urges UK to Vote Remain", *RTÉ Ten* (22 June 2016); available from http://www.rte.ie/entertainment/2016/0622/797363-with-or-without-eu-u2-urges-uk-to-vote-remain/ (accessed 12 July 2016).

19. Rebecca Omonira-Oyekanmi, "The Myth and Reality of Brexit and Migrants", in *The Brexit Crisis: A Verso Report* (London: Verso, 2016), chapter 9 (epub).
20. McLaughlin, "Bono! Do You Ever Take Those Wretched Sunglasses Off?", 316–17.
21. Theodor W. Adorno, *Problems of Moral Philosophy*, translated by Rodney Livingstone (Stanford: Stanford University Press, 2001), 169.
22. Judith Butler, "Can One Lead a Good Life in a Bad Life?", *Radical Philosophy* 176 (November/December 2012), 11.
23. Andy Greene, "The Edge Breaks Down U2's Upcoming 'Joshua Tree' Tour", *Rolling Stone* (9 January 2017); available from https://www.rollingstone.com/music/music-features/the-edge-breaks-down-u2s-upcoming-joshua-tree-tour-111050/ (accessed 25 April 2017).
24. Ibid.
25. "Bono: Trump has 'Hijacked the Party'", *Charlie Rose* (20 September 2016); available from https://www.youtube.com/watch?v=2bY8qGvhIFk (accessed 27 April 2017).
26. Katie Atkinson, "U2 & Drake Preach Love amid Tense Political Climate at iHeartRadio Music Festival", *Billboard* (24 September 2016); available from http://www.billboard.com/articles/columns/music-festivals/7518892/u2-drake-iheartradio-festival-politics-donald-trump (accessed 27 April 2017).
27. Jon Blistein, "Watch U2 Blast Donald Trump during San Francisco Show", *Rolling Stone* (6 October 2016); available from https://tinyurl.com/w443707 (accessed 27 April 2017).
28. Paul Virilio, *The Administration of Fear*, translated by Ames Hodges (Los Angeles: Semiotext(e), 2012), 30.
29. Ibid., 32–33.
30. Ibid., 27.
31. Ibid., 44.
32. Ibid., 15–16.
33. Greene, "The Edge Breaks Down U2's Upcoming 'Joshua Tree' Tour".
34. Paul Virilio and Sylvère Lotringer, *Pure War: Twenty-Five Years Later*, translated by Mark Polizzotti (Los Angeles: Semiotext(e), 2008), 97.
35. Greene, "The Edge Breaks Down U2's Upcoming 'Joshua Tree' Tour".
36. Virilio and Lotringer, *Pure War*, 134.
37. Paul Virilio, "Speed and Information: Cyberspace Alarm!", translated by Patrice Riemens, *CTHEORY* (27 August 1995); available from http://www.ctheory.net/articles.aspx?id=72 (accessed 29 April 2017).
38. Philip Auslander, "'Just Be Your Self': Logocentrism and Difference in Performance Theory", in *Acting Reconsidered: A Theoretical and Practical Guide*, edited by Phillip B. Zarrilli (London and New York: Routledge, 2002), 53–54.
39. Roland Barthes, "Diderot, Brecht, Eisenstein", in *Image – Music – Text*, translated by Stephen Heath (New York: Hill and Wang, 1977), 74–75.
40. Hilary Osborne, "Bono Used Malta-based Firm to Invest in Lithuanian Shopping Centre", *The Guardian* (5 November 2017); available from https://tinyurl.com/u2-paradise (accessed 6 November 2017).
41. Jonathan Dean, "U2 Interview: Bono on death, taxes and their new album Songs of Experience", *The Times* (19 November 2017); available from https://tinyurl.com/hsf7sf25k (accessed 10 August 2018).

42. Steven Quinn, "U2 and the Performance of (a Numb) Resistance", *Social Semiotics* 9.1 (1999): 69.
43. Auslander, "Just Be Your Self", 58.
44. Quinn, "U2 and the Performance", 68.
45. Ibid., 74.
46. Ibid., 77.
47. Auslander, "Just Be Your Self", 59. To the end of this sentence, Auslander adds, "to which Derrida refers".
48. Noel McLaughlin, "Another Green World? Eno, Ireland and U2", *Popular Music History* 9.2 (2014): 189.
49. Auslander, "Just Be Your Self", 60.
50. Niall Stokes, "Boys in Control", in *The U2 File: A Hot Press U2 History 1978–1985*, edited by Niall Stokes (Dublin: Hot Press, 1985), 24.
51. Quinn, "U2 and the Performance", 79.
52. "'Herstory'", *U2.com* (29 June 2017); available from http://www.u2.com/news/title/herstory?hootPostID=d4a02bd7b85ab6fc301ddb756edf601a (accessed 1 August 2017).
53. Ibid.
54. Ibid.
55. Ibid.
56. Andy Greene, "Bono Talks 'Joshua Tree' Tour, Trump, Status of U2's Next Album", *Rolling Stone* (30 May 2017); available from https://www.rollingstone.com/music/features/bono-on-joshua-tree-tour-trump-u2s-next-album-w484398 (accessed 5 March 2018).
57. Chris Richards, "U2 Goes MAGA at FedEx Field", *Washington Post* (21 June 2017); available from https://tinyurl.com/post-style-u2 (accessed 2 August 2017).
58. Ibid.

5 The Rosary and the Microphone: Social Justice and the Stage

U2 are well known for their live performances. Their tours have been well-received, and are almost unmatched in terms of sheer spectacle. Since the early 1990s, U2 have made a point of emphasizing their live performances by releasing concert films for each tour in support of each album (currently, only the *Joshua Tree 2017* tour and the *eXPERIENCE + iNNOCENCE* tour have yet to be treated to a home video release).

These home video releases are important as they bring the concert experience to those fans who are unable to attend a live performance. But they also allow for the fostering of an intimate relationship between fans and the band. Fans get to see U2 perform their craft in close-up, while experiencing the spectacle of live performance from all viewing angles, and with optimum sound.

It is clear that the live performance context shows a thriving U2. While Bono has had his share of vocal difficulties, the band seem not to have trouble with performing to a large audience on massive stages, dwarfed by massive mediating screens. Bono has lost his voice in concert on a few occasions, as early as the late 1980s and as recently as 2018. Unlike live performance, their difficulties in producing albums that pass their own critical muster are well-documented in the popular press, and demonstrated by long delays between releases.

The band's evolving stage design demonstrates their continuing relationship with fans, but the stage also plays into their project of promoting social issues. While the stage allows greater intimacy with the audience (both the primary audience who attends the concert and the secondary audience that experiences the band through the mediation of the concert film), it also works to harness the desire of the audience towards global concerns, *away* from the band.

Live concert performance is also where U2's audience experiences Bono in the role of various personae, which makes for an interesting paradox. Fans at a concert are in (relative) near proximity to the singer, except that the singer is not himself (inasmuch as he is himself as "Bono"). Bono's personae, though, are yet another manifestation of the band's public face, and are present particularly on the stage.

U2's changing stage design demonstrates a change of philosophy for the band, and indicates a way of including the audience in their performance, effectively demonstrating inclusivity and the fostering of a *potential* new way of living with one another. The stage becomes a signifier of a greater concept, rather than simply being a performing space for a band. The stage becomes a sort of beacon that signifies a new way forward, away from simply a part of the spectacle of a live concert performance.

In the 1980s, the band utilized a basic and conventional stage design. In their earliest concert performance film, *U2 Live at Red Rocks: Under a Blood Red Sky*, from 1983, the stage set-up is as one might expect: the band perform on a rectangular stage with the drums in the back and the lead singer, guitarist and bass player positioned in a straight line along the front of the stage, with the guitarist stage right and the bass guitarist stage left. This particular placement of musicians has basically remained constant throughout their career. Notably, the stage does not feature any video screens, and the only element that differentiates the stage for this particular performance is a backdrop which shows the cover of *War*, the album that is being promoted during this tour. Notably, Bono wears a black t-shirt emblazoned with "U2" over the image of a waving white flag. The shirt seems to foreshadow a striking moment in the concert, and an early example of U2 using props on stage to interact with the audience and to make a particular point. In this case, the point seems to be a political one. During the performance of 'Sunday Bloody Sunday', Bono emerges from the back of the stage with a white flag on the end of a flag pole, which he brings to the front of the stage. He goes on to hand the flag pole to those in the front row of the crowd, and he implores them to "hold it high". He holds it steady for them when they begin to wave the flag around. This is Bono beginning his semiotic project: because 'Sunday Bloody Sunday' is not a rebel song – not a song in support of the Irish Republican Army and Northern Irish separation from the United Kingdom – nor is it a song in support of Loyalist forces, the flag signifies *nothing*. It is not a signifier of *lack*, but it is traditionally a signifier of surrender; here it is a signifier of a kind of retreat from any sort of conflict in hopes of moving in a new, as-yet-unknown direction.

In July 1987, the band performed a concert in Paris in support of *The Joshua Tree*. The concert film was subsequently released as part of a twentieth anniversary edition of the album in 2007. For that concert, the band utilize (again) a conventional stage design, performing outdoors (similar to the concert at Red Rocks). The sound system is located on either side of the stage proper, covered in coloured fabric: the backdrop of the stage and the fabric covering the two sides of the stage over the loudspeakers come together to create the image of a silhouette of the original Joshua Tree from one of the album photos. In addition to this aesthetic addition, Mullen Jr's drum kit is raised from the rest of the band on a riser and there is a small protruding rectangular stage at the front of the main stage. This allows Bono to get closer to the audience and, perhaps, any press photographers that desire better pictures of the band.

With the *Zoo TV* tour, the stage setup becomes much more elaborate – and seemingly intentional – than before. It is intentional in the sense that there is a specific reason why the stage is designed in a particular way, apart from utility or convention. Here, there is much more intentional design than just an album cover or silhouette-printed fabric. The stage remains rectangular, with the conventional setup of The Edge on Bono's right and Adam Clayton on his left, and Larry Mullen Jr slightly raised on a drum riser at the rear. But the materials that make up the stage are a focus of attention: scaffolding holds up screens and small cars are suspended as spotlights. Also, the rectangular stage protrusion remains, and this time for the *explicit* reason of allowing photographers to take better pictures of Bono in the guise of The Fly. In addition to this, there is a walkway that extends from stage right, leading to a smaller square stage that seems to be a sort of island in the sea of the crowd. Notably, there are multiple cameras around the stage and a camera crane on the walkway from the main stage to the smaller stage. The visual material captured by these cameras – and others – populate the multiple screens that are all over the stage. The screens come in various sizes, from walls of screens to smaller square screens similar to what one might have in a home living room. A writer for U2's own fan club publication *Propaganda* writes, "Unlike other rock tours where sophisticated video equipment accompanies the band in order to make them more accessible to the audience, the *Zoo TV* tour almost seems to make U2 less accessible, more obscure and enigmatic in their stage presence, competing for attentions with a manic host of moving images".[1] Bill Flanagan describes it as follows: "The lights dim and President Bush appears on screen to tell the audience 'We will, we will rock you!' while Adam, Edge, and Larry slip onto the stage in the darkness. The intro to 'Zoo Station' blasts out of the dark as the Vidiwalls fill up with blue snow and static".[2] The idea of the band venturing out into the crowd via a walkway and "B stage", as demonstrated in the *Zoo TV* tour stage, is an element that becomes common in subsequent tours.

During the *Zoo TV* tour, the main stage can be described as a bit of a "mess". In one sense, it is compelling as a vision of a postmodern city (as, say, critic Paul Rosenfeld might suggest, with its expression of a sort of "skyscraper mysticism").[3] It is also dark, confusing and distracting. In the *Zoo TV: Live from Sydney* concert film, the camera focuses not on The Edge, for instance. Rather, the camera looks past The Edge and focuses on the guitarist on the screens that are on the stage. The viewer sees a doubly mediated version of The Edge: the viewer engages with The Edge on the stage screen *and* on the screen with which they are viewing the concert film. The camera's focus is on the stage screen, not on The Edge himself: the real guitarist is *looked past*.

This is not possible with Bono: he directly engages with the crane-mounted camera that is stationed on the walkway to the B stage. He grabs the camera by its apparatus and looks directly into it. In fact, the camera is fitted with a harness with handles which allows Bono to more easily grab it and push it away. He takes the camera and draws it towards his groin, thrusting towards it in what is, frankly, a confusing scene. Such gestures add to the visual confusion of the tour, potentially leaving the viewer somewhat shaken. Bono's gestures on the walkway appear during a performance of the *Achtung Baby* track, 'Until the End of the World'; the viewers' and fans' concerns are perhaps assuaged with the next track, 'New Year's Day' from *War*. Things settle, at least for a time, and the "authentic" U2 return, peeling away the disorienting layers of mediation and personae.

For the next tour called *PopMart* (after 1997's *Pop* album), Willie Williams, the band's stage designer, moved away from utilizing multiple screens that obscured the band during the *Zoo TV* tour, to using a single screen in order to obscure the band. The *PopMart* tour stage features a fifty-metre wide screen which takes up most of the back of the stage. While conventional thought would be that the screen would enable all those in attendance to see the band, the screen actually serves (again) to obscure the band. While the *Zoo TV* tour screens serve to hide or obscure the band, the large screen in *PopMart* effectively dwarfs the band, erasing them. The band are hidden in the massive sea of pixels that make up the screen.

The Large Screen Video Display (or LSVD) is the sort of display that might be at a sporting event, and of which the screen in *PopMart* is a gross exaggeration. According to Greg Siegel, the LSVD is a "hypermedium", and it not *only* works as a "*medium-that-channels* that which is out of reach" but also as an "*intermediary-that-obstructs* (and *constructs*) ... that which is already at hand". He writes, "The stadium spectator's willful, if intermittent, withdrawal from the immediacy of the real ... in favour of the hypermediation of LSVD contrasts with the television viewer".[4] For the audience attending a *PopMart* concert, there is almost no way for them to resist the hypermediation of the screen; if *Zoo TV* encourages the audience to "watch more TV", then *PopMart* gives them the means to do so. Siegel quotes Eichberg in suggesting that the hypermedium allows for hypervisuality, a mode of seeing that is, in fact, novel and not conventional:

Increasingly, we see large screens inside the arenas used to present the events in visual detail. They are able to enlarge on selected scenes; they reproduce processes in slow motion and split the visual impression up into a multiplicity of pictures. It is no longer the visuality of the traditional modern stadium – it is hypervisuality.[5]

In addition to the screen, the stage features a golden arch emerging from the centre of the stage from which the speakers are hung. The speakers become a key visual element in the design of the stage: coloured orange, the speakers hang from the arch above the very centre of the stage. Towards the end of the concert performance, for the encore, the band would arrive from off-stage in a large motorized mirror-ball lemon, mounted on a motorized vehicle. The lemon would open vertically, revealing the members of the band who were standing inside of it, and who would then walk down a stairway from the lemon platform to the separate B stage below. Concert t-shirts from the tour feature a stylized shopping cart orbiting around a lemon-shaped planet.

The tours changed the way with which the audience engaged with the band through screens. Whereas the band are eclipsed (in the *Zoo TV* tour) or enhanced (in the *PopMart* tour) by video screens, the first two tours of the 2000s feature the individual members of the band showcased on four dedicated screens at the top of the stage. For instance, one screen focuses solely on Bono throughout the concert. A fan who might wish to follow Bono throughout the show could pay attention to a single screen: in this instance, the screens are not a focus but rather a sort of supplement to the concert experience. The screens do not *hinder* the visibility of the band.

During the *Elevation* tour, in support of *All That You Can't Leave Behind*, the band utilize a conventional stage (again, with the band's conventional placement on it), but instead of placing the band at the front of a stage, the band are placed on a stage that is positioned towards the back of a surrounding walkway loop shaped like a heart, with the heart's bottom point oriented farthest away from the drummer and penetrating deeply into the crowd. If the 1990s version of U2 – as expressed semiotically through their stage design – seems to signify confusion and artifice, the 2000s version of the band, as expressed for the first time with the *Elevation* tour, seems to express a return to "authenticity", with the ability afforded the band members to walk more closely to and among the audience, who surround the stage.

Beginning with the *Elevation* tour, the band resurrect a version of their earlier "authentic" selves. After the "inauthentic" or "complicit" version of U2 that came with the triptych of *Achtung Baby*, *Zooropa* and *Pop* and the accompanying *Zoo TV* and *PopMart* tours, the band emerge in the 2000s as, again, authentic

– albeit now global superstars and thus complicit with the popular music performance/celebrity machine.

Nevertheless, this new authenticity is expressed through a renewed sense of accessibility even in the context of pop music superstardom. Instead of the band playing to large stadium venues with audiences of tens of thousands of people, the band played multiple nights at smaller indoor arena venues, with perhaps an audience of around fifteen thousand fans at each concert. During the *Elevation* and *Vertigo* tours, the band also allowed fans to buy cheaper tickets closer to the band. These ticketed seats were situated *behind* the stage. This not only allowed more fans and concert goers to be seated close to the band, but also allowed the band to sell more tickets in a seating area that was not available in previous tours due to the elaborate stage setups. For instance, a television screen takes up the complete length of the rear of the stage in *PopMart*, removing a wide swath of seats available to prospective concert attendees, not to mention the accompanying ticket revenue. While the use of the back of the stage allows for financially accessible tickets (the tickets were cheaper as the vantage point was from behind the band), it also provides for *more* tickets. And the potential for higher ticket sales results in potentially higher revenues. In relation to this, for those two tours (and for the following *U2 360°* tour as well), the band employ a stage design that features a walkway for Bono and the other band members to further interact with the audience. The stage design also allows the band to sell tickets to fans that wish to be *closer* to the band: those who wish to be in the standing-room-only area within the perimeter of the walkway (shaped as a heart during the *Elevation* tour and a circle during the *Vertigo* tour) and directly in front of the main stage would have to pay for a premium ticket. The sales of premium tickets – with premium ticket prices – would result in higher revenues.

For the *Elevation* tour, the band began the concerts with all house lights on, which was different from the conventional concert format. Usually, a concert begins in darkness, with all of the house lights turned down. In *Elevation*, the band members are fully visible to the audience – as is the infrastructure of the stage – and the audience is fully visible to the band. The fans and the band can see each other. This is a rarity in rock performance, where the band are the sole focus during a performance, singled out by lighting.

The band also express this new authenticity in the notion of *immersion*. In the *Vertigo* tour, the stage is made up of concentric circles that emanate from Mullen Jr's position behind the drum kit. The walkway forms one of these concentric circles around the circular stage (replacing the heart-shaped walkway used during the *Elevation* tour). During the songs, lighting embedded in the circles that decorate the stage and make up the walkway create various effects.

Visually, these effects work to include the people who are both in the premium standing-room-only section and those outside of it. Effectively, the concentric circles *include* the audience in the concert experience, in the creation of the music. They *immerse* the audience in the performance.

In addition, the lighting that is inherent in the arena, that is, the screens that are attached to the edges of the stands all around the performance space, are brought into the concert performance. Those screens, which might normally be used to show advertising or game scores during a sporting event in that arena, are now used as additional lighting for the concert experience (this is interesting logistically in that the band somehow *interface* with the location's own systems in order to use them to enhance the concert). The facility's technologies are used as lighting for the concert, resulting in a truly immersive concert experience for the fans. During a performance of 'Vertigo' during the *Vertigo* tour, the screens around the arena pulse with the same red with which the lighted walkway pulses, creating a beat that flows throughout the space, immersing the audience in the same, all-encompassing experience. The audience is truly at one with the band, all beating with the same heart, so to speak.

The design philosophy (one that might be referred to as "inclusive") finds its climax or ideal form in the *U2 360°* tour design. There, the stage is moved to the centre of the performance space, with the crowd surrounding the stage and the walkway encircling the complete stage (to continue the earlier thread, this allows for even more "exclusive" tickets to be sold, as the area within the perimeter of the walkway is much larger than in the heart of *Elevation* or circle of *Vertigo*). Furthermore, a large screen returns in the *U2 360°* tour: here the screen expands and contracts horizontally, much like a living organism. The screen faces the entire audience, encircling the central spire of the stage like a ribbon. Kimi Kärki claims that the *U2 360°* tour is an "interesting example of a techno-utopian staging that approaches the technology as a religion, both by form and by content, as something paradoxically both intimate and far-reaching – a strange and captivating utopian dream".[6] Certainly, the stage highlights yet another tension in U2's presentation, between intimacy and being out of reach.

U2 Live in Paris

During *iNNOCENCE + eXPERIENCE*, and its sibling tour, *eXPERIENCE + iNNOCENCE* (in support of *Songs of Experience*), the stage set-up changed. The tours in the 2000s (besides the *U2 360°* tour) and the 2010s are arena tours, generally focusing on multiple concerts in these somewhat smaller concert venues (as compared to stadiums). The stage happens to be situated in the centre of the arena, showing that the band are incorporating the strategies for optimizing both audience numbers and the accessibility of tickets of the previous tours. Here, however, the band are playing on what might be considered a conventional rectangular stage situated at one end of the arena, without a backdrop of any kind, allowing for a full arena of available tickets. The stage also consists of a prominent walkway leading from the centre of the rectangular stage to a smaller circular stage at the other end of the arena. What really sets this stage configuration apart from the other more conventional designs is a set of huge screens that are set into an apparatus that itself contains lighting and a walkway. The screens act as accompaniments to the songs; the screens do not only display the band as they perform, but they also display other videos supporting the narrative of the concert performance. This apparatus, with its walkway and screens, can be suspended into the air, which allows the band to walk back and forth from the main stage to the B stage at will. But the apparatus can also lower so that the band can walk through it from one stage to the other. During a performance of 'Cedarwood Road', Bono walks between the screens while suspended in the air, and The Edge walks on the walkway directly below him at the same time.

David Pattie argues that the stage itself is a site of meaning-making. For U2, the stage is a primary site of engagement with their fans. It is literally a "global platform", a stage that travels around the world, in order for the band to convey their message and to fulfil their project. In particular, this global platform, and its particular drive for social justice, is on display in U2's *iNNOCENCE + eXPERIENCE: Live in Paris* concert film, recorded live on 7 December 2015, and broadcast on HBO the same day. The concert is especially pertinent in that it acts as a politically charged site for global sentiments after the Paris terrorist attacks in November 2015, which included a mass shooting at the Bataclan concert hall. Because of the terrorist attacks, the first scheduled concerts were postponed by a month. The promotional material in advance of the rescheduled concert on the band's website describes the show as "Our best for Paris", and promotes the Twitter hashtag, "#STRONGERTHANFEAR". In addition to these promotional items, the stage itself (along with its screens) expresses the band's global cosmopolitanism and drive for social justice in the face of global terrorism and local unrest.

The audience of a band shares a kind of "collective memory". This collective memory can sometimes be created solely by the band or the people who work for the band in the roles of artists, designers and so forth. Alternately, this collective memory can be built through experiences that the band and its audience share. This shared memory is built by many different elements in popular music, such as the recorded music itself, media packaging, live concert experiences as well as music video and live concert films. Pattie theorizes that music video and live performance can be read as similar performative events in which the artist is perceived as authentic: the live performance "prizes the performance of the artist's self, in a manner that is designed to appear candid and truthful – or, in other words, authentic".[7] Pattie continues, "the relation between the performer, the stage persona, and the idea of the real person exists within the performance event".[8]

Pattie concludes that, even in places where "processes of authenticity are not where they seem to be", or where "performance as constructed mediation seems to clash with the ... spontaneity of the live event, the ideology of authenticity is still present".[9] That is, when the audience is watching a music video in which, for instance, the musical performer is acting some role, they still feel that there is some authentic connection with the performer. Similarly, when the audience present at a live concert focuses not on the live band that is playing in front of them but rather on the screens that magnify them, there is still the desire for an authentic experience, an experience with the authentic band. Pattie points out that the audience knows who is responsible for the sound produced in live performance, no matter how mediated the band or performance might be, or, by extension, how many layers of mediation there might exist between the band and the listener.[10]

Pattie explores the evolution of U2's live performance, and their increased use of technology, stating that "simplicity was a point of pride" in their early performances. But this changed: "it seemed as though U2 had taken to heart the idea that post-Cold War culture was thoroughly mediated".[11] He describes how, in much of U2's later career, the technology serves to immerse the audience in the event of the live concert.[12] In fact, U2 begin to use *mediating* technology explicitly during the *Zoo TV* tour, video screens that serve to obscure rather than to reveal. The use of immersive technologies – primarily visually-based – continued through the 1990s, moving to larger screens. In the *U2 360°* tour and in *iNNOCENCE & eXPERIENCE*, the band use mediating televisual technologies as significant parts of the stage design, in that these elements physically move all through the performance, providing important pieces to the narrative. The evolution, from the original *Joshua Tree* tour to the *Zoo TV* tour – from the absence to the presence of mediating televisual technologies on stage – would have been visually stunning (and potentially disorienting) for fans who did not expect such displays from the "authentic" U2. But, because of that drastic change in the early 1990s, a U2 concert is now characterized by its use of mediating televisual technologies. U2 would be "inauthentic" without it.

Pattie writes, "leaving aside the fact that a 'real' U2 is clearly present, paradoxically, in the midst of the ironic mediatisation of the event (which is, after all, heavily authored ...), the old, authentic version of the band surfaces at such moments ... [in] the IMAG [Image Magnification] images of the musicians themselves, engaged in the creation of the music".[13] In other words, U2 are clearly present in the performance space even while being mediated. And the band, in all its "authenticity", is present also through its mediation. The audience might see the band singing and playing their instruments without the aid of any sort of magnifying screens, and the audience also sees the band performing in the form of magnified images.

Conversely, Bono himself has talked about how the IMAG system distances the band from the audience. Discussing *The Joshua Tree 2017* tour with Andy Greene, he says,

> It's all very well going back to where you started in terms of not using IMAG [screens]. That's the way we became the band that wrote *The Joshua Tree*. It's great to play like that, but it's hard for some people since they're used to IMAG. I just felt, "Can't we just concentrate on the music?" People weren't taking out their phones, which was amazing. [It] was just listening, so I really have to make the singing be the connective tissue, from my point of view. There's [*sic*] no images available ... you're just these four dots at the start of the show. Then, presto, just add water and you become giants.[14]

So, *without* the screens, the relationship between the band and the audience is both intimate and distant at the same time. Bono suggests that the audience is listening to his singing voice when the screens are not on; they are not engaging with a mediated version of the band through screens, whether they be the massive IMAG screens or those of their cell phones. The intimacy originates in the idea that the audience is simply listening, and it is through that engagement with the "four dots", basically Bono's voice as "connective tissue", that the band enter into an intimate relationship with the audience. And then, suddenly, the band become huge – and potentially break that intimacy – once the IMAG screens are engaged.

Pattie continues, "At these moments ... what is displayed is not the moment where agency disappears into mediation, but the moment where mediation reveals agency; at these points, technology does not distance – it immerses". Immersion, here, is the important idea. Pattie explains that the technology works "toward an experience of immersion, in which band and audience trade on, reactivate and develop a shared performance history".[15] The band, through mediation, foster this idea of a shared history with their audience.

But in the case of the *iNNOCENCE + eXPERIENCE* tour, immersion does not seem to be the result. While it can be argued that the technology serves as "image magnification", here the video literally *obscures* the artists. This is nothing new: televisual images obscured the band in *Zoo TV* and *PopMart* in the

1990s (small screens and a humongous screen, respectively). While the video during the *iNNOCENCE + eXPERIENCE* tour *does* show the band as they are *currently* playing live in concert, the band could be hidden in another room if they needed to be. But it should be noted that this is *not* what is happening in this case: the band are present. But they are present in the physical space between two screens that both show and obscure the band from the audience.

Disreality

In his discussion of the discourse between lovers, Roland Barthes talks about the concept of "disreality", a sort of "withdrawal of reality" experienced by the lover.[16] In a way, Barthes' experience of disreality is similar to the experience of depersonalization, the separation of a person from the external world, and from their own subjectivity. The section of the book in which Barthes explores this idea betrays the writer's own social anxieties, such as not wanting to talk to others and so forth. He writes, "So long as I perceive the world as hostile, I remain linked to it: *I am not crazy*".[17] This is analogous to live performance in popular music: there is a tension that exists between outward concern, empathy and inclusion, and the (exclusive) focus of popular music fandom. Barthes' own reluctance to communicate with others demonstrates a similar discomfort that exists in what can be considered a "charitable" impulse that is cultivated in the context of a multi-million-dollar live performance.

But it is clear that Barthes is making a distinction between disreal and unreal: it is not that what he experiences is not real (unreal) but rather that "I no longer have any meaning (any paradigm) available to me". The disreal cannot be uttered (unlike the unreal, which is uttered in novels and poems).[18] In his exploration of disreality, Barthes writes of the experience of sitting in a café and looking through the glass window at a poster. For Barthes, the window acts as a barrier, or a mediator, of the visual experience of the poster.[19]

Later, Barthes writes, "The first time I saw X [that is, his lover] through a car window: the window shifted, like a lens searching out *who to love* in the crowd; and then – immobilized by some *accuracy* of my desire? – I focused on that apparition whom I was henceforth to follow for months".[20] This object of desire, for Barthes, seems to enter into the realm of the disreal, that which cannot be uttered, but that which is also mediated (through the car window in this latter case, the café window in his earlier discussion) and fundamentally separate from the subject.

How does this fit, then, with U2 and their performance during the tour? During 'Even Better Than the Real Thing', the band are performing on the walkway in the centre of the arena, surrounded on either side by screens which effectively obscure them completely. If the screens are dark and lights are on between them, then the audience is able to see the individual band members. But during 'Even Better Than the Real Thing', they are obscured by colourful footage of themselves performing, and it is only in fragments of darkness that the viewer sees the actual physical bodies between the screens. Bono announces this portion of the concert by stating that it is the "heartbeat of innocence and experience". This occurs after the band perform the song 'Invisible', during which Bono states emphatically, "There is no them, there's only us", a call seemingly to unity and to destroy the division between fan and celebrity.

As David Dark suggests, there have been those who find U2 "insufferable" from the earliest days of the band (Dark calls U2 an "Irish arts collective"); such a sentiment has increased as the band have gained a larger audience, as well as greater monetary success. Dark suggests this is because people like to have boundaries or categories in order to *order*: "The placeholders are mind-numbingly familiar. Keep religion out of politics (or vice versa). Are you an artist or an activist? Sacred or secular?" He states, "they are still wrestling out loud with and awash in the contradictions of wealth and consciousness". Instead, he calls what the band does a "divine comedy":

> This vision of comedy – divine comedy – is behind a healing truism that Bono has offered in words of appreciation for opponents of fascism everywhere, both structural and that fascism of the heart Bruce Cockburn refers to as "fascist architecture of my own design", the self-seriousness that can't and won't see.[21]

He suggests that U2 are anti-fascist, against Cockburn's "fascist architecture of my own design". That is, they are working against a sort of hyper-selfishness, a belief in personal supremacy, not wanting to work towards cooperation and instead demand obedience to one's own wishes and whims. Dark makes a startling comparison between Bono and Roman Catholic monk and writer Thomas Merton, who writes, "The whole illusion [in the experience of living] of a separate holy existence is a dream".[22] In other words, "There is no them". There are two possible agendas that emerge out of this for U2: the audience needs to work against this idea of "anti-love", this "fascism" of each person's life; and everyone needs to recognize that "there is no them".

This is not a new idea if one considers Bono holistically. It is possible to see U2 as never separating the two elements of religion and rock. Consider, for instance, the mention of Christian sacraments – bread and wine – in 'Until the End of the World' and 'When I Look at the World'. At the end of the *Vertigo 2005: Live from Chicago* concert film, Bono drapes his rosary on the microphone and mentions his priest friend at the University of Notre Dame, a concrete example of this conflation of religion and popular music. In the song, 'God Part

II', from *Rattle and Hum*, John Lennon is named as synonymous with Christianity, even being posited as the epitome of its true expression. Michael J. Gilmour suggests that the central tenet of U2's music is encapsulated in 1 John 4:7-8: "Beloved, let us love one another, because love is from God; everyone who loves is born of God and knows God. Whoever does not love does not know God, for God is love". Bono seems to recognize something of God (in that "everyone who loves is born of God") in the figure of John Lennon. This is especially evident in Lennon's song, 'God', the direct inspiration to U2's 'God Part II'. Gilmour explains, "Lennon tells the world to love one another but so does the New Testament, which for Bono is a critical oversight by his singer-songwriter predecessor".[23] In 'Acrobat', Bono sings that he would participate in the Eucharist – that is, the sharing of the Lord's supper, a ritual instituted by Jesus Christ the night before his Passion – if there was a community that would have him. Presumably, then, the stage is Bono's "church", his place of communing with others and with God. In a video describing U2's performance during the Super Bowl Halftime Show in 2002, Bono states, "We play 'Where the Streets Have No Name' whenever we need God to walk through the room".[24] W. David. O. Taylor broadens the scope, recounting Bono saying, "I have a church that I'm a part of and it has road crew in it, and when U2 goes on tour, it's like a whole city moves around the whole world. It's a big parish". The world is U2's parish.[25]

U2's audience never engages with Bono when he is not, in some sense, performing: the audience always encounters the "rock star" and never Paul Hewson. He showcases his particular, peculiar, brand of Christianity whenever he is in public; in fact, he embodies this particular, peculiar, brand of Christianity. The Christianity that is embodied in Bono is a Christianity that is tinted with rock. Gilmour expresses U2's co-mingling with religion with much deft:

> U2's music often includes religious content but it is a highly creative, restless and wondering relationship with religious mysteries. They look for the baby Jesus under the trash and would take bread and wine if there were a church they could receive in, but their articulation of sacred themes is often playful and always incomplete, as if they never quite find what they are looking for.[26]

For U2, then, it is both religion and rock music, not one or the other. Just as in the early days of the band and their experience with the Shalom Fellowship, there is just no way for the group to let the two elements – religion and music – be separated, or, for that matter, to let one go. Rather, religion and rock music seem conflated so much that they are intrinsically one and the same. The stage is, indeed, Bono's church, where he encounters the Divine, and from where he encourages others to encounter that Divine in the faces of those around them, and those well beyond the confines of their local circles.

Iain Thomson suggests as much, though he arrives at that end via a different path. In discussing U2 as a particularly *postmodern* band, especially after *Achtung Baby* and into *Zooropa* and the accompanying *Zoo TV* tour, Thomson specifically explores the song 'Even Better Than the Real Thing'. The song can be read in a number of ways. First, 'Even Better Than the Real Thing' can be read as a song between two lovers, in which the protagonist is requesting another chance at making the relationship work. Thomson suggests that there is another reading that is more appropriate, especially in light of the idea of U2 as a postmodern band. He suggests that the song is addressed to the broader audience and "seeks to transform this entire audience into the beloved".[27] Thus, U2 are attempting to create a communal experience, and one that is based on the idea of communal love. The idea is that communal love is better (as in the title of the song) than the love between two individual lovers. Thomson states, "Heard in this communal register, the erotic meaning that 'I'm gonna make you sing' has when addressed to a particular lover becomes transformed, elevated into a celebration of communal singing as an ecstatic experience that transcends even the feeling of real love between two individuals".[28] Connecting to Gilmour's idea (that Lennon's notion of love is appropriated by Bono as a fundamentally and intrinsically Christian idea), Thomson states that:

> the communal experience of universal love, a love transcending the bounds even of the community in which it is experienced, and so working (ethically, spiritually, erotically, politically) to both reinforce and expand the bounds of those communal bonds by extending the feelings of unity, sympathy, and belonging beyond the contingent limits of a group – toward that universe experienced in love which both inspires and beckons for such an unlimited embrace.[29]

This is U2's project, then, to not only transform the entire audience into the beloved, but also to transform the world into the beloved for the audience. And, for Thomson, this points to U2 as "Christ-emulating rather than 'Christian theology' following".[30] Interestingly, Thomson refers to U2's ideology as "Christ-ianity" (rather than the conventional "Christianity"), in order to convey the idea that U2's religious impulse might be initially informed by institutional Christianity, but is manifest or played out in a much broader way than institutional doctrines or dogmas would allow, and may even be manifest in the face of those doctrines or dogmas.

Ironically, during the performance of 'Even Better Than the Real Thing' from *iNNOCENCE + eXPERIENCE: Live in Paris*, that call – "There is no them" – is followed by a performance that signals a sort of division, social anxiety and depersonalization, not necessarily something conventionally desirable in live performance. The relationship that the viewer of the concert film has with the band is doubly mediated: the viewer sees the band through the window of the mediating screen (television, phone, computer monitor) *and* the screens on either side of the catwalk on which the band actually perform. As the song progresses, Bono uses a line from The Doors to introduce the band members as they emerge from between the screens (thus removing one layer of mediation): "break on through to the other side".

Consider Barthes' words again, when he writes about seeing his lover for the first time through the car window. He suggests that the window – the mediating screen – shifted in its searching and identifying "who to love". The screen through which Barthes sees his lover situates that lover into a disreal space, which then changes his focus after the "accuracy" of his desire immobilizes him. The screens do this for U2 as well, but with a difference: the *accuracy* of the desire of fans might first be focused on the site of celebrity – on the band themselves – but that desire then gets shifted to concerns of the world, at the time. Just as Virilio is also experiencing the dromocratic world through the mediating screen, Barthes experiences the world (and disreality) through the café window or through the car window. Disreality includes, then, the push for Europe not to ignore the plight of immigrants. In shows prior to the Paris attacks, U2's live concert presentation makes a point of criticizing the European Union's response to the refugee crisis: the huge screens on stage show an image of what appear to be drowned refugees floating in a blue sea, in a circle formation and wearing yellow life-vests, in a parody of the European Union flag. In another sequence, the video screens show a fly-over of a ruined city with the accompanying question of how one might return to a home or place of origin that can no longer sustain their living. How could one return home when there is no home to which to return?

The terrorist attacks that postponed U2's first concert in Paris occurred on 13 November 2015, during which three suicide bombers exploded outside of the *Stade de France* (in the suburb of Saint-Denis in the north of Paris) while a football game was taking place, resulting in additional casualties. In other parts of the city were incidents of mass shootings and another suicide bombing, killing forty people (including the suicide bomber). A further eighty-nine people were killed when gunmen entered the Bataclan theatre during a concert by the American band Eagles of Death Metal. The gunmen began shooting concert goers before taking a large number of hostages. Police intervened to free the hostages; the three perpetrators were killed by the detonation of their explosive vests. In all, 137 people were killed (including the seven perpetrators) and over 350 people were injured.

The message of concern for refugees is muted during the performance on 7 December, after the Paris attacks; the band work to shift the viewing audience's concerns to proclaim solidarity with the people of Paris and the victims of the attacks and their families. U2 even use the Twitter hashtag "#STRONGERTHANFEAR", using a lyric snippet from the song 'Raised by Wolves'. The title evokes the story of Romulus and Remus and the founding of Rome. In the story, the boys are raised on the milk of wolves, but go on to quarrel with each other as they are building the walls of the city on the shores of the Tiber River. Their quarrelling leads Romulus to kill Remus. Like this story, the Ireland of Bono's youth was divided by sectarian violence, resulting in Irish people killing their fellow Irish brothers and sisters. The song deals with local concerns for the band, that is, the violence in Bono's youth in Ireland; the negative sentiments of the song are transformed with the establishment of the hashtag as a tool of solidarity. In a way, the hashtag acts as a Barthesian window to transform the lyric into disreality and change the "accuracy of desire" from the local to the global, from an expression of local conflict to a reflection of global solidarity in the face of terrorist threat.

'Stronger than Fear' is also a call for response to the refugee crisis, couched in a statement of defiance against terrorists. In the days after the Paris attacks, there was much debate concerning the influx of refugees and the possibility of infiltration by terrorists; that, with the mass acceptance of migrants, terrorists would have free access to Europe, with potentially disastrous results. The hashtag, now "disreal", suggests European strength to improve migrant and refugee acceptance in the face of terrorist threat, that Europe – and France, in particular – is stronger than the fear of infiltration, and is able to overcome such fears in the name of the greater global good, as suggested by the band.

Disreality, then, is a state of being that allows for the redirection of desire from the local – or the present reality – to the global, or the world outside of the concert venue, all within the context of live performance and the stage itself. Those very screens both obscure and reveal (and mediate) the band for those in attendance at the Paris concert, and those watching the live show on HBO. The mediation does something other than immerse: it *deflects*. It is the "accuracy of desire" that changes course, fulfilling the band's cosmopolitan impulse, an outward view and a global care.

There is another factor at work: U2's audience is drawn to what might be considered the band's "flash", as Barthes would call it. In *The Pleasure of the Text*, Barthes explores the notion of the "erotic" in the written word, in literature, and takes from the idea of so-called "erogenous zones" to try to understand why one gains pleasure from reading a text. For Barthes, "erogenous zones" do not exist. This is because, for him, the erotic exists where the skin flashes between two pieces of clothing: this is the site of erotic desire. He writes, "it is this flash itself which seduces, or rather: the staging of an appearance-as-disappearance".[31] In the case of U2, the audience is drawn to the band's "flash", that is, their very presence – in the live concert experience – and absence – hidden behind the screens – at the same time. As per Barthes, the concert experience (and the particular concert performance, along with the specific staging and video) becomes a site of desire, a kind of "erogenous zone" that brings the audience pleasure.

But perhaps it is not only the audience that experiences pleasure, but U2 as well. This makes sense considering how much of U2's activity takes place in front of an audience. If the band did not receive pleasure from the audience, they would rue the activity in which they are so often engaged. Barthes writes about a text in which he takes some sort of pleasure: "The text chooses me, by a whole disposition of invisible screens, selective baffles: vocabulary, references, readability, etc.; and, lost in the midst of a text (not *behind* it, like a *deus ex machina*) there is always the other, the author".[32] Barthes' comments point to a sort of theoretical agency on the part of the author, lost in the "midst of the text", not unlike the *Zoo TV* era band, lost to the sight of the audience in the chaos of the television sets and their programming: perhaps they not only desire their audience but they *choose* it.

Barthes precedes the above statement with the idea of the text as a "fetish object", but with a twist: "this fetish desires me". U2, in a way, exercise their theoretical agency without doing so explicitly. U2, as the authors of meaning, are dead, but through mediation, they are still active. They choose whomever is in their audience at any given time. There is a reciprocal relationship: fans desire the members of the band; the band desire their audience in order to create a new world, and a new way of being in the world.

U2 are fighting against the doxa of the world: opinion or "nature", as Barthes would suggest. U2 are *paradoxa*: against or in dispute of nature, wanting instead to create a new nature or a new doxa in the form of Barthes' "third term".[33] Perhaps they know that the world cannot be changed (at least, by them): "an utopian idea (the idea of a future culture, resulting from a *radical, unheard of, unpredictable* revolution, about which anyone writing today knows only one thing: that, like Moses, he will not cross over into it)".[34] Could it be that U2 know that they will not change the world, at least in their lifetime? Is what Barthes calls "future culture" too far from present culture to be accessible? Is the present culture unable to be transformed into this utopian idea? Perhaps it is because U2 are not radical or unheard of, and are, for the most part, entirely predictable. This might be another reason why the band are relegated to the realm of complicity. They are the opposite of radical; if they were radical, they would not be successful players in the realm of late twentieth-century popular music. This can be disheartening to those who look to U2 as agents of change.

Personae

Bono is a fictional character. He is embodied – played – by a man who was named Paul Hewson at birth, though his close family call him Bono to his face. Bono is a fantasy that does not exist. Fans and audiences suspend their disbelief when they come across the figure, when they engage with him in concert or through media. They look to Bono for an authentic experience, even though they are coming into contact with a fictional character, a person under (at least) one layer of mediation. And in this engagement with Bono, he hopes that fans and audiences will see the world through Bono's Fly shades, so to speak. He provides a possible new world for his fans and audiences: this world also does not exist. More specifically, the world does not *yet* exist. And by suspending its disbelief, the audience *believes* that these new sorts of worlds are possible, that the world could be "even better than the real thing".

In a televised performance and interview with the BBC at the Abbey Road Studios in London in December 2017, Bono mentions that his family calls him Bono; his wife Ali calls him "Bono" and not Paul, even at home. An interesting question is why the two more vocal – or more accessible – members of the band (that is, Bono and The Edge) continue to use stage names rather than their real names. It could very well be that they require stage names because of their apparent visibility, and the fact that their voices are always heard. The Edge's singing voice is prominently featured in both recorded songs and live performance. For instance, he is the only singer on 'Van Diemen's Land' from *Rattle and Hum* and in live performance during the chorus of the song 'The Fly' from *Achtung Baby*. They are under more scrutiny from media and fans, and thus use the stage names in order to maintain some sort of mediated distance between themselves and the greater world, fans and critics. In a performance of 'An Cat Dubh/Into The Heart', from the *Vertigo 2005: Live from Chicago* concert film, Bono calls up a young boy from the audience to accompany him on the stage. After asking the boy his name, Bono says, "My name is Paul, but I call myself 'Bono'".

Originally, the character of The Fly was meant to represent how the media viewed the popular music celebrity. The character was conceived during the recording of *Achtung Baby*, and made his physical appearance on stage during the *Zoo TV* tour. Bono states, "I felt like I didn't recognize the person I was supposed to be, as far as what you saw in the media". He goes so far as to suggest that being in the spotlight violates one's most personal self, but that a celebrity must be willing to accept that.[35] What Bono is doing with The Fly is creating his own misinformation; that is, he is constructing himself in the same ways that the media would. Bono reveals what U2 were up to in the early 1990s:

> We used to have this thing about our image: "What image? We don't have an image. We're playing with images, like the desert or whatever, and we dress in a way that is sympathetic with the music, but it's not an image". And finally, I just said, "... maybe it is". In fact, if it is, let's play with it, and let's distort it and manipulate it and lose ourselves in the process of it. But let's write about losing ourselves in the process of it, 'cause that's what's happening to everybody else on a smaller scale anyway.[36]

Part of the impetus for creating The Fly was to allow Bono and the band to say (the same) things in new ways. Bono adds, "I always felt it was our responsibility to abuse our position". Because U2 had made a lot of money at that point in their career, they felt a strange responsibility to *use* it (he suggests that *use* is really *abuse*): "If you waste that, you're just a wanker, you don't deserve anything". The use (or abuse) that Bono wishes for The Fly is to be able to continue to effectively communicate while being in Bono's position. If Bono has made so much money, and has been seemingly misrepresented by the media, how do he and the band push back against that? They do so by creating that misinformation, by embodying all of the worst ideas of rock superstardom, to be bigger than they themselves actually are and to erase the line between reality and imagination. Sean Sennett quotes Adam Clayton on personae: "they each accentuate a part of yourself anyway ... it's a lot more interesting if the persona is an exaggerated version of you. I'd prefer to see that than some false cartoon persona that makes you seem more interesting than you really are".[37]

The Fly is certainly not (only) a cartoon. Stephen Catanzarite, in his book *U2's* Achtung Baby: *Meditations on Love in the Shadow of the Fall*, suggests that The Fly is a biblical Adam-like character that has fallen from grace.[38] In Judaeo-Christian belief, Adam is the first human being created by God, along with Eve (the first woman created from Adam's rib). With Eve, he commits the first sin against God and thus ushers sin into humanity's experience. In Catanzarite's interpretation of the album, The Fly is a proto-Adam who has become separated from Eve, whom he realizes he loves and cannot live without. While Catanzarite's reading is not altogether convincing, he does get to the bottom of who The Fly is: he is a *basic* human. He is basic in that he holds closely to his intrinsic loves, selfishness and the desire for attention, or the need to be a spectacle.

In a conversation with B. P. Fallon, who joined the *Zoo TV* tour as DJ as a "warm-up" act for the crowd before the start of the concert, Bono talks about The Fly persona, and how the signature sunglasses were originally a thrift-store find gifted from Fintan Fitzgerald (the head of wardrobe for that tour):

> When everyone would be getting a bit depressed or bored or bleak about what was goin' down, I'd pick up the glasses, put them on and go "Now I can see *everything*, now I can *really* see it". Y'know, The Fly couldn't see a *thing* really 'cos the goggles were so dark, but he wasn't looking *round* the room, he was looking *through* the walls and through the ceiling up into the stars.

When asked whether Bono enjoyed playing The Fly, he responds, "Yeah, I get to be the poser that I've always wanted to be".[39]

In early September 2017, the band officially released their first new music after the election of Donald Trump as the President of the United States. Posted to the social media site Facebook, the band released the video of a live performance of a song called 'The Blackout', from the then-forthcoming *Songs of Experience* (which did not yet have a release date). The video features the band in a live performance of the song. It begins with The Edge's distorted guitar, a repeating musical gesture that is evocative of the very beginning of 'Zoo Station' from *Achtung Baby*. But the feeling of *déjà vu* is not limited to the guitar parts, but also to Bono's vocals: he sounds like The Fly. The resurrection of The Fly persona is not only reflected in vocal inflections, but also in visuals: the live video is in black and white, which makes Bono's ever-present sunglasses appear particularly opaque so that the audience cannot see his eyes. This is in stark contrast to the glasses he normally wears, which are often tinted blue or yellow, but continue to allow one to see the singer's eyes.

The Fly also appears – albeit briefly – in the "lyric" video, an official video that displays the lyrics of the song as they are sung. Such videos generally do not possess the conventional narrative or thematic content of other promotional videos. The purpose of a lyric video is to convey the actual printed lyrics in a visually compelling way. His image shows up as a page in a book; the book's pages are flipped in succession by an unseen force, revealing the lyrics animated on each page as they are sung. The page that features Bono as The Fly persona is quickly scrunched up and seemingly discarded. In this case, The Fly appears for a moment only to be destroyed.

The Fly is only one of the personae that is made manifest during the *Zoo TV* tour. The other personae are the Mirror-Ball Man and Mr MacPhisto. The Mirror-Ball Man could be described as an American Christian television evangelist as was made popular in the 1970s and 1980s, known for being media savvy and known for their moral failings or financial scandals. Mr MacPhisto is a devilish figure who is well past his prime. Both of these figures are similar and demonstrate U2's engagement with the abuses that are often perpetrated in the name of the Christian Gospel. Additionally, Bono often implicates himself in the abuses that he describes, erasing the barriers between the personae he enacts and the presentation of his "true" self.

For instance, the engagement between U2 and American Christianity began even before the *Zoo TV* tour. In the *Rattle and Hum* film, at the beginning of 'Bullet the Blue Sky', an American flag lights up, made from fireworks. Bathed in red light, Bono sings the song wearing a wide-brimmed hat, evocative of an American cowboy hat. He completes the costume with a vest. During The Edge's guitar solo, Bono picks up a large blinding spotlight and shines it on The Edge, and alternately shines it into the audience. After the guitar solo, Bono begins another monologue in which he criticizes American Evangelicalism in the form of greedy thieving television evangelists, and the distance (both ideological and physical) between them and people suffering in abject poverty in El Salvador. This might be Bono at his most "authentic", turning the spotlight on the band (essentially himself), and the audience.

But the band's engagement with the Gospel in live performance is not always explicitly negative. At the end of 'Bullet the Blue Sky', in the *Zoo TV: Live from Sydney* live concert film, Bono embodies the character or persona of the fighter pilot. Following 'Bullet the Blue Sky', the pilot begins to sing 'Running to Stand Still', a song that seems to discuss heroin addiction. In the concluding part of that song, Bono mimes thrusting a needle into his arm and injecting himself with the drug, after which he begins to repeatedly sing the word "Hallelujah", a particularly powerful moment in the concert. Though he might be mimicking the bliss or euphoria of the high associated with heroin use, it is a moment when the barrier between the mundane and the sacred is broken. Though it might simply be a dramatization, it also suggests a call to a higher power in the midst of suffering or, at the very least, in the midst of this secular ritual of the concert experience. As this part of the song ends, Bono is enveloped with billowing smoke that is lit with bright orange and yellow lights that evoke fire (the billowing smoke lit with the yellow lights looks very much like a fiery explosion). Bono's character begins to play plaintive notes on the harmonica before the very beginning chords of 'Where the Streets Have No Name' start to play, and he walks down the walkway from the B stage to the main stage. The lights go down on Bono, and when they come on again, he has changed out of his pilot costume and has taken up his more conventional persona, "Bono" (at least as indicated by a plain black blazer jacket and no sunglasses). At the start of 'Where the Streets Have No Name', the lights on the stage turn on and shine very brightly towards the audience. The bright lights and the colour red shown on the monitors and screens around the stage are a well-established sign of the beginning of 'Where the Streets Have No Name', by this time in the band's career. Furthermore, with the bright lights, the apparatus that literally supports the spectacle is clearly visible. The audience (and later, the home video viewer) can clearly see the cameras and the cranes, the crew that are attending to all of these pieces of technical equipment, as well as all of the scaffolding that supports the screens and the lights of the stage. All of the infrastructure that supports the "magic" of the spectacle is revealed in the bright light of all the spotlights. The stage is laid bare, and all is revealed. Could it be that the activities of the pilot are now clearly visible, and revealed by the light of God, whether they be the brutal civil war in Nicaragua and the American role in that conflict, or the substance abuse of an inhabitant of a Dublin block of residential towers? If 'Where the Streets Have No Name' is a song that evokes the streets of heaven, or the domain of God, perhaps Bono's "Hallelujah" is more a cry for mercy which ultimately comes in the form of the subsequent song. With God's mercy comes the ability for one to shed any pretexts (the costume and the persona of the pilot) and to be who one really, genuinely, is (Bono, the "authentic" lead singer of the band).[40] This is a ritual that is repeated night after night during the *Zoo TV* tour during the performance of these songs: after a confession, the mercy of God is released and relationships are restored, at least until the encore. At that point, the audience is introduced either to the Mirror-Ball Man or to Mr MacPhisto.[41]

During the American leg of the *Zoo TV* tour, Bono would come out on stage as the Mirror-Ball Man, dressed in a silver suit (with the rainbow sheen of old holographic stickers or the surface of a compact disc or other optical media) and a matching cowboy hat and black aviator sunglasses. He appears to be a mix between an older American rock star (like Elvis Presley) and a television evangelist preacher, complete with a southern drawl. He would even throw fake money into the crowd. In the *Outside Broadcast* concert film, a "Zoo TV correspondent" comes on stage to interview him at the very end of a performance of 'Desire'. He proclaims to the crowd and to the correspondent that he has a vision, and that this vision is "Television! TELEVISION!" All the while, the screens behind him show the American flag while fake money rains on the audience. As for the Mirror-Ball Man's values, they are bound up in his beliefs. He says to the correspondent, "I believe in love! Money! Poetry! Electricity! Cheap cosmetics!" Bono puts it this way: "He had the confidence and charm to pick up a mirror and look at himself and give the glass a big kiss. He loved cash and in his mind success was God's blessing. If he's made money, he can't have made any mistakes".[42] B. P. Fallon quotes Bono describing the Mirror-Ball Man as a figure who is "into money and he's selling a religion where you can believe in anything really", which, for Bono, is a quintessentially 1990s persona. He continues by characterizing the Mirror-Ball Man as a seller of a "religion without God ... a religion where everybody can have what they want and make a lot of money as well – pyramid selling, anything you find on the obscure channels late at night in the US. He has no shame though he talks a lot *about* shame". Fallon then asks Bono how much of himself resides in this character. Bono responds, "Performers ... *lie* for a living, they are *insincere* for a living". He likens himself to an actor who pretends that he is someone else, compared to those people who do not need to pretend: "there is just something a little untrustworthy about people who don't [need a mask], people who try to come off as true ... I tried that in the '80s ... *now* when I put on a mask it's in the hope that it reveals more than I ever could without it".[43] Bill Flanagan describes the scene and some of Bono's influences for these characters at length in *U2 at the End of the World*. Bono takes on the characters that he wishes to fight against: Flanagan describes engaging with Bono, in conversation late at night, about what Bono hopes to achieve with the spectacle of the tour. Bono suggests that the spectacle, along with personae and costumes, is about accepting the "stupid glamour" of popular music (and the shenanigans of a worldwide tour) without jettisoning the "truth" in the music. Flanagan explains, "[Bono] compares it to Elvis Presley in a jumpsuit singing 'I Can't Help Falling in Love with You' to a weeping woman in Las Vegas. It might have been hopelessly kitsch, but if the woman believed in the song *and Elvis believed in the song*, it was not phony. Maybe rock & roll was at its truest in the space between those apparent contradictions". In other words, it is about being real in the midst of artifice and irony. Bono's performance is ultimately dependent on authenticity in the midst of inauthenticity.

According to Flanagan's account, Bono continues by suggesting that part of this authenticity is wrapped up in the act of accepting that much of the performance of popular music is compelling for the audience *and* for the band members, even though much of that performance is about "swagger" and posturing. This is despite the fact that the band are living an affluent life; Bono suggests that the members of the band are being paid exorbitant amounts of money to play music, something that they would do for free. And so, rock performance is attractive. Bono asks the important question, "how do you write about some of the stuff that I'm interested in writing about and be in big business? Suddenly I felt gagged. If I wrote a song about the Gulf War, then that would be making money out of the war! ... So I decided the only way was, instead of running away from the contradictions, I should run into them".[44] Bono is acknowledging the tensions inherent in the U2 project. For instance, though the Mirror-Ball Man no longer has a place in Bono's arsenal of personae, the band still sit in that same position of making money even as immigrants and the disenfranchised, those segments of global society to whom the band want to give voice, continue to struggle.

The other persona in the later part of the *Zoo TV* tour is the devilish character of Mr MacPhisto. Flanagan recalls how the band refer to particularly conservative Christians as "squeakies". They are referring to the sort of pious Christian that strongly refrains from smoking and drinking, for instance. Flanagan recounts a concert in what he calls "a hotbed of evangelical enthusiasm", Cardiff, Wales, in which a concert attendee had trouble with Bono's Mr MacPhisto persona. As Bono invited a woman on to the stage in order to dance with him, she began to berate him for his costume, even attempting to wipe the makeup off his face and demanding to know what he was trying to accomplish. His response: "'It's Ecclesiastes,' he whispered while waltzing her around romantically for the crowd. She didn't buy it, she was angry. 'Did you ever read *The Screwtape Letters?*' Bono asked her. She said she had". C. S. Lewis wrote *The Screwtape Letters* as a record of correspondence from a senior devil and mentor, Screwtape, to his nephew, a rookie by the name of Wormwood. Flanagan quotes Lewis who described the mentor as follows: "Screwtape's outlook is like a photographic negative; his whites are our blacks and whatever he welcomes we ought to dread". Flanagan continues to describe Bono's engagement with the "squeaky": "While waltzing with the angry evangelical Bono invoked Screwtape and told her, 'That's what this is'".[45] Bono calls Mr MacPhisto "a sort of old English Devil, a pop star long past his prime returning regularly from sessions on The Strip in Vegas and regaling anyone who would listen to him at cocktail hour with stories from the good old, bad old days. There was a certain pathos to him".[46] The Edge recounts an instance of Mr MacPhisto playing to the sorts of evils that Bono and the rest of the band would rather rail against: "One highlight was [of Mr MacPhisto] calling The Minister of Fisheries in Norway, Jan Henri Olsen, to congratulate him on whaling, which was forbidden by the European Union but legal in Norway. He actually took the call and invited Bono to come and have a whale steak with him".[47]

When one considers the character, though, in the context of the *Zoo TV* tour, Mr MacPhisto is an *aging* star, one who was at the top of his game in the past and is now on the decline. As the performance continues, Mr MacPhisto tosses his horns, stumbles as he walks in his glitter platform boots and wipes away some of his white face makeup along with the sweat on his face. His English accent becomes less prevalent and his smile goes away. By the end of the concert, he is no longer who he was when he came out of the back-stage dressing room to the strains of 'Daddy's Gonna Pay for Your Crashed Car'. In fact, he is being transformed back into Bono as the end of the concert approaches. He is no longer a threatening character, if he ever was.

The song 'Hold Me, Thrill Me, Kiss Me, Kill Me', featured on the soundtrack for the 1995 feature film *Batman Forever*, includes both The Fly and Mr MacPhisto. The official video consists of images from the feature film (which is to be expected for this sort of promotional video, as promotional material for the feature film as well). The video also features an animated narrative (perhaps well-paired with the comic book origins of the Batman film) that showcases the band as animated characters in their *Zoo TV* tour forms. Here, Bono appears as a modified version of himself, with holes for eyes (thus the need for the large sunglasses) as The Fly and as Mr MacPhisto (the other comic book villains from the film also make brief appearances as animated characters). At one point, the Bat signal, the spotlight that is used in the fictional Batman universe to call Batman in times of need, and which shines Batman's logo into the sky in order to alert him of the need for his assistance, is replaced with an outline of Mr MacPhisto's horns and evil-looking eyes. The graphic would later feature in the centre of Bono's megaphone during live performances in late 2017 and early 2018.

In the video, an animated Bono is portrayed as taking questions from reporters to comment on how honest and how genuine he is as a rock star. His response to this is "So what?" He wrestles with the halo that has appeared over his head with the questions from the press, stretching it and compressing it until it emerges as a pair of sunglasses. He puts the sunglasses on to transform himself into The Fly and smiles. In the following sequence, he is on top of a building suddenly surrounded by reporters (presumably similar to the ones who thought that he was so righteous before) who take pictures of him without his glasses, and perhaps see that his eyes are simply holes that reveal the world behind him, or perhaps reveal a soul that is intrinsically empty. Bono falls off the building as he stumbles away from the flashes of the cameras. As he is falling, one of his bandmates throws his sunglasses to him, and he catches them in his hand and is able to then swing himself from an electrical wire to safety. Bono as The Fly then confronts Mr MacPhisto.

This version of the band is among the villains, though, as an animated Batman flies into the scene in his bat-shaped aircraft: the band, with Mr MacPhisto, shoot at Batman with their guitars that have suddenly become guns just before they all jump into a yellow Mr MacPhisto-themed car (this is an animated promotional video for a comic book movie after all).

The viewer then sees what might be the actual band (though still animated) walking around on street level. Bono is reading a book as he walks and is suddenly struck by a careening car that is being driven by a figure that resembles

Elvis Presley. As Bono is thrust into a pile of garbage at the side of the road, it is revealed that he has been reading Lewis's book, *The Screwtape Letters*.

Animated Bono is then seen recovering, it seems, in a hospital, but when the band pulls the curtains that are around his bed in order to see him, he has resuscitated as Mr MacPhisto. They are shocked and afraid. The final scene of the video shows Mr MacPhisto removing his face as if it is a literal mask to reveal that *he* is Batman. But then Batman removes his mask to reveal that he is Mr MacPhisto, and so on.

The video shows all aspects of the band at this point in their career as being one and the same: Bono is portrayed as a genuine and caring star, *and* as shallow and empty (with literally nothing behind his eyes). Bono then takes agency and transforms that halo or public perception into something else, the sunglasses of The Fly, thus hiding his shallowness and emptiness, not to mention destroying his perceived authenticity. This is not the full extent of the transformation, though: when he is struck by the car (arguably, driven by a *true* master of celebrity, the immortal Elvis Presley himself) and about to die, he is instead saved by a lightning bolt that transforms him into Mr MacPhisto, in turn destroying whatever vestiges of the authentic Bono remain.

During the 2018 *eXPERIENCE + iNNOCENCE* tour, 'Hold Me, Thrill Me, Kiss Me, Kill Me' returns during an intermission, in the form of a new animated video. In the video, the band members are afloat on a raging sea, clinging to a broken raft, but are saved when a helicopter-like flying machine mysteriously rescues them (using some sort of technology to elevate the band members into the ship). Once inside, they encounter a shadowy figure who gives them her business card which reads, "Wormwood & MacPhisto Inc., BESPOKE ATONEMENT SERVICES". She gives Bono the gift of style, along with a pair of The Fly sunglasses. She gives Mullen Jr the gift of strength and a vial labelled "Eternal Youth". To Clayton, she gives the gift of ambition and a pair of wings. To The Edge, she bestows god-like talent and a guitar. They take their gifts back to the world, flying through a field of logos and graphics from throughout their career (suitcases containing hearts, concentric target-like circles, and so on), and then into a sky full of alcohol bottles and pills. But then, Clayton's wings burn off and the band begins to fall to earth. Luckily, they fall into a car driven by the stranger from the ship, who drives them to a Las Vegas-like city. During their journey, they ask the stranger about the meaning of life, and (now male) he answers, "Wisdom is the recovery of innocence at the far end of experience". When the car stops, the band emerge to a bank of cameras. With each flash of the cameras, Bono's sunglasses change from those of The Fly to the present round blue sunglasses. At that point, the video states that the story is "to be continued".

Interestingly, the stranger's quote, "Wisdom is the recovery of innocence at the far end of experience", is from American philosopher David Bentley Hart's book, *The Experience of God: Being, Consciousness, Bliss* (2013). Responding to U2's use of his words during the intermission, he responds,

> the very structure of all experience – whether innocent or not – is founded upon an original experience of the supernatural, and that in fact we possess a tacit knowledge of supernature before we know anything of "nature". Innocence is not simply ignorance, but is a kind of immediate experience of the mystery of existence, of the wonderful strangeness of being. But that original knowledge, which we possess with such immediacy in the state of childhood innocence, can become an object of reflection only as we acquire words and concepts, and as the original experience of the question of everything is crystallized into finite experiences and small local questions about this or that. This often involves, of course, a great deal of pain and disenchantment, as well as discovery. And this very process, necessary as it is, makes the original moment of awakening more remote from consciousness, ever more difficult to recall.[48]

This is the interesting power of the Mr MacPhisto performance: the "squeaky" from Birmingham is upset with Bono because of his apparent representation of a devil character. His defence is that he is mocking the devil rather than praising him. And in that mockery, Bono seems to become (at least according to the music video for 'Hold Me, Thrill Me, Kiss Me, Kill Me') what he is mocking, until that fades away. He becomes Bono again. But is this new Bono perceived as empty inside or as genuine, or is the new Bono simply complicit with all of it? Just as the animated versions of The Fly and Mr MacPhisto emerge alternately from the darkness, the audience does not know which version of Paul Hewson they will ultimately encounter.

During the encore portion of the *U2 360°* tour, as seen in the *U2 360° at the Rose Bowl* concert film, Bono dons a black jacket that is covered with red laser lights along the seams at the sides of the jacket as well as the seams on the sleeves. He sings 'Ultraviolet (Light my Way)', from *Achtung Baby*, into a microphone that seems embedded in a frame evoking a steering wheel, also covered with red laser lights, and hanging from above the stage. The microphone not only serves as a novel design for the amplification technology, but also something for the singer to play with: throughout the song, he swings from the microphone, swinging over almost the complete length of one side of the circular stage. As he performs, the stage is covered both in a dark blue – or "ultraviolet" – light contrasting with the powerful narrow streams of light coming off his jacket, and the bright red of the "wheel" microphone. Bono's playful swinging on the microphone, along with the original context of the song (with its release on *Achtung Baby* and its performance during the *Zoo TV* tour), evokes his Mr MacPhisto persona, especially considering how Mr MacPhisto presents himself towards the end of the *Zoo TV* tour performances. Here, Bono is pleading – while swinging, pulling and being pulled by the microphone – for someone to show him the direction in which he should go, for someone to make clear the way to go. While the colour red is used extensively during the *Vertigo* tour, the red during the concert is more akin to Mr MacPhisto than to *Vertigo*. Part of this might be due to Bono's enigmatic performance, and his enigmatic presentation. Like the stage during the *Zoo TV* tour, Bono seems to hide himself in the smoke and behind the lights that emanate from his jacket. These elements serve to ostensibly hide the singer from the audience that has come to see him perform. What might otherwise be considered "playfulness" on Bono's part comes across instead as a struggle or conflict in which the singer is losing.

Also, the performance seems spectacle for the sake of spectacle. That is, the performance is akin to Mr MacPhisto's gold-glitter boots: like the devilish character from the early 1990s, Bono is playing to the crowd while being hidden by lights. Ironically, these same laser lights have the potential to show the crowd exactly where Bono is located, but are unable to because of both the smoke and the power of the lasers reflecting off the other band members. Bono is particularly aloof in the performance in the concert film. He seems not unlike Mr MacPhisto who is struggling with forces that he cannot control: age and the waning of fame. About this portion of the concert, which Neil McCormick calls a "coda", he writes that it "represents U2 at their most raw and vulnerable, stripped to the metaphorical bone, when we have all been exhausted by the outpouring of collective emotion and ready just to get down to the dirty truth".[49] But in this case, the "dirty truth" might simply be that even if an audience is in the physical presence of Bono, he is no more accessible than any other stranger. Perhaps the song is about God and the cruelty of God's restraint or reserve, the oft-experienced supposed absence of God (literally ultraviolet, that light on the spectrum that cannot be seen by human eyes). Rothman suggests that Bono's jacket with laser lights is a metaphor for these ideas: "It's a pained, incomplete aura – trashy, but beautiful".[50]

During the 2018 *eXPERIENCE + iNNOCENCE* tour, Mr MacPhisto returns, this time appearing less like a cartoon or buffoon, and more menacing. Appearing in a black blazer and top hat (and, true to form, without Bono's signature sunglasses), Mr MacPhisto introduces the track 'Acrobat'. He is no longer the "aging" rock star, but now the one who is exerting a lot of effort in order to appear a certain way, while acting in another way. While introducing the song, Mr MacPhisto looks into a camera of what appears to be an Apple iPad (or similar). On the large screen above the stage, an animated and grotesque face appears as an "augmented reality" mask on top of Bono's actual face. But the technology is not perfect; the mask flickers on and off throughout the introduction. This works to obfuscate who the villain actually is. After all, there is some Mr MacPhisto in Bono. Mr MacPhisto/Bono continues, "When you don't believe I exist, that is when I do my best work. Don't believe what you hear. Don't believe what you see".

Related to Mr MacPhisto is the character of the Shadow Man, a persona that Bono takes up during performances of 'Exit' from *The Joshua Tree*, during the tour in support of the album's thirtieth anniversary in 2017. As the Shadow Man, Bono is dressed in a black suit (complete with black vest, not unlike what he might have worn during the original *Joshua Tree* tour) and black hat. This character seems to have some things in common with the Mirror-Ball Man, in that he appears to be a sort of evangelist. During one performance, in Chicago in June 2017, the Shadow Man asks the crowd to "Put your hand against the screen", something that a television evangelist of the 1980s would ask, in order for the supposed healing powers to flow from their ministries through the screens into people's lives. The Shadow Man then adds, "Send me ten dollars". He seems to be a cross between an effeminate dandy character and a lunatic street preacher. Bono describes the Shadow Man as an American gothic character, a way for him to deal with the darkness that seems inherent in the song.

The character is heavily influenced by American writer Flannery O'Connor: "It's quite a character. I'm actually using some lines from [the O'Connor book] *Wise Blood* … The bit from *Wise Blood* is, 'Where you come from is gone, where you thought you were going is never there. Where you are is no good unless you can get away from it'".[51] This is a curious quote for Bono to use: is the place where one comes from in the lifted quote from *Wise Blood* the version of America in 1987? Is the place where they were going to – that is never there – the idealized vision of America, an idea of America that does not exist? Bono and the band would agree that the idealized vision of America is only an idea and not something that exists, but it certainly *informs* the America that does exist. And how does the band then use the idea that "Where you are is no good unless you can get away from it"?

It could be that the Shadow Man from 'Exit', Bono's character in a black suit and black hat, is a thematic foreshadow of the next album, *Songs of Experience*. In the performance of 'Exit' from the tour, a clip featuring a con-man character from a 1950s television show promises to build a wall in order to keep his companions safe. The con-man's name is, ironically (and conveniently), Walter Trump.[52]

Notes

1. "Zoo TV Station Talent", *Propaganda* 16 (1 June 1992); available from https://www.atu2.com/news/zoo-tv-station-talent.html (accessed 5 February 2018).
2. Bill Flanagan, *U2 at the End of the World* (New York: Delta, 1995), 61.
3. Paul Rosenfeld, *By Way of Art* (Freeport: Books for Libraries Press, Inc., 1967), 64.
4. Greg Siegel, "Double Vision: Large Screen Video Display and Live Sports Spectacle", *Television & New Media* 3.1 (February 2002): 53.
5. Ibid., 53. Siegel is quoting Henning Eichberg, "Stadium, Pyramid, Labyrinth: Eye and Body on the Move", in *The Stadium and the City*, edited by John Bale and Olof Moen (Keele: Keele University Press, 1995), 340.
6. Kimi Kärki, "The Technological Reach for the Sublime on U2's 360° Tour", in *U2 and the Religious Impulse: Take Me Higher*, edited by Scott Calhoun (London: Bloomsbury, 2018), 111.
7. David Pattie, *Rock Music in Performance* (Basingstoke: Palgrave Macmillan, 2007), 109.
8. Ibid., 163.
9. Ibid.
10. Ibid., 36.
11. Ibid., 34.
12. Ibid., 37.
13. Ibid., 38.
14. Andy Greene, "Bono Talks 'Joshua Tree' Tour, Trump, Status of U2's Next Album", *Rolling Stone* (30 May 2017); available from https://www.rollingstone.com/music/features/bono-on-joshua-tree-tour-trump-u2s-next-album-w484398 (accessed 5 March 2018).
15. Pattie, *Rock Music in Performance*, 38–39.
16. Roland Barthes, *A Lover's Discourse: Fragments*, translated by Richard Howard (New York: Hill and Wang, 1978), 87.
17. Ibid., 89.
18. Ibid., 91.
19. Also, Barthes is exploring the difference between mundane space (perhaps the space of the café in which he exists alone) and amorous space, the space that is occupied by one and their lover, the locus of their desire.
20. Barthes, *A Lover's Discourse*, 192.
21. David Dark, "Why Does U2 Irk So Many People? A Look at their Struggle for Pop Hits and Social Justice", *America Magazine* (17 July 2017); available from https://www.americamagazine.org/arts-culture/2017/07/17/why-does-u2-irk-so-many-people-look-their-struggle-pop-hits-and-social (accessed 3 August 2017).
22. Thomas Merton, *Conjectures of a Guilty Bystander* (Garden City, NY: Image Books, 1968), 156.
23. Michael J. Gilmour, "'God', 'God Part II' and 'God Part III': Exploring the Anxiety of Influence in John Lennon, U2 and Larry Norman", in *Reception History and Biblical Studies: Theory and Practice*, edited by Emma England and William John Lyons (London: Bloomsbury T&T Clark, 2015), 236.

24. NFL Network, "U2's 'Beautiful Day' & Super Bowl XXXVI Halftime Show Helps Heal America after 9/11", *YouTube* (3 December 2017); available from https://www.youtube.com/watch?v=ZPHGOMXQyDQ (accessed 6 March 2018).

25. W. David O. Taylor, "Foreword: Bono as the Religious Everyman", in *U2 and the Religious Impulse: Take Me Higher*, edited by Scott Calhoun (London: Bloomsbury, 2018), xii.

26. Gilmour, "'God', 'God Part II' and 'God Part III'", 234.

27. Iain Thomson, "'Even Better than the Real Thing'? Postmodernity, the Triumph of the Simulacra, and U2", in *U2 and Philosophy: How to Decipher an Atomic Band*, edited by Mark A. Wrathall (Chicago and La Salle: Open Court, 2006), 92.

28. Ibid., 93.

29. Ibid.

30. Ibid., 94.

31. Roland Barthes, *The Pleasure of the Text*, translated by Richard Howard (New York: Hill and Wang, 1975), 10.

32. Ibid., 27.

33. Ibid., 18, 28.

34. Ibid., 38–39.

35. Alan Light, "Bono, Behind the Fly: The Rolling Stone Interview", *Rolling Stone* (4 March 1993); available from https://www.rollingstone.com/music/news/bono-behind-the-fly-the-rolling-stone-interview-19930304 (accessed 7 March 2018).

36. Ibid.

37. Sean Sennett, "U2: Making Music to Blow their Minds", in *Off the Record: 25 Years of Music Street Press*, edited by Sean Sennett and Simon Groth (St Lucia: University of Queensland Press, 2010), 251.

38. Stephen Catanzarite, *U2's* Achtung Baby*: Meditations on Love in the Shadow of the Fall* (New York: Bloomsbury, 2007), 53–57, 64–70.

39. B. P. Fallon, *U2 Faraway So Close* (Boston: Little, Brown and Company, 1994).

40. Of course, the audience only sees Bono, not Paul Hewson.

41. As an aside, the band sings "Hallelujah" during the very last song in *Elevation 2001: Live in Boston*, right at the end of 'Walk On'. Right after thanking all of the Bostonians for attending the concert, Bono shouts, "And unto the Almighty", with the response of the sung "Hallelujah". This is another moment when the thin membrane between the mundane and the divine seems to break. The concert space is transformed into a sacred space for that moment.

42. Neil McCormick, *U2 by U2* (London: HarperCollins, 2006), 294.

43. Fallon, *U2 Faraway So Close*.

44. Flanagan, *U2 at the End of the World*, 56–57.

45. Ibid., 434.

46. McCormick, *U2 by U2*, 304.

47. Ibid., 305.

48. Scott Calhoun, "Stealing David Bentley Hart's Wisdom for U2's Traveling Show", @U2 (6 August 2018); available from https://www.atu2.com/news/stealing-david-bentley-harts-wisdom-for-u2s-traveling-show.html (accessed 6 August 2018).

49. Neil McCormick, "U2: Secrets of Stadium Rock", *Telegraph* (17 August 2009); available from https://tinyurl.com/U2-100002560 (accessed 3 February 2018).

50. Joshua Rothman, "The Church of U2", *The New Yorker* (16 September 2014); available from https://www.newyorker.com/culture/cultural-comment/church-u2 (accessed 28 August 2017).

51. Greene, "Bono Talks 'Joshua Tree' Tour, Trump, Status of U2's Next Album".

52. Jon Pareles, "Review: U2 Revisits 'The Joshua Tree' in the Here and Now", *New York Times* (15 May 2017); available from https://www.nytimes.com/2017/05/15/arts/music/u2-joshua-tree-30th-anniversary-tour-review.html (accessed 5 March 2018).

6 *Linear*: A Way Forward

How to Dismantle an Atomic Bomb was released in November 2004. The song 'Vertigo' was the first single from the album and was featured extensively in an advertisement for Apple's iPod digital music player. The album won a number of Grammy Awards including "Album of the Year" in 2006. 'Sometimes You Can't Make It on Your Own' received awards for "Song of the Year" and "Best Rock Performance by a Duo or Group with Vocal". In all, the band won nine Grammy Awards for the album in 2005–2006. Of the album, Rob Sheffield writes, "This is grandiose music from grandiose men, sweatlessly confident in the execution of their duties".[1] The sense is that the press were wondering what U2 would do to respond to the "over the top" experience of *Pop* and the *PopMart* tour of the late 1990s, complete with mirror-ball lemon and giant television screen. The response was the hugely successful *All That You Can't Leave Behind*. After the success of that album, U2 were then able to do whatever they wanted. Of course, this was the case after the success of *The Joshua Tree*; the band did not have to worry about commercial success in terms of financial freedom or any sort of financial constraints at any point after its release. But the discourse of "pressure" was certainly on the band after *Pop*. However, such pressures were assuaged with *All That You Can't Leave Behind*. So, *How to Dismantle an Atomic Bomb* was released into the context of a band not needing to prove itself to an audience, or in a commercial context. And in some ways, this might have made U2 as a band irrelevant, in that they had nothing more to prove. They might have been read as "coasting". But they were accused of something worse than coasting: the band were accused of becoming explicitly commercial. Bryan Wawzenek writes, in 2015,

> U2 took more than a few shots for their embrace of a corporation, but the gambit worked. 'Vertigo' became a blockbuster single (and the name of the band's gargantuan 2005–2006 tour) and *How to Dismantle an Atomic Bomb* was released to enormous sales, topping the charts in countries around the world – becoming one of the biggest-selling records of '04 and eventually moving more than 3 million copies.[2]

A large part of the "corporate embrace" to which Wawzenek refers was the release of a branded Apple iPod digital music player. The main characteristic was its black colour with a dark red scroll wheel. The band appeared on stage at an Apple "special music event" with then-CEO Steve Jobs to introduce the device in October 2004. In addition to the device, the band released a "digital box set" available only through the iTunes Music Store called *The Complete U2*. The set contained over 400 tracks.

The band released the concert film *Vertigo 2005: Live from Chicago* in November 2005, and the concert film *Vertigo 05: Live from Milan*, which came as a bonus to the audio compilation *U218 Singles*, which was released in November 2006.

No Line on the Horizon was released in February 2009, and its accompanying concert film, *U2 360° at the Rose Bowl*, was released in June 2010. Adam Sherwin laments the poor commercial performance of the album, which sold only 65,000 copies in the UK in its first week of release. Such sales figures could be problematic for a band that "are determined to maintain their status as the 'world's biggest', not least because it gives singer Bono leverage in his discussions over Africa debt relief with world leaders". It does seem strange to think that the commercial prospects of a rock band might impact humanitarian efforts around the world. Nevertheless, about the first single from the album, 'Get on Your Boots', Sherwin writes that "Radio stations … did not give a warm reception to the track". In fact, it did not break into the top ten charts.[3] Critically, though, the album performed rather well. David Fricke, reviewing the album for *Rolling Stone*, gives it five stars (the highest possible rating), and writes – unabashedly – that the album is "their best, in its textural exploration and tenacious melodic grip, since 1991's *Achtung Baby*". Fricke calls *No Line on the Horizon* "transitional", akin to *The Unforgettable Fire* and *Zooropa*. For Fricke, though, the album is more an exploration of Bono's own place in the band, and in the world. He writes, "Bono knows exactly what a lot of you think of his social activism and flamboyant freelance diplomacy": he knows when he has gone "too far", and the lyrical content of the album expresses much of the insecurity that the lead singer holds. Fricke concludes his review as follows: "Bono knows he was born with a voice. He also knows that without Mullen, Clayton and The Edge, he'd be just another big mouth".[4] This is the crux of the matter: much of the press (and popular fandom, to be fair) consider Bono a "big mouth", but Fricke is a bit more subtle with his categorizations. The spirit of Fricke's observations are made twelve years earlier by Jay Cocks: "The band shares a kind of ecumenical, nonspecific spirituality".[5] Here, though, Fricke is referring to a different sort of "spirituality", the ability of the band to achieve humanitarian goals together.

Released as an accompaniment to the deluxe edition of *No Line on the Horizon*, U2 sought the talents of long-time photographer and collaborator Anton Corbijn to produce a long-form music video for the songs on the album, called

Linear. Patrick Burgoyne quotes Corbijn as saying, "It is not an extended music video or a U2 documentary, it's a new way to listen to a record – a new way to use film to connect to music".[6] *Linear* constructs a U2 that represents a "way out", a divergent way of thinking from the oppression of the state to a utopian "beyond". This utopian space is a space of Barthesian "idiorrythmy", a space of living together, or coexisting, while respecting each other's space and need for solitude from time to time. While the film does not feature the band visually (except for a single segment), the music from *No Line on the Horizon* is central. The band, and the band's music, are a "guide" throughout the film, suggesting a way forward, a way that is compassionate, bringing to light both global concerns and personal desires.

There seems to be an interesting thing happening with U2 in the 2010s, their so-called fourth period. The band appear complicit with corporate entities and seem to be in a comfortable place. Many, for instance, think that the band are no longer innovating or creating interesting music, as they might have been doing during the 1990s, which was arguably the band's most creative period. But they are using that "comfortable" space to effect change. The change to which they are seeking to contribute is a theoretical one, a much more daring project. They are working towards a sort of "zone that falls between two excessive forms" (to use Roland Barthes' language): Barthes suggests that this zone is "neither the monastery, nor the family, the idea being to eschew those grand repressive forms".[7] This space demonstrates a possible future. *Linear* anticipates this in the figure of the protagonist: late in the narrative of the film, he manages to secure a row boat in order to cross the ocean to northern Africa. The boat can be thought of as a particularly special space, moving at a rhythm radically different from his previous day-to-day existence.

Kate Briggs explains that, in his lectures on "How to Live Together", delivered at the Collège de France in 1976 and 1977, Barthes is exploring "a form of living together that would accommodate rather than dictate the individual rhythms of its small scale community. Allowing for something like solitude, as Barthes puts it, with regular interruptions. What kinds of structures, spatial or temporal, would enable this?"[8] Barthes' solution is expressed in the term, "idiorrythmy". Barthes is trying to work out "the fantasy of a small-scale community offering the ideal negotiation of inter-personal distance, of companionship and solitude; the fantasy of the neutral as a non-conflictual way of being in the world; and, in the last years, the fantasy of writing a novel that would finally speak of and for the ones you love".[9]

Barthes describes, particularly, the scene that illustrates the opposite idea to that of "idiorrhythmy":

> From my window (December 1, 1976), I see a mother pushing an empty stroller, holding her child by the hand. She walks at her own pace, imperturbably; the child, meanwhile, is being pulled, dragged along, is forced to keep running, like an animal, or one of Sade's victims being whipped. She walks at her own pace, unaware of the fact that her son's rhythm is different. And she's his mother! → Power – the subtlety of power – is effected through disrhythmy, heterorhythmy.[10]

For Barthes, the opposite of "idiorrhythmy" is "rhythm". He suggests that the term "rhythm" was "never applied to the regular movement of the waves. The actual meaning is rather: a distinctive form, a proportioned figure, an arrangement".[11] In other words, waves are not strictly rhythmic. Rather, waves fit into his definition of idiorrhythmy: "a median, utopian, Edenic, idyllic form".[12]

U2 are certainly invested in the same things as Barthes in his earlier study, wanting their audience to "coexist", particularly in the face of religious sectarianism. As mentioned, during the *Vertigo* tour, Bono would don a headband imprinted with the word, "Coexist", with a crescent in the place of the "C", a Star of David in the place of the "X" and a Christian cross in the place of the "T". The headband, then, signifies coexistence between the three Abrahamic religions, Islam, Judaism and Islam. The graphic was originally a piece of graffiti that one of Bono's friends had come across by a Polish artist named Piotr Mlodozeniec; Bono states, "It seemed such a powerful symbol of tolerance".[13]

Linear opens with the city of Paris descending into night, the lights of the city outlining its landmarks and noticeable thoroughfares. The viewer then sees passing city features at street level, as if from a moving vehicle. These visuals are accompanied by the track, 'Unknown Caller'. The lyrics of the song seem a desperate call to quit or escape the current conditions, to *move forward* or to reset oneself and begin again. The lyrics also refer to numbers: Bono sings about seeing the numbers three and thirty-three on a clock face, perhaps another reference to Jeremiah 33:3 on the cover of *All That You Can't Leave Behind*. The 'Unknown Caller' of the title could be God (remember the idea that 33:3 is the "phone number" for God). The reference here, though, might also be to the actual time when the narrative is taking place, at 3:33 in the morning. The first segment takes place in the middle of the night or in the very early morning.

As the song continues, the vantage point oscillates between the shops and storefronts of the inner city moving from the left to the right along the field of vision (as one might encounter being a passenger in a vehicle) to front-facing views (as if one is driving a vehicle). The visuals finally become still, resting on the protagonist, a male police officer. Up to this point, the viewer has perhaps unknowingly been with the officer on his evening patrol along the city streets, with its restaurants and clubs. The viewer has experienced the streets of the city from the officer's vantage point. The officer is sitting on his police-issued motorcycle, looking at a spray-painted wall which says, "NIK LA BAC" (which refers to a strongly derogatory statement against the police). The segment ends with the police officer lifting his helmet visor and turning off the ignition of his motorcycle.

The officer lives in what Barthes calls an "autarky", a "self-contained existence": the officer is "a being with its own boundaries that he sees no need to overstep; he has absolutely no recourse to ... mankind [or humanity]".[14] About the example of the sanatorium as an autarkic space, Barthes writes, "Once the structure (the Living-Together) is established, it's ever-lasting; it runs on and on – like a homeostat ... For the visitor [to a sanatorium]: repulsion and attraction. Fascination: death; not because it's a place where people die, but because it's never-ending".[15] So, Paris seems like this for the officer. He is "Living-Together" in the space of, say, immigrant communities in the Paris suburbs (the officer is of North African origin). For those outside of this community (or even outside of the community of those who would live in tension with authorities and, thus, spray paint "NIK LA BAC" on a city wall), there is a certain fascination if not of death, but of tension and violence, in that the tension and violence do not necessarily end. The life in this autarkic space or *milieu* is not the same as outside of it. Those outside of it do not effectively engage in "Living-Together" either; in this case, there is a sort of self-sufficiency that seems to be insufficient. The officer seeks to be released from the never-ending nature of that *milieu*.

As the next song 'Breathe' begins (and after a momentary fade to black), the officer gets off his motorcycle, pours gasoline over it and sets fire to it. As he walks away from the burning motorcycle, he discards his helmet. The camera then remains focused on the burning motorcycle, alternating between various viewing angles for the remainder of the song. As the song comes to an end, the light over Paris moves from dark to light, and the officer, now without his uniform, is seen getting on a new motorcycle. It appears that he has decided definitely to leave the police force (if burning his police vehicle was not sufficient proof of his intent).

In his discussion of idiorrhythmic spaces within Roman Catholic religious organizations, Barthes addresses power: more accurately, "the tension between power and marginality". He continues to outline the power of the Church over marginality:

(1) through its obedience to a Superior, (2) through the serving priest, who was initially Cistercian, then later Dominican or Franciscan, (3) through the tendency among pensionnaires – as a means of avoiding suspicion – to join the third order or follow the Rule of Saint Augustine (rule for semireligious men and women).[16]

The police officer dismisses the power of his position and chooses the side of marginality, to be removed from his place of authority. He does this first by making clear that he is no longer going to be obedient to his superiors or supervisors. This is made certain (and permanent) through his destruction of police property, by destroying his motorcycle and discarding his police helmet. He destroys the part of his uniform that is most recognized while he is in service to the public. His helmet states who he is in block letters: "POLICE". Barthes' second point states that the Church holds power through a serving priest, as part of a particular order. In a similar way, the protagonist is a police officer, part of the "order" of police services, serving the public. Finally, those Christian communities in the Middle Ages are governed by the Rule of Saint Augustine, which calls for chastity, poverty and obedience, as well as other aspects such as detachment from the world, fasting, abstinence and prayer, and how to function in community (for instance, when to speak). The police officer is governed both by his duties as a police officer in serving the public, but also in terms of how to behave as a member of a civil society. It is certain that burning a road vehicle that belongs to the state would work against both those codes of behaviour.

In Barthes' study, then, there is a tension between power and idiorrhythmy. The protagonist in *Linear* fits within Barthes' idiorrhythmic spaces, but while possessing a subject position at the *periphery* of French society, the country in which he lives. The police force wields both a perceived and actual power over the marginalized population of immigrants in the Paris suburb (with their denunciation of the police as a homogeneous group), much like the Church and its "domesticated form of idiorrhythmy" in Barthes' study. The police officer fights off this power, thus resorting or surrendering to what might be called an *undomesticated* form of idiorrhythmy that the viewer is yet to discover. The new way of "Living-Together" is yet to be revealed, as the power of the state has been suddenly usurped. This is not to be a coming together of "us versus them", but rather a case of "There's only us".[17]

After an abrupt but brief black screen, the music begins again. The third segment is the first in colour and the first to feature a song that is not from *No Line on the Horizon*. The song, 'Winter', was written for the soundtrack to Jim Sheridan's 2009 film *Brothers*. In this segment, the protagonist is now travelling through the streets of the city that he used to serve and protect. The protagonist begins his journey (to some as-yet-unknown destination), by travelling on major thoroughfares, his progress indicated by highway signs. He is then shown travelling upward on an empty and narrow mountain highway, taking curve after curve before entering into Spain (again, indicated by the highway sign). Once in Spain, his progress continues to be indicated by passing signs. The segment ends with a fade to black.

Continuing his discussion of "Living-Together", Barthes suggests that what he calls the "fundamental problem" of idiorrhythmy is "an ethics (or a physics) of distance between cohabiting subjects". In exploring these ideas, Barthes expresses his own personal feelings towards others: he finds other people's bodies difficult though he admits that he often desires them. That is, he finds it difficult to *be* in close physical proximity to others. This can be confusing for Barthes, and he wishes to somehow control this confusion. So, he states, "I fantasize a state that ought to make it [that confusion] go away: *hesuchia*: respite from desire, a vacancy without distress, equanimity". *Hesuchia* is Greek for tranquility or peace. With the idea of *hesuchia* in mind, Barthes then sets out the rules that would allow him to achieve this tranquility or peace which results in "rules of distance with respect to other bodies". But this also results in Barthes losing his desire to live, now that he no longer has the desire for other bodies. In an attempt to find a solution to this, Barthes looks to Christian monasticism, where the rules of distance are the last step; the members of monastic religious communities *change*, or redirect, their desire.[18]

This is what might be happening here with the protagonist, or the biker. He enables or enacts literal "rules of distance" by putting physical distance between himself and all of those that were around him. His primary subject position (at least from the vantage point of the viewer) is as a police officer. But he has let that subject position go; he has left that community. In fact, he has done more than that: he has left the urban community as well, the community in which he was living. He has left all of Parisian society, not only the community of authority but also the marginal community of which he is a part. Though sated by "rules of distance", the viewer does not yet know where the biker's desire is directed. Before that, though, "The body is completely isolated, meticulously enveloped by distance". The highway signs make this apparent.

There is an interesting sonic moment here as well. At one point (as the biker comes around a corner on the mountain road), Bono's voice is heard without any processing or effects applied to the recording: Bono's vocals are "dry", so to speak. This is aurally striking, especially after hearing his voice with the usual reverb or echo applied. The "dry" voice is much more intimate: the viewer hears the singer as if he is actually present, not in the context of a studio but as if he is in the same room as the viewer. The untreated voice is used to deliver a lyric that suggests the coming of age of a man at the age of twenty-one. That person comes to the realization that he is able to kill another human being. For the next sung phrase after the "dry" passage, Bono's voice is treated to almost a plethora of effects: his voice echoes to excess. This is coupled with Bono's emotional expression at this point. The narrator of the song seems to lament the fact that he has realized that he would do anything to protect those who are on his side, or who share his view of things. The lyrics describe a situation in which one group of people have power over another group, and the narrator is willing (and able) to do whatever it might take to end one person's life in the stead of another person's life. This is obviously a wrong thing, at least as suggested by the excess of effects put on the singing voice. That is, having power over another and using such power to end a life is an excessive position. Consider the opposite, as outlined in John 15:13, "No one has greater love than this, to lay down one's life for one's friends". This idea is the opposite of the one outlined by the narrator in the song. The narrator's view is *excessive*.

During 'White as Snow', the protagonist stops on the side of the road for a rest. He removes his jacket and helmet, revealing his shirt soaked with sweat. He unbuttons his shirt and proceeds to lay on top of the motorcycle, his hands clasped behind his neck and his feet propped on the handlebars. He gazes up at the blue sky and observes the clouds slowly coming together to form the shape of the continent of Africa. In the middle of the segment, the protagonist is seen from above: he stretches his arms out to the sides and cocks his head to his right, gestures that evoke the image of Jesus Christ crucified, a common image found in visual art and elsewhere. The view shifts again to the sky where the clouds reconfigure into a numeral "1". This seems a moment of epiphany for the biker; this is one of the clearest sequences of symbols in the film, but what they might signify is difficult to interpret. The biker then dons his gear, gets back onto his motorcycle and continues his journey. The scene fades first to white (with the brightness of the sun) and then to black to mark the end of the segment.

The evocation of Christ by the protagonist on the motorcycle also evokes the biblical story of Lazarus's death:

> When Mary [the sister of Lazarus] came where Jesus was and saw him, she knelt at his feet and said to him, "Lord, if you had been here, my brother would not have died". When Jesus saw her weeping, and the Jews who came with her also weeping, he was greatly disturbed in spirit and deeply moved. He said, "Where have you laid him?" They said to him, "Lord, come and see". Jesus began to weep.

> So the Jews said, "See how he loved him!" But some of them said, "Could not he who opened the eyes of the blind man have kept this man from dying?"
> Then Jesus, again greatly disturbed, came to the tomb (John 11:32-38a).

Christ mourns with those who mourn. Christ (and Christ's death) seems to be the connecting element between the continent of Africa and the notion of unity symbolized by the numeral "1", literally "one". In that semiotic moment, escape from the biker's urban situation, an act of nonviolence, couples with death, an act of terrible violence but one that, in the Christian narrative, is imbued with deep love, bringing together a continent with the notion of unity. The epiphany seems to call for an impulse to move outward, to become, literally, one with the *other*. Also, these elements seem to be an explicit indication of Bono's own philanthropic project: Bono's ONE campaign hopes to eradicate extreme poverty and disease, particularly in Africa.

Barthes describes a space without conflict as "idyllic". It is straightforward to consider the biker's countryside pause as fitting into such a space. And Barthes states something striking here: "[The idyll is] the form that erases social or parasocial reality, on the one hand, by leaving it in place, not subverting it, allowing it the differences between its homogeneities and, on the other, by scotomizing [referring to the ability to forget trauma] the abrasion, the friction, the chafing between those distinct homogeneities".[19] The conflicts that the protagonist is leaving behind – the conflicts between the police in authority and the immigrant communities which he served (and of which he is a part) – are erased or forgotten. This is an unfortunate suggestion; in terms of U2's greater project here, it would be better if social realities were at least subverted and at most overturned and corrected. By his leaving, those social realities (which might be identified as inequalities) are left in place, but furthermore, they are forgotten. Barthes suggests that this "idyll" is not a utopia. At least, U2 are not proposing a clearly or classically utopian vision here: in a utopia, conflict is acknowledged and neutralized. With the protagonist relaxing on the side of the road, relishing in the leisure of cooling off and dozing off, the conflict is left behind, erased and forgotten. Or it is so at least for the moment.

But what does the sequence of images mean, then, if the initial conflict is erased or forgotten? It could be that this is the beginning of what Barthes identifies as the change of desire that monastic communities so successfully achieve. The Parisian conflicts seem long ago: not only does this segment begin some three songs into the film, but also far from the urban visuals that the viewer was privy to so early on, including the violence of a burning motorcycle in the second segment.

But what about the dream, the idea that the biker is somewhere between sleeping and waking when he sees the sequence of images in the sky on the side of the highway? The biker might be experiencing something of a "neutral" position. Rudolphus Teeuwen suggests that Barthes' neutral finds its characteristics in a sweetness that Teeuwen specifies exists in "sleep, weariness, abstention, retreat, tact, apathy, androgyny, tolerance, and skepticism" (among others) and not in "arrogance, conflict, and anger".[20] Along with this is the idea of an "exemption from struggle, a time-out from meaning", as if waking from a dream without remembering it.[21] Elsewhere, Barthes writes about the first fifty pages of Marcel Proust's novel, *In Search of Lost Time* and its focus on sleep: organization and disorganization at the same time – or half waking: "it is a sleep which can be written, because it is a consciousness of sleep: the whole episode ... is thus held suspended in a sort of grammatical scandal".[22] This form rests on the *disorganization* of time, which does not mean destruction, but rather a shifting. Barthes calls the writing, if not enough to call it an essay or a novel, *rhapsodic*.[23] Are U2 illustrating yet another option in living together? Or is there something more complex going on? Is this a disorganization of time in which the narrator self (or, say, the protagonist self) is not the *real* self? About *In Search of Lost Time*, Barthes suggests that the protagonist there "is simply *another* Proust, often unknown to himself".[24] The biker is not the one writing this story: the credits for *Linear* cite Bono and Corbijn as the writers of the story. Are they presenting to the viewer versions of another Bono and Corbijn, even unknown to themselves? Is the project simply providing what Barthes would call a "system of moments" which follows "illusory logic"? The strategy, then, might be to place the viewer in a rhapsodic state that leaves the viewer contemplative about the passage of time, and the biker's place in it (and, by extension, the viewer's place in that same narrative).

This might simply be a neutral, a "neither/nor", that leaves the viewer (and the biker) in a moment of bliss, in a better place. This better place is one devoid of any sort of anger or conflict, but instead full of tolerance (even if this tolerance is accompanied by an apathy; even the apathy might suggest that one does not worry about what is happening in their community). It is not about being uncaring, but about not being concerned that someone might be infringing on one's space or one's time. Rather, it is an apathy of coexistence: one has no interest in making an issue where there is no issue to be made.

The next segment features the album's title track, 'No Line on the Horizon'. This track also contains the phrase from which the film gets its title, *Linear*. Here, the viewer is situated high in the air, following the protagonist on his continuing journey on the highway towards some unknown destination. At times, the camera actively follows the motorcycle, whereas there are other scenes in which the camera is still and the motorcycle moves through the frame. The viewpoint or camera angle alternates between being at a very great height and being relatively close to the vehicle.

There are a few instances of the motorcycle travelling through a tunnel when the camera is forced to trace the route of the protagonist over the covering land. The protagonist is effectively hidden from the viewer in these scenes. More so than just hidden, the protagonist in these scenes is *enclosed*, protected from the gaze of the recording camera and the viewer. About enclosure, Barthes states, "any encroachment on the part of neighbouring animals is immediately resisted".[25] He continues, "The idea of territory incorporates the opposition public/private … Private space is the same thing as territory". In a sense, when the protagonist travels on the road, he is part of a private space, the "sphere" surrounding his motorcycle: his helmet encloses him in his own protected world. He moves in a solitary "sphere" of one, and he is further protected – enclosed – when he enters the tunnel. Even the viewer cannot follow him there, but instead relies on the extrapolated path taken by the camera, hoping to meet him on the other side of the hill, or on the other side of the enclosing ground.

But in terms of idiorrhythmy, Barthes states, "The function of idiorrhythmy is not to protect a 'purity', that is to say an identity. Its arrangement in spacial terms: not concentration, but dispersion, spacing". And the protagonist's emerging from the other side of the tunnel demonstrates this: he enters into a tunnel, into the further enclosed world, but then emerges, signifying his move back into *potential* "Living-Together". Like the monasteries that Barthes describes, the enclosure or territory of the protagonist is "only a fairly loose marking out of the confines of the space".[26] He is not closed off, but momentarily private (while in the tunnel), and protected or enclosed only when he is wearing his helmet or within the travelling "sphere" of riding his motorcycle. Otherwise, his territory is wide open.

The song is pivotal for the film: through its lyrics, the song describes the protagonist and names him as a traffic officer on the Parisian rue du Marais who needs to leave the city. The song's lyrics refer to memory and nostalgia: the narrator is remembering a woman who is deeply desirable and indefinable. She is described as being like the ebb and flow of waves. She evokes *rhuthmos*, that *original* definition of "rhythm" that Barthes accounts for at the start of his study of idiorrhythmy. *Rhuthmos* is "the pattern of a fluid element (a letter, a *peplos*, a mood), an improvised, changeable form".[27] The woman described in 'No Line on the Horizon' seems to embody idiorrhythmy itself.

'Fez – Being Born' has the protagonist stopping at a small diner. After parking his motorcycle and removing his helmet, he walks in, removes his jacket and looks over to the young woman who is behind the counter, and who proceeds to take his order. The young woman appears bored throughout the scene. He looks at her longingly after she takes his order and turns from him to proceed to the kitchen. He looks at her longingly again when he receives his salad. She returns to her place behind the counter. While she bites her nails, the server watches the biker eat. The camera focuses on him eating his salad in close-up, perhaps signifying the scrutiny that he is facing under the gaze of the server.

The lyrics here also describe and inform the narrative of the film. They seem to describe the biker's journey thus far in the film; the lyrics indicate that the time is now approaching evening, as the biker has travelled in the heat of the day. The lyrics also suggest his final destination, the Bay of Càdiz, and across the water to Africa (in the film, the biker seems to head to Tarifa, crossing the Strait of Gibraltar). It is unclear in the lyrics, though, whether the narrator arrives in Africa; rather, through a seemingly violent event, the narrator of the song falls literally head over heels and is "born" into a new life, perhaps a life after death as a result of an accident. None of this occurs in the filmic narrative as the protagonist eats his salad; the biker is having his life sustained rather than destroyed in the company of the server in a relatively serene scene in the diner. The final fate of the protagonist occurs sometime after the credits roll and the film ends.

Like the protagonist here, Barthes suggests that humanity lives off needs and desires. The protagonist needs his salad – a stand-in for any sustaining meal in which he might partake – and he clearly desires the server, as indicated by both his lingering gaze on the server as she walks away and the subtle nod of approval that accompanies his gaze. Barthes states, "Now, Living-Together is a field of desire, and idorrhythmy is the subtle (non-scientific, notionally or only ineffectually institutionalized) form of that desire. But alongside that desire, what happens to needs? How do needs get satisfied? Who takes care of domestic tasks?"[28]

Barthes continues by exploring (particularly Christian) communities in which the taking care of domestic needs and the taking care of desires are considered equal. He refers to "sublimated domesticity" in which an elder exchanges some spiritual wisdom with a younger "disciple" who provides a small service which enables the elder's seclusion. In cases where desire does not equal need (arguably that is the case in this segment of the film), Barthes writes, "Clearly, this communitary problem repeats the major structural problems of all societies: the division of labor, exchange, class divisions, the reconstruction of a social microcosm at the margins of society, the circumscription of an idle, privileged group".[29] The diner, then, becomes a microcosm of the "major structural problems of all societies", with the server serving, and the protagonist receiving, in the dual forms of consuming the food and consuming the body of the server through his gaze. The protagonist thinks nothing of this exchange of "spiritual goods", to use Barthes' term, and nor does the server, who spends her time biting her nails, not noticing anything but the particularly mundane sequence of events: the entrance of a man, the ordering of food, the delivery of food and the consumption of food (and, of course, the consumption of the server).

The next segment features the song 'Magnificent'. Here, the server turns on the television in the diner, which features the band themselves performing the song. The image on the television is not clear, though: the image jumps, it is interrupted by moments of static and the colours shift. The band are heavily distorted. In the clip that the viewer is watching, U2 are doubly mediated: the viewer is seeing the band through the mediation of the television in the diner in addition to the mediation offered by the Corbijn film.

In the middle of the song, the scene changes back to the protagonist and the server in the diner. They look at each other for a moment before both turning again to look at the television. The band are again featured on the television screen, and, once the performance is finished, the segment fades to black.

For Barthes, the frame is important: he first discusses the ways that lives (and living) are constrained by the square or rectangle. Consider the shape of rooms in which people live, a shape which he argues does not exist in nature. He draws this discussion, then, to cover the idea of the frame, including the film screen. In a sense, then, Barthes could be exploring the implications of the television screen as well. He writes,

> It's as if imaginary perversion actually called imperiously for the frame, the rectangular outline, the border. Cf. Loving enchantment, love at first sight, to be suddenly enamored = to be kidnapped by the image. Now, as a general rule, that image is framed. The object of love (the object to be loved) abruptly appears (a) as a cut-out silhouette – or as a particular, fetishized part of the body, (b) in a frame, (c) in a setting, in the process of doing something.[30]

There are eleven segments that make up the film, covering eleven songs, and the band are visually absent in all of them except for one. The segment in which the band are present comes in seventh in the sequence of eleven. Nevertheless, U2 are the "objects of love" of *Linear*, and the band do *abruptly* appear. The band do not appear here as a cut-out silhouette (though, in 2004, they did appear in a television advertisement for a special edition U2-branded iPod in silhouette, in the style of Apple iPod digital music player advertisements at the time). The setting of the *Linear* performance appears to be a studio recording of some sort, with Mullen Jr playing the drums in a room separate from the rest of the band. The band appear to be in the process of recording: the viewer sees the band in the process of doing something (as do the duo in the diner).

But this frame is further distanced from the *Linear* viewer, as this viewer is watching the band through multiple screens, multiple mediations. This *breaks* the frame. Referencing comic strips, Barthes mentions subversions of the frame, mentioning a cartoonist that "gets his characters talking to or fighting each other across two different frames".[31] The band, here, are "talking" to the *Linear* viewer across two different frames. The first is the frame of the television set in the diner. The second is the frame of Corbijn's *Linear* film. Because the band are communicating to the viewer across two frames, they effectively break or subvert the notion of the frame completely. They are not bound by the diner's television frame at all, as they are communicating with the *Linear* viewer, past the diner occupants, and away from their potential gaze. They seem to be busy with other matters, in any case. When the camera moves away from the band, it features the protagonist and server acknowledging each other; the "loving enchantment" that the viewer has towards the band is broken and the viewer is *forced* to see the momentary acknowledgement of the two figures in the diner. This subversion happens "by more subtle means, by retaining the shape and inventing a distinctive play of superimposition for it, or one of effacement, of overstepping its limits".[32] Double mediation oversteps the limits of the screen, forcing the viewer to see the couple *seeing* each other.

The next segment, featuring the song 'Stand Up Comedy', has the viewer focused on the reflection of the passing landscape on a part of the motorcycle engine, with nothing else appearing in the frame. The protagonist is back on the road, moving closer to his destination. The shiny metal plate upon which the camera is focused is curved with a flat portion at its centre. Therefore, the reflections are more distorted on the edges of the plate (and of the frame), while the reflections are in focus at the centre where the plate provides a flat surface upon which the passing scenery can reflect. At the very end of the segment, the motorcyclist is seen riding past a sign that indicates that Cádiz is seven kilometres away. Presumably, the biker is approaching his final destination.

In his discussion of utopia, again in the context of "Living-Together", Barthes mentions the notion of distance as being valuable. In his discussion, he defines this distance as "tact", by which he means "distance and respect ... not to direct the other, other people, not to manipulate them, to actively renounce images".[33] Kate Briggs expands on this idea by explaining Barthes' own term *délicatesse*:

where the neutral is imagined as a utopia (in grammar, the neutral or neuter is neither masculine nor feminine, neither active nor passive; in politics, Barthes sees it as a refusal to take sides on complex conflictual questions phrased in such a way as to permit only yes/no answers), *délicatesse* is the name given to the small-scale, everyday practice of values such as goodwill and attentiveness, what Barthes also calls "sweetness" (*la douceur*), values in the form of behaviours that parry the already decided, the apparent self-evidence, the all-purpose explanation – and attend instead to those small, fleeting and fragile moments in life where, as Samoyault puts it, "individualities truly express themselves in their truth".[34]

The image that Barthes is discussing here is the presupposed image that one has of another person, but it can also refer to how one perceives the world. Barthes' utopian vision is expressed in *hupar*, a Greek word that refers to a sort of clear vision or dream. This is not what one sees in the reflection of the engine plate: rather, one sees something more along the lines of a "subtle shimmering of different intensities", something that Barthes suggests is at work in discourse, in voices.[35]

So, Barthes' ideas might help the viewer in this way: the shimmering reflection of the world in the plate is not so much a utopian vision, or *hupar*. It is, instead, the multiple facets of discourse, and points to the idea of tact and distance, the notion of *actively renouncing images and allowing them to shimmer*. This is a compelling image of "Living-Together", of coexistence. The viewer sees the world as unfixed, as in flux, as *idiorrhythmic*.

Emma Mason discusses the "shimmering", what she calls "twinklings", as a concept that "baffles the paradigm" of binaries: "The glimmer of the 'twinkle', with its indeterminate wavering light, is suggestive of such 'baffling'".[36] Mason quotes Teeuwen in describing what is happening in the "baffling":

> Although not designed as a genre of writing, *The Neutral*'s present and future mode of existence is that of writing: a truly utopian writing, a "third form", neither creative nor academic, neither nonsense nor entirely clear, always investing language with more nuances than easily fit a goal simply of communication, always deferring finality by means of the neither-nor.[37]

Barthes' "neithor-nor", the idea of a shimmering, unfixed neutral, is central. Mason establishes these "twinklings" as elements in Barthes' writing that engage readers, while working to "undo and suspend the oppositional thinking that structures and produces meaning".[38]

The next segment features the song, 'Get on Your Boots', which is the first single released from *No Line on the Horizon*. Here, the protagonist arrives at what appears to be a club or a bar called "Bay Bay" (perhaps a play on the word "baby"). He enters the flamboyant interior, complete with billiard table, mirror ball and coin-operated child's horse ride (as one might have encountered at shopping malls in the past). The interior is lit with reds and purples, and appears otherworldly after the natural scenery of the previous segments. Immediately, a woman who is sitting across from the protagonist begins to dance provocatively for him. The bartender brings the protagonist a drink as he watches her dance. He seems uncomfortable, and it is clear that he does not take pleasure from the spectacle. She lifts the back of her dress revealing a part of her buttock which has the number six on it (perhaps a tattoo?). He then removes his keys from his pocket, as if offering her his motorcycle, and places them on the table. His keys are on a miniature billiard ball keychain; the ball also has a number six on it.

He then leaves the woman and enters what appears to be a "peep booth", a private room with a peephole in order to gaze upon semi-naked or nude women. Through the peephole, he watches a number of scantily clad women dance for him. But the women are all moustachioed. This, of course, adds a sense of whimsy and a sense of the fantastic to this segment. On the wall behind the women are a neon "99" (which might be a broken "69", perhaps a colloquial reference to the act of oral sex) and the words "SEÑOR-ita". After watching the spectacle, the protagonist leaves.

This segment seems more humorous than sexual: the women are clearly not transvestites or transgender, as the "SEÑOR-ita" sign might otherwise suggest. Rather, they are sexualized women under the male gaze that are *not*: they resist that gaze, it seems, by playing to it but not providing the protagonist with what he might expect. This is reflected in the neon sign as well: the broken "6" communicates that what is expected is not what is delivered. This space is not one of bodily erotic pleasure, but one of unexpected prank.

For Barthes, the room – that is, the room that is one's own space, evoking the privacy of the bedroom – is a protected space for fantasy. It is not subject to any sort of surveillance, and it is separate from any other structure. It is its *own* space: the room at the "Bay Bay" is certainly its own space, separate from the reality of the outside world, seemingly functioning by its own gender rules. Barthes states, "Indeed, the luxury of the bedroom derives from its freedom: a structure protected from all norms, all powers; as a structure – an exorbitant paradox: it's unique".[39] The room at the "Bay Bay", then, is protected from all norms, including those of male power. The women are under the power of the male gaze for the few moments that the protagonist does not notice the woman's facial hair, and before she is joined by other women. Once he sees her face, it as if the relationship is switched. He is under the power of the gaze of the women, as is the viewer of *Linear*. What the viewer expects, a sexualized spectacle of women in their underwear, becomes that, but something more and something unexpected. The structure of the room is protected from male power: that power is subverted by the "SEÑOR-itas" therein. But the subversion of male power seems to start even earlier than that. The protagonist does not enjoy the provocative dancing of the woman in the main area of the bar, and gives up his motorcycle to her, symbolized by his leaving his keys on the table after waving them in front of her. He loses – or, more accurately, he voluntarily relinquishes – his mobility and a symbol of his male power. The police motorcycle was the sign of his civic power as a police officer and he burns that in a forceful move against that civic power. His personal motorcycle, though, allowed him travel and movement. He gives that up even before being subjected to a further marginalization during the peep show.

But this room is not necessarily something negative. The room, free from societal power, likewise strips the protagonist of societal power, but also from societal pressure. He loses his masculine power, perhaps, and relinquishes access to his motorcycle and mobility, but he is also freed. These societal pressures include the pressure to wield masculine power, civic power and the pressures that accompany the privilege of mobility. This freedom then allows the protagonist to *live* with the others in the "Bay Bay". The humorous engagement of the "SEÑOR-itas" might emasculate, but it does not denigrate.[40] It is an episode of a forceful equalization of power between the protagonist and the others.

Women with moustaches appear in the official promotional music video for 'Get on Your Boots' as well as in *Linear*. This is a curious link that might help in understanding what is going on with the moustachioed women in the club in the film. In the music video for 'Get on Your Boots', the band are featured playing the song in a collage of outer space, popcorn, thrill rides, lava and erupting volcanoes, armies and weapons of war, American flags, flowers and, of course, beautiful women, some of them with moustaches. Like in *Linear*, the facial hair is not realistic and looks very much like costume disguises. At one point in the song, Bono exclaims that women are the future; this is the idea upon which the "herstory" sequence in *The Joshua Tree 2017* tour is built. Here, a giant woman is featured watching over soldiers in a military parade. She blows on them and they are scattered by the power of her breath, in a similar way that children might scatter a crowd of toy soldiers as they play with them on the ground.

The track 'Get on Your Boots' can have a number of meanings. First, there is the idea that women need to mobilize, to put on their boots and get to work, so to speak. Through their actions, military intervention and activity can be laid aside – scattered – in deference to other options for world peace and in the face of domination and global power play. Second, the idea of putting on boots might suggest the taking on of male power: the moustaches suggest that there is a drastic change being displayed. The expectation is that these women in the video are simply present for the pleasure of the male spectator. This is certainly a conventional position for women in music video, and such a position in turn interpellates spectators that consume the music video format. As the women are moustachioed, they are no longer providing what is expected in the conventional male-gaze/female "to-be-looked-at-ness" relationship. They subvert it.

In the music video, during the bridge section of the song, Bono repeatedly lifts and lowers his microphone stand forcefully to the drum beat. The glass that makes up the "fourth wall", or the screen through which the viewer engages with the video, cracks in time with the thrusts of Bono's microphone stand. The repeated cracking of that mediating screen functions in the same way as the double mediation in the diner in *Linear*. Here, the band are overstepping the frame yet again by literally breaking it. In addition to breaking that external barrier between viewer and the world of the music video, Bono appears at moments to be under water, and he appears shirtless (though the viewer only sees his bare torso from above the shoulders). The breaking of the screen corresponds to the submersion in water: the surface level of water is broken in the same way as that barrier between the band and viewer. Bono is, perhaps, emerging from baptism into a new life – a life in which women are in charge, ready to move towards a new future, and where Bono has died to an older way of being. For that matter, the idea of Bono being shirtless, or having his shirt removed from him, removes his own status as celebrity. It should be noted that Bono is not particularly muscular, or a figure who is here seen as sexualized or hyper-masculine. Bono laid bare (though still not exposed to the viewer) is Bono equalized with the male viewer under the *new* power of women of the future.

After the segment in the "Bay Bay" comes the segment for the next song in *Linear*, 'Moment of Surrender'. The protagonist is now outside, in the coastal town of Tarifa. He unbuttons his shirt and puts on a scarf as he walks the cobblestone streets. This segment is in black and white, and the camera is shaky as it is hand-held. The viewer feels as if they are walking beside, in front of and behind the protagonist, accompanying him as he wanders the streets, with his duffel bag over his shoulder. This segment is quite a departure from the events of the "Bay Bay". At one point, the protagonist rests against a wall under a light, perhaps contemplating his next move. His moment of contemplation lines up with the moment in the song when Bono sings its title, which suggests that this is also the protagonist's moment of surrender to unknown forces. Finally, the protagonist arrives at his destination (for now): the beach. He kneels down on the beach, in front of the sea, wraps his scarf tightly around his neck, pulls his jacket over himself and lays his head on his duffel bag to sleep.

The lyrics of 'Moment of Surrender' explicitly evoke the Roman Catholic tradition of the Stations of the Cross, a series of contemplations based on fourteen moments in the Passion and crucifixion of Jesus Christ. The prayers that accompany these contemplations constitute an act of devotion to Christ. The lyrics also refer to the time between the death, resurrection and ascension of Christ and the day of Pentecost, that is, the day of the delivering of the gift of the Holy Spirit as companion and guide to the people of God, according to the biblical account. Bono conflates the Stations of the Cross with subway stations through which he is travelling, suggesting a process of movement *through* the various contemplations (of course, he chooses to mix the sacred of the Stations with the profane of subway stations). The protagonist is moving on his own contemplative journey.

It is during this song that the protagonist finds himself at the penultimate destination on his journey: he is on the beach in Tarifa across the Mediterranean from his destination of Morocco and North Africa (this is the closest point in Spain to the city of Tangier in Morocco, a forty-minute ferry ride away). The moment just before he reclines to spend the night on the beach (when he gets on his knees before the sea) is, in some way, the protagonist's second "moment of surrender", the moment when he resigns himself to continue the dangerous journey to his destination.

This is also a moment of surrender to the sea, which is a recurring example of this utopic "Living-Together", the idiorrhythmy of the sea. These are the last moments that the protagonist will feel what Barthes calls *Xeniteia*, or the feeling of being a foreigner in one's own country. Barthes states that this is "Feeling like a foreigner in your own country, within your social class, your caste, the institutions you've been placed in".[41] With the sea in front of him, the protagonist has hit a limit, a physical constraint, that keeps him in this sense of *Xeniteia*. It seems this was the initial catalyst for the beginning of his travels: his inability to handle the tensions between communities – and his role in the middle of the conflict as a police officer (in the institution he had been placed in) – certainly would have made him feel as if he was a foreigner. It is plain, also, to see that the biker does not have French ancestry: the actor Saïd Taghmaoui is French from Moroccan parents. Barthes concludes, "And so we come back to the Utopia of the affective group, the fantasy of the idiorrhythmic community. It would allow for a certain form of *Xeniteia* with respect to a common fatherland, the great Other, while at the same time sheltering its subjects from the anxiety of affective abandonment, affective expatriation".[42] Barthes then suggests that monastic life shows idiorrhythmy and utopia particularly because the timing of monastic life is regulated and sure. His discussion sheds light on what the protagonist is experiencing on the beach:

> The community prepares to brave the night (imagine a countryside far away from anywhere, with no lights, so where nightfall really means the threat of darkness). Living-Together: perhaps simply a way of confronting the sadness of the night together. Being among strangers is inevitable, necessary even, except when night falls.[43]

Except, of course, that the protagonist is alone on the beach, without strangers or those he knows. This lack is palpable.

The final track on *Linear* is called 'Cedars of Lebanon'. The segment begins with the protagonist waking up on the beach. He gets up and gazes out to sea, not appearing particularly confident of his decision that has brought him to this point. He then gets up and grabs his belongings and approaches a row boat that is nearby on the shore. The scene switches briefly to a map that appears to be outdoors, perhaps on a sign or building close by. The map indicates the close distance between the Spanish coast and the north of Africa. Finally, the protagonist is shown rowing the small boat in the water. A sign indicates that he is in fact attempting to row across the Strait of Gibraltar.

Barthes calls a sort of separation idiorrhythmy: his idea of an initial separation – that is, the separation of a community from society – is demonstrated in the Christian monk. Once separated, there can be an additional separation, in the form of idiorrhythmy. Barthes suggests that those people who live within this secondary marginality are seen by society as mad (his examples are such figures as Dendrites, those who live in trees in order to be closer to the heavens, and Stationaries or Stylites, those who live in society but do not communicate with it). The protagonist is like this, especially when the viewer discovers that he is attempting to row across the Mediterranean: this is an abnormal activity. His journey conversely mirrors the immigrant journey of refugees from Syria further to the east across the same sea, except that the biker is not fleeing from danger. He was in a position of power and, while he was perhaps caught within a tension of class and ethnic conflict, he was not the powerless actor in that conflict. It is because of frustration and discomfort that he leaves, rather than due to any physical danger to himself or any sort of threat to those that he loves.

His journey, then, is madness, and he can be considered a madman. Barthes defines a madman as "someone who's devoid of all power. Whence his excessive position, excessive because it's neutral: being neither for nor against power (neither master nor slave), he strives to remain outside of it. A position that's untenable".[44] At least, the position is untenable in the current, physical world. But the viewer does not see where the protagonist ultimately ends his journey, and whether or not he is successful in reaching Africa.

Overview of *Linear*

The officer begins as an "autarky", that is, a self-contained existence, or he lives in an autarkic space. He does not engage in "Living-Together" and wishes to exit the *milieu* of tension and violence, of dying and death. He moves from his position of power to that of marginality, making it clear that he will no longer obey his superiors, that he will no longer participate in his function of service to society as a police officer and that he will even forsake his title as a member of a civil society. His destruction of property owned by the state (the police motorcycle) makes that clear. He will not be subjugated to the power that is inherent in this sort of "domesticated idiorrhythmy", state control through authority and power.

The biker enforces "rules of distance" by putting distance between himself and his primary subject position as a police officer. He has left the Parisian community behind, thus being marginalized even from those who are in the margins. And his desire is for something yet outside the frame: the viewer does not know where the biker is going. The trip is like a monastery: his desire (for a place in society, a desire which is a source of both tension and confusion) is deflected away from the communities of authority (the police) or the marginal (the immigrants) but to the "idiorrhythmic", though what this entails for him is unknown.

The trauma that the biker leaves behind is scotomized, or forgotten. In that forgetting, the transformation of desire is begun. He travels by motorcycle – in an enclosed world of his helmet and vehicle – but then emerges into potential "Living-Together". He is enacting idiorrhythmy, being momentarily private or in solitude but is then thrust fully into the public sphere.

The biker stops at a diner which is like a microcosm of the world, displaying the structural inequalities inherent in society. And then U2 are on the television screen: U2 are the objects of desire for the whole film. The band are the reason for the film to exist. But in the double mediation of the television in the diner, the "loving enchantment" with the band is broken. Again, double mediation oversteps the limits of the screen, and breaks it.

The film visually demonstrates to the viewer the idea of "Living-Together" as acknowledging the world – and the people in it – as being in flux, allowing them to shimmer. The film illustrates the ideas of tact and distance.

Then there is the segment in the "Bay Bay", which, along with the sequence of images when the biker is on the side of the road, is the most difficult portion of the film. The room that the protagonist enters, complete with "SEÑORitas", is a protected space, free from societal norms, including male power. In fact, in his (rather male) act of gazing on the women, he loses his mobility and is subject to further marginality. But in this marginality, he is privy to equalization. While humorous, the segment is positive in its demonstration of the power to equalize.

On the biker's mad journey (being outside of the structures of power, which is ultimately an untenable position), he begins in the suburbs of Paris and travels across France into Spain, and then across the waters of the Mediterranean to the north of Africa, a reverse journey of many migrants with whom U2 concern themselves. The immigrant and refugee flows come from Syria and the Middle East towards Greece and Italy, and then those immigrants might travel across the various borders of the European Union to settle in large urban centres like Paris, in large suburbs full of apartment blocks and rife with tension. Does this possible reverse path of movement as indicated in *Linear* – that is, the flow of immigrants and refugees into Europe through the Mediterranean – always result in tensions, such as those in which the biker finds himself at the start of the film? These tensions force him to leave.

Looked at from this perspective, the film seems to suggest an unsatisfactory trajectory for those seeking refuge in Europe. The film shows a French citizen moving back to his origins, a flow that is in the opposite direction than expected, or as expressed in later career songs like 'Red Flag Day' or 'Summer of Love', both of which seem to describe movement in the Mediterranean away from geographical locations that are prevalent with conflict and human suffering. Even if the biker is of North African heritage, he serves as a police officer in Paris, which suggests at the least some comfort in and commitment to Parisian and French culture. For the biker, North Africa seems to promise a fulfilment of the lack that he has when he is on the beach in Tarifa. If the police officer is wanting to escape the societal pressures and tensions that exist between immigrant communities and those that hold societal or civic power (such as the police), is it possible for an immigrant or refugee to thrive in those similar conditions? Also, what can the biker expect when he arrives at his destination in North Africa? Is his partner going to make his stay worthwhile? Will he be able to overcome the societal tensions that he might encounter at his new destination or will he be forced to flee from there as well?

The film *Linear* closely accompanies U2's *No Line on the Horizon*, in that it acts as a long-form music video. There are no lines of dialogue and no diagetic sound in the film: the only sound in the film is provided by the songs of the album. The film employs both travel and binaries as overarching themes. The film moves from an urban setting to a rural one (and back), it moves from black and white to colour (and back), it moves from Europe (Paris) and ultimately to Morocco and North Africa (at least as the suggested end destination, which the viewer does not see). The main character is a motorcycled traffic patrol officer who escapes his job and his city, and the shallowness of his world, though he rides a classic symbol of liberation and rebellion in the motorcycle. This shallowness is expressed in the cityscape that is showcased in the beginning montage, during which clubs and bars in the urban centre of Paris are passed by, as if on the officer's motorcycle. He moves from the shelter and mundanity of the city to the open road: it is not hard to consider that the police force represents the establishment and the idea of conformity. The protagonist escapes that establishment, burning the police motorcycle and eventually discarding his uniform. The beginning and end of the film, in which the protagonist is in a "city" (he departs from Paris and travels to the Spanish town of Tarifa in order to cross the water to Morocco) are in black and white, while the sections of the film in which he is travelling, stopping at rest-stops to eat or, in a curious segment, to gaze at mustachioed women at a bar, are in colour. It is most interesting that, once he gets on a rowboat to Africa, the film does not once again change into colour. Of course, all of this assumes a certain "positivity" associated with colour as opposed to the "seriousness" of black and white. Ultimately, though, the film is disorienting: when the viewer finally sees U2 performing in the film, they are doubly mediated. That is, the viewer sees them through the eyes of the protagonist who is watching the band perform on a blurry television set with poor reception. Even if the viewer was to see a crystal-clear image of the band, it would still be "apart" or "separated" from the viewer, mediated twice by the context of the story (once through the *Linear* viewer's own screen and once through the one in the film). The fact that the image is also distorted adds even more distance.

Throughout the film, the gaze of the viewer remains on the protagonist as he struggles with his authoritarian role as a Paris police officer in the face of immigrant unrest. The viewer's gaze, though, does simply that: it does not judge the protagonist but rather travels with him. In other moments, the viewer's gaze becomes that of the protagonist: in these moments, the "reportage", to use Kracauer's term, becomes personal. The viewer can feel the draw of escaping the life in which the protagonist finds himself, to somehow move forward towards something new, to travel outward away from shallow insularity.

Barthes seems to echo U2 with some of his thoughts in his lectures. Consider his rumination on the idea of pairs: "what's opposed – what produces meaning – isn't so much the One and the Two but rather: the integrated (which is perhaps better than composite) One and the disintegrated (disassociated, divided, conflicted) One".[45] Frederic Jameson would call these things the complex and neutral terms.

In a short commentary on the home video release of Alfonso Cuarón's 2006 film, *Children of Men*, philosopher Slavoj Žižek considers the image of a boat as rootless. Žižek is bringing to mind the boat that the film's protagonist/antihero Theo and the refugee Kee take to meet members of the "Human Project" and safety. For Žižek, "the condition of the renewal is you cut your roots".[46] This is a Marxist idea, that it is only through a break from culture and tradition that one is able to thrive. Michel Foucault discusses the utopic potential of the boat in his discussion of heterotopia:

> the boat is a floating piece of space, a place without a place, that exists by itself, that is closed in on itself and at the same time is given over to the infinity of the sea and that, from port to port, from tack to tack, from brothel to brothel, it goes as far as the colonies in search of the most precious treasures they conceal in their gardens, you will understand why the boat … has been … the greatest reserve of the imagination. The ship is the heterotopia par excellence. In civilizations without boats, dreams dry up, espionage takes the place of adventure, and the police take the place of pirates.[47]

The protagonist police officer does the opposite of Foucault's admonition at the end of his essay: he takes the "place of pirates" on the boat leaving the police behind.

Notes

1. Rob Sheffield, "U2: How to Dismantle an Atomic Bomb", *Rolling Stone* (9 December 2004); available from https://www.rollingstone.com/music/albumreviews/how-to-dismantle-an-atomic-bomb-20041209 (accessed 20 February 2018).
2. Bryan Wawzenek, "Revisiting U2's Unfocused 'How to Dismantle an Atomic Bomb'", *Ultimate Classic Rock* (17 November 2015); available from http://ultimateclassicrock.com/u2-how-to-dismantle-an-atomic-bomb/ (accessed 20 February 2018).
3. Adam Sherwin, "New U2 album No Line on the Horizon given lukewarm reception". *The Times* (3 March 2009); available from https://tinyurl.com/TIMES-u2-album (accessed 6 August 2017).
4. David Fricke, "U2: No Line on the Horizon", *Rolling Stone* (20 February 2009); available from http://www.rollingstone.com/music/albumreviews/no-line-on-the-horizon-20090220 (accessed 8 August 2017).
5. Jay Cocks, "U2: Band on the Run", *Time* (27 April 1987); available from http://www.u2.com/news/title/rocks-hottest-ticket-time-magazine/news/ (accessed 6 August 2017).

6. Patrick Burgoyne, "U2 Linear: it's not a music video", *Creative Review* (14 April 2009); available from https://tinyurl.com/8dcfc8a283b (accessed 21 February 2018).
7. Roland Barthes, *How to Live Together: Novelistic Simulations of Some Everyday Spaces*, translated by Kate Briggs (New York: Columbia University Press, 2013), 9.
8. Kate Briggs, *This Little Art* (London: Fitzcarraldo Editions, 2017), 38–39.
9. Ibid., 112.
10. Barthes, *How to Live Together*, 9.
11. Ibid., 7.
12. Ibid. Related to this, Barthes discusses "acedy", which refers to "no longer being capable of investing in other people, in Living-with-several-other-people and yet at the same time being incapable of investing in solitude. → Throwing it all away, but without even somewhere to throw it: waste without a waste bin" (23). This hints at, but is not, Living-Together, and this is not idiorrhythmy, both of which look for a *new* way. Acedy is an in-between in that it refers to being incapable of both community and solitude, but does not show a positive way forward; it does not answer Barthes' ultimate question of "How to Live Together".
13. Neil McCormick, *U2 by U2* (London: HarperCollins, 2006), 423. As an aside, The Edge was sometimes afraid that Bono would come across as a "school teacher" with all of the lecturing about human rights, coexistence and so forth, particularly during the *Vertigo* tour (424).
14. Barthes, *How to Live Together*, 36.
15. Ibid., 37.
16. Ibid., 40.
17. Ibid., 40–41.
18. Ibid., 72–73.
19. Ibid., 89.
20. Rudolphus Teeuwen, "An Epoch of Rest: Roland Barthes' 'Neutral' and the Utopia of Weariness", *Cultural Critique* 80 (2012): 4.
21. Ibid., 7.
22. Roland Barthes, "*Longtemps, je me suis couché de bonne heure ...*", in *The Rustle of Language*, translated by Richard Howard (New York: Hill and Wang, 1989), 280.
23. Ibid., 281.
24. Ibid., 282.
25. Barthes, *How to Live Together*, 57.
26. Ibid., 58.
27. Ibid., 7.
28. Ibid., 75.
29. Ibid., 77.
30. Ibid., 115.
31. Ibid., 116.
32. Ibid.
33. Ibid., 132.
34. Briggs, *This Little Art*, 324. Briggs is translating an entry on "Délicatesse" in Tiphaine Samoyault, "Lexique Roland Barthes", *Roland Barthes: L'inattendu, Le Monde Hors-Série* 26 (Paris: Société éditrice du Monde, 2015), 113.

35. Barthes, *How to Live Together*, 168.
36. Emma Mason, "Punctive Grace: Reading Religion in Barthes' *Mourning Diary*", *Textual Practice* 30.2 (2016): 335.
37. Teeuwen, "An Epoch of Rest", 8.
38. Mason, "Punctive Grace", 335.
39. Barthes, *How to Live Together*, 54.
40. Of course, any instance of the male gaze is potentially problematic, and it should be strongly noted that the male gaze is not erased in this segment.
41. Ibid., 128.
42. Ibid.
43. Ibid., 129.
44. Ibid., 92.
45. Ibid., 96.
46. See the *Children of Men* DVD extra.
47. Michel Foucault, "Of Other Spaces", *Diacritics* 16.1 (Spring 1986): 27.

7 *Songs of Innocence* as Barthes' Ideal Novel

In September 2014, the band released *Songs of Innocence*, the beginning of what might be called the band's fourth period, though it is unclear what this period of the band's history will exactly look like, ultimately. The two albums that have been released in the 2010s thus far – *Songs of Innocence* and *Songs of Experience* – seem to inhabit a similar world, and seem to extend the "commercial" trajectory of the band begun in the 2000s, after the daring of the 1990s albums. If the 2000s were U2's age of "return to authenticity", and a kind of surety in their place as legends (if not really taste makers) in popular music, then the albums of the 2000s do nothing to dismiss or eclipse those earlier ideas. The difference is more subtle: the band toy with corporate complicity with the release of *Songs of Innocence* for free on Apple's iTunes music service: the album was marked as purchased in all iTunes accounts and automatically downloaded on customer devices (for those who had activated the option to download to all devices a purchase made on a single device). This was not well-received. About this, writing for *Pitchfork*, Rob Mitchum states, "U2 have aligned with their old friends Apple to insert *Songs of Innocence* into all of our libraries without consent. This indisputably queasy approach to the 'surprise release' gambit might be the most interesting element about the band's latest album".[1]

Of the album – and the band at this stage in their career – David Fricke comments, "No other rock band does rebirth like U2. No other band – certainly of U2's duration, commercial success and creative achievement – believes it needs rebirth more and so often".[2] The band released the concert film *U2 iNNOCENCE + eXPERIENCE: Live in Paris*, from the tour in support of *Songs of Innocence*, in June 2016.

While the automatic download on iTunes was convenient for those who wanted the album, the particular method of distribution caused the album to appear on their devices seemingly without their knowledge or consent. In a way, the album is anathema to Barthes' notion of a novel being free from power, as Adam Thirlwell suggests below. Additionally, the album finds meaning in what it *does not* do: allow choice in its distribution. As such, U2's album is an *imperfect* example of Barthes' ideal novel, expressing both passion and intimacy, while conveying a loss of innocence on many levels. This is ironic considering the title of the work, *Songs of Innocence*.

Tiphaine Samoyault refers to the Barthesian idea of "Marcelism", or the "special interest" that readers might have in the life of Marcel Proust. She then suggests the idea of "Rolandism", a look at a life as a succession of figures, which turns Barthes' life into a "Life", that is, a literary experience, a novel.[3]

Here, then, is a Barthesian evocation of remembering and resuscitating in U2's *Songs of Innocence*. The term "evocation" is used because the album does just that: it evokes Barthes' idea of the ideal novel, the *Vita Nova*. This figure (that can be thought as being "in succession" with the other elements that are analysed in this book) might be read as a "Life", a life after death of the author. These speak to the "Rolandism" of real life, of popular culture, of a narrative of the world. Not only does the "Life" show the vitality of Barthes' theoretical *oeuvre* into the twenty-first century, but it also demonstrates a resuscitation of his very life into the present.

There are a few ways for the listener to conceive of the lead singer of U2. He is either a man named Paul Hewson, or he is a man named Bono. Perhaps another way to think of this is that the man named Paul Hewson *puts on* the persona of a rock star named Bono. That is, Paul Hewson is real and Bono does not really exist. As has already been stated, the audience suspends its disbelief in engaging with the figure of Bono as real. This does not take into account The Fly or Mr MacPhisto; this is just about Bono. Even his wife Ali Hewson seems to refer to Paul Hewson as Bono, which problematizes the notion of Paul Hewson as the real person and Bono as the performance. Perhaps it simply points to the conflation of the rock star and the person. As Bono has said in concert performance, "There is no them, there's only us".

If Paul Hewson lives in the real world, Bono lives in a world that is *not yet*, a potential world. The band ask the audience to see the world through their eyes, through the lens of potential. Paul Hewson is the author of Bono; Bono is the narrator of the story of this new world. What Bono proclaims – the possibility of a new *potential* world – is written by Paul Hewson. As author, Paul Hewson writes this new sort of novel, a novel that perhaps arises out of the grief from the death of his mother, and the struggles of early life, and informed by the later death of his father. Through death (and even Bono's own experience of mortality, as expressed in the liner notes for *Songs of Experience*), Hewson creates something new: the possibility and potential of a new life and new world, both for himself and for his audience. Paul Hewson, then, writes something of a new life, with Bono as his narrator, the one that lays out the way forward, and who acts as an architect of a new, positive way.

Vita Nova

As early as November 1977, French semiotician and theorist Roland Barthes began to think about a new project, in the form of a novel called *Vita Nova*. This project emerged from the grief that engulfed him after the death of his mother, his life-long companion, in October 1977. During the summer of 1979, Barthes began sketching out the novel, informed by his lectures on *The Preparation of the Novel*, delivered at the Collège de France beginning in December 1978.

Adam Thirlwell suggests that Roland Barthes' desire to write a novel late in his life is ultimately a story of conversion, a decision to move in a "new way". Thirlwell describes Barthes' ideal novel as a combination of two ideals: "language as a form of passionate suspension". That is, speaking of one's passions in a language that is not a form of power, and in a way that foils the "paradigmatic, oppositional, structure of meaning".[4]

Thirlwell looks to Barthes' essay (delivered as a lecture in October 1978), "*Longtemps, je me suis couché de bonne heure...*". The title of the lecture refers to the opening line of Marcel Proust's *In Search of Lost Time*. In using Proust's words, Barthes wishes to identify with the protagonist of the novel, an author who, at the start of his work, wants to write a novel: "the narrative of a desire to write".[5] After the death of Proust's mother in 1905, Barthes suggests that the author entered into "a period of despondency, but also of sterile agitation".[6] According to Barthes, Proust is stuck between writing metaphor (what something means), which would result in an essay, or metonymy (what can follow, or come before, what one says), which would result in a novel (Barthes asks the question, "What can be engendered by the episode I am telling?"). Barthes continues, "Proust is seeking a form that will accommodate suffering ... and transcend it". This is, in fact, a sort of "third term" for Barthes.[7]

In the essay, Barthes seems to acknowledge that all humanity is threatened by death, and plagued by a life of repetition. But there can occur an event that changes all of this: a "middle of life's journey". For Proust, this was his mother's death. The middle of life for Barthes is "the moment when you discover that death is real and no longer merely dreadful". And so, for Barthes, the *Vita Nova* is a new practice of writing that contains a couple of elements. It contains the pathos of love and death, what Barthes calls a "moment of truth"; and it must be animated by (something to do with) love: "kindness? generosity? charity? ... pity (or compassion)".[8]

Barthes then concludes that his new project will permit him to "*say* whom I love ... and not to say *to* them that I love them". Barthes intends that the work would be representative of pathos; and that it would "exert no pressure upon the other (the reader)". He concludes with the question, "Should it not express at once the world's brilliance and the world's suffering, all that beguiles and offends me?"⁹

In late 1977 until September 1979, Barthes begins to commit, to small sheets of paper, daily thoughts after the death of his mother. These notes are collected in a book called *Mourning Diary*, published in 2010. In his entry for 30 November 1977, Barthes mentions something called *Vita Nova*, a project that represents a "radical gesture", which is, by its nature, discontinuous from what comes before it. Barthes suggests two possible paths for the continuation of the work: to embody liberty, hardness, truth (he suggests that this is a reversal of what it was before); or to embody laxness and charity (he suggests this is a reinforcement of what it was before). In both of these paths, he suggests that he himself would embody these traits. In a lecture given at the Collège de France on 19 January 1980, he talks about a "Complete Break, a Reinvented Way of Life, the Organization of a New Life": "There are two elements to this fantasy: *To shake off* ... the past, the present that adheres (=freedom, a liberating breaking of ties: mythical image of shedding one's skin, of desquamation, of rebirth, path to immortality)+*to create something new*: total, grandiose, triumphant".[10]

In a note in Richard Howard's translation of the *Mourning Diary*, Nathalie Léger clarifies that Barthes is exploring "a radically new life longed for by the mourning for the dear departed, explicitly [referring] to ... the invention ... of a poetic and narrative form in order to express love and mourning".[11] Central to the idea of *Vita Nova* is the notion, after the writing of Proust, of the "collapse of any subject-object distinction". Léger clarifies the source of this idea: "It was during this trip to Morocco [during the month of April 1978] that Barthes underwent, on 15 April, a spell of vertigo analogous 'to the illumination experienced by Proust's narrator at the end of *Time Regained* [the seventh and final volume of Proust's novel, *In Search of Lost Time*]'".[12] It is in the writings of Proust and Tolstoy that Barthes finds what Jonathan Culler translates as "moments of truth". Culler states that it is in these moments "where suddenly literature coincides with an emotional event for the reader who suffers".[13]

In the context of this mourning, Barthes seems to turn to the Protestant Christian faith of his mother, at least as a referent for some of his thinking. In a particularly interesting and important entry, dated 10 August 1978, Barthes quotes a portion of John 11, noting that he is "Struck by the fact that Jesus loved Lazarus and that before resuscitating him, he wept".[14] It is unclear why Barthes would cite this biblical passage, though he seems to take some comfort in the idea that the protagonist of the passage mourned: Barthes writes, at the end of the entry, "Jesus therefore again groaning in himself ...", which seems to refer to Jesus' state of being as he approaches the tomb of Lazarus, while the sentence fragment also suggests a present action, that Jesus is somehow mourning along with Barthes himself who mourns (note that Barthes writes the ellipses in the entry). Barthes seems compelled by the notion of Jesus being in grief even though he was about to resuscitate the dead. This very vignette seems to be a type of "cosmopolitan Christianity", an attempt to look outward, from isolated grief to communal identification, what Siegfried Kracauer would call an "unconcealed compassion".[15]

Bono has used the music of U2 to resuscitate the memory of his own mother, who died when the singer was a child. Songs like 'Tomorrow' from 1981's *October* album, 'Mofo' from 1997's *Pop*, and 'Iris (Hold Me Close)' from 2014's *Songs of Innocence*, are the most obvious examples of this. But something more seems to be occurring with Barthes.

Emma Mason suggests that there is a certain kind of grace that one can find throughout Barthes' late writings. She explains, "As a trigger for transformation, redemption, change and conversion, grace is the dynamic influence of the divine experienced by the believer, through faith". She continues to suggest that grace has the ability to end suffering, though suffering was the source of its beginning. In Christianity, Jesus' suffering and crucifixion were the source of grace and absolution of sin. Mason, then, summarizes Barthes' position thus: "Following Henriette Barthes' death on 25 October 1977, Barthes begins to associate grace with the 'female' and maternal, both possible sites of redemption which he might access through his love for his mother".[16]

As an aside, Mason discusses the place of tears and mourning, quoting Sandra McEntire, who explains that "compunction is a grace, gratuitously given". Furthermore, for McEntire, tears are an outward manifestation of inner emotion – or interior touch of grace – "before the greatness and mercy of God". Mason suggests that the idea of the "grace of tears" would not have been alien to Barthes because of his research into Michelet and Ignatius of Loyola. But also, "*Mourning Diary* is itself a record of weeping, Barthes' tears granting the journal an emotional structure in which reader and weeper are joined in grace".[17]

Mason continues, "Barthes' focus on Jesus' anxiety and tears remind the reader that the grace through which Jesus 'resurrects' Lazarus is also that secured by his own suffering at the crucifixion: love and joy are guaranteed but only through a movement towards God mobilised by suffering".[18] Remember the image of Aaron Brown being released from prison in the promotional music video for 'Song for Someone' from *Songs of Innocence* as an example of a movement towards God mobilized by suffering. The love and joy that the newly released prisoner will experience are only available after a time of anguish.

Barthes' conversion, the working of grace, is realized in his writing and, in particular, in his plans for *Vita Nova*, literally a "new life" (Diana Knight quotes Barthes commenting on the proposed novel, that "I too was going to enter into the novel, just as you enter into religion").[19] Mason explains,

> For Barthes literature is his religion, or, as he writes in his essay "Deliberation" (1979), "literature is *like* religion". Similarly, his writing is like grace, both aesthetic and spiritual, and so defies empirical theorising for evocations of "truth". *Mourning Diary* in particular attempts to conjure this truth by searching for a neutral space in which to live with grief following his mother's death ... [Religious] references help Barthes to figure literature as worth believing in, and writing as the dynamic that enables such faith.[20]

Julia Cooper suggests that Barthes knew the notion that grief is ultimately mundane and boring: "Mourning holds very little entertainment value. It repeats the same story over and over (and over and over)".[21]

Can the vivid rememberings in *Mourning Diary* (and in U2's 'Iris', as outlined below) be likened to photographs, mediated "slices" of a sort of reality, arresting an image and enticing the viewer to discover the greater narrative? If so, do they contain what Barthes calls an "air", the notion of the soul, the shadow, that makes an image "true"? Then this is the locus of the U2 listener's desire, what keeps the listener listening, and what makes, for that listener, the songs that U2 perform "true". In his novelistic study of photography as a cultural process published in 1980, *Camera Lucida*, Barthes writes about the desire that he confronts when dealing with certain photographs. He wishes to "enter the paper's depth", a desire to see something more than simply the image that is presented. He refers to notions of desire here: "I can have the fond hope of discovering truth", though he admits he will not find it.[22]

He suggests that, sometimes, he perceives something of the truth in a photograph, what he calls "a likeness", but the likeness is imprecise or imaginary. He concludes, "I cannot penetrate, cannot reach into the Photograph". The photograph is unlike the text; that is, "our vision of it is certain", a curious thing for a semiologist to suggest. The photograph arrests interpretation: "this-has-been".[23]

Barthes' frustration is evident here: he still seeks (or, more accurately, he still desires) something more in the photograph. He wishes to discover the person in the photograph completely. It seems here that Barthes is grasping at straws, so to speak. He wants to find the truth in a photograph, and so he finds, as the locus of his desires, the air (or the expression). But then he immediately writes, "The air of a face is unanalyzable".[24] But it evokes for the observer a "little individual soul, good in one person, bad in another".[25] The air is what allows Barthes to identify his mother in a photograph taken when she was a young child in a winter garden (a glass-enclosed conservatory for keeping tropical plants in colder climates).

For Barthes, this is the culmination of his desperate search through photographs, something that began as a phenomenological study of why photographs, these "slices of reality" and pieces of paper imbued with such memory and power, are so effective, and what draws people to view and keep them. Brian Dillon explains:

> Having lost his mother, with whom he had lived most of his life, he goes looking for her among old photographs; time and again the face he finds is not quite hers, even if objectively she looks like herself. At last, he discovers her true likeness, the "air" that he remembers, in a picture of Henriette aged five, taken in a winter garden in 1898. (In the journal entry that recounts this discovery, Barthes simply notes: "Je pleure".)[26]

Mason states, "Like Jesus' tears for Lazarus, Barthes' tears for his mother also come before a resurrection, one enabled by the chemical process behind the photograph".[27] Furthermore, the photograph becomes a sort of icon for Barthes, an image that allows him to connect to the very soul of his mother, still alive and still active, able to imbue him with a sort of grace, a knowledge of his mother, alive to him in the moment and a figure able to effect change in him, an enlightenment. Barthes explains it as follows: "All the photographs of my mother which I was looking through were a little like so many masks; at the last, suddenly the mask vanished: there remained a soul, ageless but not timeless, since this air was the person I used to see, consubstantial with her face, each day of her long life".[28] This is what makes a true photograph: the capturing of the air (one's soul, or one's shadow). Sylvère Lotringer writes, referring to Barthes' sentiment of the photograph as referring to a subject "that-has-been", not what *is*,

> It was this presence at a second remove that mattered to Barthes, its sudden return from the dead, death claiming its due from the living ... In the absence of religion, where else could death have taken refuge if not in these fragile images, which "keep producing death while attempting to preserve life"?[29]

And so, as Lotringer writes, Barthes begins his *Vita Nova* novel not by writing it but by planning for it:

> Dante started writing his *Divine Comedy* (1321) after he lost his Beatrice. Barthes would similarly turn his life into a Vita Nova, a new life dedicated to writing, mobilizing all his tutelary gods, all the writers who had inspired him and who had experienced in their lives a similar predicament. Writing as if he were them would help him unravel the knot that held together emotions and creation, death and writing.[30]

About the winter garden photograph – a photograph of his mother as a child – Barthes states (much to the chagrin of the readers of *Camera Lucida*): "I cannot reproduce the Winter Garden photograph. It exists only for me. For you, it would be nothing but an indifferent picture, one of the thousand manifestations of the 'ordinary' ... in it, for you, no wound". Cooper adds that, in the winter garden photograph, the reader would not understand with the same intensity that "Barthes sees the origin of his world". Cooper then explains that "Death really is the manifestation of the ordinary to everyone except the griever. Barthes's experience of looking at the Winter Garden image cannot be reproduced because his loss cannot be reproduced".[31] There is no way that his readers would understand the experience.

Cooper goes on to indicate something particularly striking about Barthes' approach to death (again, from *Camera Lucida*, a book that she says is an eulogy for Barthes himself, as he died not long after its publication):

> "For Death must be somewhere in society", Barthes muses, "if it is no longer (or less intensely) in religion, it must be elsewhere". He suggests that with the "withdrawal of rites" and the wearing out of religious illusion, there is now an "asymbolic Death, outside of religion, outside of ritual", that has taken its place. Which is to say, death is no longer a site of meaning – of faith, of comfort, of value – but an abruptly literal thing. Since we no longer sit with death for very long anymore and since it does not get the same prolonged attention it once did, death becomes purely (and terrifyingly) literal, and a binary is entrenched between life and death, as though they weren't intrinsic to each other. For Barthes, death returns in the photograph: "Life/Death: the paradigm is reduced to a simple [camera] click, the one separating the initial pose from the final print".[32]

Throughout *Camera Lucida*, Barthes suggests that photography is not only the site of death's return (as Cooper suggests above), but it is also the medium *which kills*. Through photography, the subject is arrested, fixed and becomes transformed into the realm of "that-has-been", but is no longer. If Cooper's musings above are correct, Barthes would have longed for a return to the numinosity of death and the rituals surrounding the event: the abruptness of presence and then absence at the moment of death (or at the click of a camera's shutter) are what effectively *killed* Barthes. Of course, this would not be his literal cause of death – he died of complications after being struck by a van – but one could see that his spirit was crushed by experiencing a loved one's death that is devoid of faith, comfort, or value.

Barthes, then, needs to work harder. He needs to try to inject into an experience of "asymbolic Death" faith, comfort and value. This is no small task, especially when he is the one enthralled in the mundanity of grief, the sense of the same suffering over and over. In fact, he takes his grief and the supposed "promise" of "asymbolic Death" and applies it to everyone around him: "Now, everywhere, in the street, the café, I see each individual under the aspect of ineluctably [or inescapable] *having-to-die*, which is exactly what it means to be *mortal*. – And no less obviously, I see them as *not knowing this to be so*".[33] Everyone is under the impression that they will live forever but this is not the case. It is not only photography that hands down the sentence of death, but also life itself that makes sure that all will die. How, then, does Barthes attempt to solve the problem, to vanquish death, to make sure that death no longer has power over him and those that he loves, even those who have already succumbed to the power of death? Is there a way for death to lose out, for those who are *having-to-die* to continue breathing, to continue living even under the shadow of ineluctable death?

Barthes suggests, via his lecture of 2 December 1978, that the book, *Vita Nova*, would be, ultimately, "a means to vanquish Death: not his own, but the death of loved ones; a way of bearing witness for them, of perpetuating them by drawing them out of non-Memory".[34] Non-memory is a compelling idea, though unclear: it might be that Barthes is hoping to call the memory of his mother from the grave – to resuscitate her memory.

Later, on 22 July 1979, Barthes states that "All the 'rescues' of the Project [that is, according to Léger, *Vita Nova*] have failed". He continues: "It's as if [it] now occurred quite clearly … the solemn impact of mourning on any possibility of creating a work of any kind".[35] Lotringer puts it this way: "Writers don't 'prepare' for a novel by writing about what makes novelists write – they just write it".[36]

Translator Richard Howard suggests that these fragments that make up *Mourning Diary* are an exploration of whether "another kind of utterance might, eventually, be constituted out of this deprivation, this dispossession, this travail": that is, what Howard calls this "notation of bereavement".[37]

'Iris (Hold Me Close)'

The account of the biblical story of Lazarus from John 11 can be thought of as a literal prefigure of *Vita Nova*, an account in which a person is resuscitated from death and an episode during which death is vanquished. It is also an episode that gives licence to Barthes to grieve as Christ did in his life, and, presumably, as Christ mourns the actual death of Barthes' mother. *Vita Nova* never came to be: Barthes failed in his construction of the work.

U2 seem to pick up on the idea of Barthes' (non-existent) *Vita Nova*, with *Songs of Innocence*, and, in particular, the song 'Iris (Hold Me Close)'. With little advance notice, U2 released the album *Songs of Innocence* in September 2014, in conjunction with Apple as a promotion for the technology company's iTunes music service. In a review, Jim Carroll writes, "[the album] was all back to the northside". That is, the album seems to return the band to their geographic and spiritual roots. He continues, "The Dublin which informs 'Songs of Innocence' no longer exists so it's a world created in a fog of nostalgia".[38] Carroll's description is curiously evocative of Susan Sontag's description of Barthes' later writings, what she calls "para-fictional pyrotechnics of exchanges ... between text and semi-obscured references", not unlike a fog of nostalgia. She also notes "the celebrations of illusion in his last book, on photography", referring to *Camera Lucida*, published in English in 1981.[39]

Brian Boyd recounts a compelling moment, one that seems to resuscitate Barthes' own words, when Bono remembers his mother, who died when the singer was fourteen years old. Boyd writes, "Standing up and walking around the room, [Bono] highlights a lyric in the song. 'I sing this verse which has "Iris standing in the hall, she tells me I can do it all", and then there's a typical mother's line when she says to me, "You'll be the death of me". But it wasn't me. I wasn't the death of her. I was not the death of her'".[40] Drawing from Mick Wall, Lynn Ramert notes that Bono's mother was an influence in her absence, and that her death led him to be raised by a father with whom he often disagreed.[41] Bono's guilt is almost palpable in Boyd's account: his misspent youth was supposed to be the figurative "death" of his mother but, instead, something else took her from him. This is reminiscent of Barthes' account of his mother's plaintive words as she approached death: "My R, my R".[42] It is as if Barthes was guilty in that he could not care for his mother at this point in her life, and that he had failed to care for her – to sustain her – in the ways that she did him. In the same way, he failed with his *Vita Nova*, unable to resuscitate her memory.

Joshua Rothman suggests that the song 'Iris (Hold Me Close)' is not an example of comfort at all: "it reaches for something it doesn't quite understand, and possibly doesn't even want; it becomes ambiguous and mournful. It expresses a particular combination of faith and disquiet, exaltation and desperation, that is too spiritual for rock but too strange for church".[43]

Songs of Innocence is trying to work through the problems of death and the creative process. In an interview from 2015 during the *iNNOCENCE & eXPERIENCE* tour, Bono claims that he does not remember much about his mother, but that his daughter Eve Hewson reminds him of her. In his childhood home, there was little reference to his mother, either in terms of visual representations like photographs or simply as a topic of conversation. But Bono continues,

> "Years later, this film turned up, by a friend of a friend of the family. It is black and white footage of her playing rounders on the beach in Rush.
> "I put it on and, apart from the cheesy music, it was very, very moving. And it is in the show now", he explains. "And she also, I think, turns up in the lemon dress that she wore to her sister's wedding".⁴⁴

Bono reflects on this differently in *U2 by U2*. He states,

> I have very few memories of my mother because my father never talked about her after she died. So it was a very strange experience to receive, in the post, from a very distant relative, early Super 8 footage of my mother, aged 24, younger than me, playing a game of rounders in slow motion. The beautiful, young Irish girl, with a narrow waist, curvaceous figure, dark gypsy hair. The film was early colour and it looked extraordinary. It was a wedding, where she was the maid of honour in this beautiful lemon dress.⁴⁵

During the *iNNOCENCE + eXPERIENCE* tour, the band play 'Iris (Hold Me Close)' with the footage of Bono's mother appearing on the large screens. As The Edge plays the opening harmonics of the song, the video screens show Bono's mother at the wedding wearing the bright yellow dress, smiling. Bono repeatedly speaks her name, as if trying to get her attention. The screens then change to display stars and constellations and lines connecting the stars, suggesting connections between people and the power of memory to transport these people from times past to the present, like light travelling from a cosmic event in times past to the earth in the present. The stars also evoke Fallon's conversations with Bono about The Fly: he sees through his large sunglasses, and though he cannot see anything in the room, he looks beyond it to see the stars. This is the moment of looking not at what is in the arena, in the concert space, but what is beyond it. The world that Bono is looking at is the literal "communion of the saints", the lives of those no longer alive. Once Bono begins to sing the bridge of the song, the footage of his mother running and playing the game on the beach is shown on the screens. The film clip then loops to just show her running, and the image of Bono singing there in the arena is superimposed on the repeating clip of his mother running. He is unable to catch her; his hand reaches her body but cannot grasp her; she slips through his grasp like a ghost.

Bono's working through of his grief is a major element in U2's musical output. Also in *U2 by U2*, Bono is asked if the band's early single 'I Will Follow' was about the death of his mother, and Bono answers that it was about God's love (an unconditional *agape* love) but it *might* be about his mother. Bono states, "It's a song about unconditional love, which is what a mother has for her child ... Which echoes the scriptures ... But if you step out of that for a second and think it's a song about my own mother, it becomes a suicide note".[46] This is chilling, but demonstrates the complexity of Bono's writing, as well as the complexities that appear when one explores issues of mortality. 'Tomorrow' from *October* is clearly about the death of his mother, and the fact that she is not going to return to him and his family in this life. In fact, Bono calls it an unconscious narrative account of his mother's funeral.[47] The song also includes an explicit call for the listener (or perhaps the narrator?) to accept love from Jesus Christ who, it is assumed, will bring peace to the grief left in the wake of his mother's death. A complement to that song is *Pop*'s 'Mofo', in which the narrator looks for something to fill a God-shaped hole, not a mother-shaped hole, or at least that is what is expressed at the start. Bono states, "The song would come to a shuddering halt and there I was, just speaking to my mother in front of fifty thousand of my closest friends. Some nights it would really surprise me what an emotional place I would get to ... I'm looking forward to meeting my mother".[48] The song continues to the place where the narrator is asking for his mother to enlighten him; his biological mother might be conflated here with the mother of the Church, Mary, the mother of Christ. While there is little indication that Bono subscribes to a particular Marian view of Christianity, he has often carried a rosary – prayer beads used in Roman Catholic devotion – during which events in Christ's life are meditated upon, and during which the Magnificat (the words of the angel's announcement of Mary's pregnancy with the saviour of God's people) is repeated. Finally, in the song 'Lemon' on *Zooropa*, Bono sings about how a woman wore lemon, perhaps referring to his mother's lemon dress, which he mentions in the interview with Egan.

What are U2 attempting to do with these songs, this working through grief? On the one hand, the songs are simply analogous to Barthes' late writing. But on the other hand, they are a way for the band to show that they are suffering through the same issues that everyone else suffers through. Grief is universal and so U2's struggle with grief is simply an equalizer. It is the first step in allowing the audience to see that the band are accessible (in as much as the band are *actually* accessible). Once the audience is convinced of this accessibility, then the audience can be convinced that the political or social ends that are presented by U2 can be the audience's ends as well. As U2 have often suggested, the audience and the band are united, and should work towards coexistence with everyone, and the fostering of the "good life" for all persons as well.

Lotringer recounts that, on the day of Barthes' death, he had an unfinished document on his typewriter with the title, "One Always Fails to Speak of What One Loves".[49] Andrew Gallix suggests that he had wished that to be the title of his never-completed (never begun?) *Vita Nova*.[50] Elsewhere, Gallix suggests that, prior to Barthes' famous essay, "The Death of the Author" in 1967, "The key to a work of literature was sought, ultimately, in the life – often the private life – of its author".[51] Barthes suggests that the author's intentional authority – or the idea of the "Author-God" but not necessarily the existence of the writer – are undermined in contemporary literature by the power associated with the reader, who makes their own meaning, a meaning that is not necessarily inherent in the text. Gallix points out that, in *Sade Fourier Loyola* from 1971, Barthes brings the author back:

> Barthes mentions an "amicable return of the author", he hastens to add that this is not a resurrection of the Author-God. First of all, this is the author as he or she is experienced by the reader: "the author who leaves his text and comes into our life" ... this author is primarily a physical presence: "he is not a (civil, moral) person, he is a body".[52]

The dead author is *physically* resurrected in the written work.

The novel, then, is where Barthes tries to intersect his own life and his writing, in order to do some of this work of resurrection. After his mother's death, Barthes writes, "It is the *intimate* which seeks utterance in me, seeks to make its cry heard, confronting generality, confronting science".[53] Therefore, Barthes' writing does not only resurrect – or utter – the *intimate*, that is, his mother, but it also works to resurrect himself. Gallix writes,

> If Barthes presents biography with a problem, it is not because he is absent from his work, but on the contrary because he is inseparable from it. Etymologically, a text is a piece of cloth, one that, in Barthes's view, is constantly in the process of being woven. In this making, "the subject unmakes himself, like a spider dissolving in the constructive secretions of its web". ... However, it is also through these very secretions that the subject resurfaces, in disseminated form, "like the ashes we strew into the wind after death".[54]

Concluding remarks

For Carroll, the band have lost a large part of their authenticity. Later in his *Irish Times* review, Carroll writes, "They're all about the money, as Bono keeps reminding us, and have become a story which now seems to belong more on the business pages than the music or arts pages".[55] Bono acknowledges the tensions that Carroll identifies. The album cover features a monochrome photograph of Mullen Jr "protecting" his eighteen-year-old son, Aaron Elvis Mullen, represented by Mullen Jr's embracing of his son's bare torso. About the visual language of the cover, Bono states, "holding on to your own innocence is a lot harder than holding on to someone else's".[56]

In the final analysis, Thirlwell suggests that *Mourning Diary* is the only artefact that the reader has that might be anything like *Vita Nova*. This is a notable fact, as what became *Mourning Diary* were notes on squares of paper, published some thirty years after Barthes' death: "It is a collection of aphorisms, sadnesses, self-analysis: a journal of savage intimacy".[57]

Regarding the iTunes release of *Songs of Innocence*, something can be drawn from The Edge's words in Boyd's interview: "As a band we were always either power or noise. But now U2 have so many grey areas. It's no longer power, which is good, or noise, which is bad. You've got to know when it's not happening with us, and the most destructive thing here is to almost get it right".[58] Just like Barthes' ultimate project, *Songs of Innocence* does not succeed as a *Vita Nova*, particularly because of its perceived abuse of power in the act of its distribution: it speaks of passion – of love for a parent in the loss of that parent – but does so in a way that does not foil structures and forms of institutional power. In many ways, the album, in the conditions that surrounded its release and distribution, is absolutely not oppositional in the way that Barthes desires *Vita Nova* to be.

But it does succeed in being grey; it echoes Proust (and Barthes) as a sort of "spell of vertigo" (like Barthes' experience in Morocco in 1978). The critics do not appreciate this: Carroll states that the memory and nostalgia, the fuel for the creation of the songs, as well as "all the highly paid producers on hand to help co-parent the album didn't result in any great songs".[59] But it does create a *grey* album: The Edge has it right. It is no longer about power, whether that be in terms of stadium rock music, corporate concert experience or the perceived distribution system that seemingly foisted unwanted songs on the public; or noise, the critics' disdain for the album, or the critics' suggestion of U2's loss of authenticity. Barthes would, at least, commiserate with U2. Both Barthes and U2 failed in their project, though they did bring their loved ones from non-memory, in *Mourning Diary* and *Songs of Innocence*. The Edge states that "the most destructive thing here is to almost get it right". Perhaps this is the closest to Barthes and his affection for a work that is *"une oeuvre blanche, colourless, neutral"*, a grey area, a destructive area that is only *almost* right ... a period of mourning.[60]

Notes

1. Rob Mitchum, "U2: Songs of Innocence Album Review", *Pitchfork* (12 September 2014); available from https://pitchfork.com/reviews/albums/19816-u2-songs-of-innocence/ (accessed 21 February 2018).
2. David Fricke, "U2: Songs of Innocence", *Rolling Stone* (11 September 2014); available from https://www.rollingstone.com/music/albumreviews/u2-songs-of-innocence-20140911 (accessed 10 March 2018).
3. Tiphaine Samoyault, *Barthes: A Biography*, translated by Andrew Brown (Cambridge: Polity Press, 2017), 18.
4. Adam Thirlwell, "My Novel, My Novel", *New Republic* (7 December 2010); available from http://www.newrepublic.com/article/books-and-arts/magazine/79745/novel-roland-barthes-realism (accessed 26 December 2014).
5. Roland Barthes, "*Longtemps, je me suis couché de bonne heure ...*", in *The Rustle of Language*, translated by Richard Howard (New York: Hill and Wang, 1989), 277.
6. Ibid., 278.
7. Ibid., 279–80.
8. Ibid., 285–88.
9. Ibid., 288–90.
10. Roland Barthes, *The Preparation of the Novel: Lecture Courses and Seminars at the Collège de France (1978–1979 and 1979–1980)*, translated by Kate Briggs (New York: Columbia University Press, 2011), 212.
11. Roland Barthes, *Mourning Diary*, translated by Richard Howard (New York: Hill and Wang, 2010), 74.
12. Ibid., 115.
13. Jonathan Culler, "Preparing the Novel: Spiralling Back", *Paragraph* 31.1 (2008): 117.
14. Barthes, *Mourning Diary*, 186.
15. Siegfried Kracauer, *Theory of Film: The Redemption of Physical Reality* (Princeton: Princeton University Press, 1960), 203.
16. Emma Mason, "Punctive Grace: Reading Religion in Barthes' *Mourning Diary*", *Textual Practice* 30.2 (2016): 328.
17. Ibid., 338. Mason is quoting from Sandra McEntire, *The Doctrine of Compunction in Medieval England: Holy Tears* (Lewiston, NY: E. Mellen Press, 1990), 55. She refers to Roland Barthes, *Michelet*, translated by Richard Howard (Berkeley: University of California Press, 1987), 196; and Barthes, *The Preparation of the Novel*, 248, 445.
18. Mason, "Punctive Grace", 338.
19. Ibid., 329.
20. Ibid., 330.
21. Julia Cooper, "The Essential Mundanity of Grief", *Hazlitt* (17 March 2017); available from https://hazlitt.net/feature/essential-mundanity-grief (accessed 19 March 2018).
22. Roland Barthes, *Camera Lucida: Reflections on Photography*, translated by Richard Howard (New York: Hill and Wang, 1981), 99–100.
23. Ibid., 106–107.
24. Ibid., 107.
25. Ibid., 109.
26. Brian Dillon, "Rereading: Camera Lucida by Roland Barthes", *The Guardian* (26

March 2011); available from http://www.guardian.co.uk/books/2011/mar/26/roland-barthes-camera-lucida-rereading (accessed 29 April 2017).

27. Mason, "Punctive Grace", 339.
28. Barthes, *Camera Lucida*, 110.
29. Sylvère Lotringer, "Barthes after Barthes", *Frieze* (1 January 2011); available from https://frieze.com/article/barthes-after-barthes (accessed 25 March 2018).
30. Ibid.
31. Cooper, "The Essential Mundanity of Grief".
32. Ibid.
33. Barthes, *Mourning Diary*, 52; original emphasis.
34. Barthes, *The Preparation of the Novel*, 9.
35. Barthes, *Mourning Diary*, 237.
36. Lotringer, "Barthes after Barthes".
37. Barthes, *Mourning Diary*, 260.
38. Jim Carroll, "On the Record: U2 'Songs of Innocence'", *Irish Times* (16 September 2014); available from http://www.irishtimes.com/blogs/ontherecord/2014/09/16/u2-songs-of-innocence/ (accessed 29 September 2018).
39. Susan Sontag, "Remembering Barthes", *The New York Review of Books* 27.8 (15 May 1980); available from http://www.nybooks.com/articles/archives/1980/may/15/remembering-barthes/ (accessed 3 April 2015).
40. Brian Boyd, "Bono's Dublin: 'A Long Way from Where I Live'", *Irish Times* (13 September 2014); available from http://www.irishtimes.com/culture/bono-s-dublin-a-long-way-from-where-i-live-1.1927184 (accessed 2 April 2015).
41. Lynn Ramert, "A Century Apart: The Personality Performances of Oscar Wilde in the 1890s and U2's Bono in the 1990s", *Popular Music and Society* 32.4 (October 2009): 448.
42. Barthes, *Mourning Diary*, 40.
43. Joshua Rothman, "The Church of U2", *The New Yorker* (16 September 2014). Available from https://www.newyorker.com/culture/cultural-comment/church-u2 (accessed 28 August 2017).
44. Barry Egan, "Bono: 'I still have the rage but I have worked it through: I'm dealing with it'", *The Independent* (17 May 2015); available from https://www.independent.ie/entertainment/music/music-news/bono-i-still-have-the-rage-but-i-have-worked-it-through-im-dealing-with-it-31228813.html (accessed 26 March 2018).
45. Neil McCormick, *U2 by U2* (London: HarperCollins, 2006), 306.
46. Ibid., 130–31.
47. Ibid., 148.
48. Ibid., 331.
49. Lotringer, "Barthes after Barthes".
50. Andrew Gallix, "The Writer Postponed: Barthes at the BnF", *The Los Angeles Review of Books* (23 August 2015); available from https://lareviewofbooks.org/essay/barthes-panorama (accessed 12 October 2015).
51. Andrew Gallix, "Roland Barthes' Challenge to Biography", *The Guardian* (14 August 2015); available from http://www.theguardian.com/books/booksblog/2015/aug/14/roland-barthes-challenge-to-biography (accessed 12 October 2015).
52. Ibid.
53. Barthes, "*Longtemps, je me suis couché de bonne heure ...*", 284; original emphasis.

54. Gallix, "Barthes' Challenge to Biography". Gallix is quoting from Barthes, *The Pleasure of the Text*, translated by Richard Howard (New York: Hill and Wang, 1975), 64; and Roland Barthes, *Sade Fourier Loyola*, translated by Richard Miller (New York: Hill and Wang, 1976), 9. As an aside, there is an interesting example of a writer being inseparable from his own work in U2's *oeuvre*. Consider the video for the song 'The Ground Beneath Her Feet', which appears on the soundtrack for *The Million Dollar Hotel*. The music video features author Salman Rushdie, who is shown writing some of the lyrics of the song in a notebook, just as Bono sings those very words. The song's lyrics are modified from Rushdie's novel, *The Ground Beneath Her Feet*, and the poem that is written by the character Rai: "All my life, I worshipped her. Her golden voice, her beauty's beat. How she made us feel, how she made me real, and the ground beneath her feet". See Salman Rushdie, *The Ground Beneath Her Feet* (Toronto: Alfred A. Knopf Canada, 1999), 475.

55. Carroll, "On the Record: U2 'Songs of Innocence'".

56. "Cover Story", *U2.com* (25 September 2014); available from http://www.u2.com/news/title/cover-story/ (accessed 9 October 2014.

57. Thirlwell, "My Novel, My Novel".

58. Boyd, "Bono's Dublin".

59. Carroll, "On the Record: U2 'Songs of Innocence'".

60. Culler, "Preparing the Novel", 111. Consider Mason's explanation here, on Barthes' desire for a future moment in which his grief might be negated, accompanied by a tentative gesture towards the religion of his mother: "Such negation – of nothingness, not praying, not blessing [not power or noise] – is itself a kind of apophatic grace capable of enlightening the suffering individual precisely because it is unknowable and neutral" (Mason, "Punctive Grace", 339).

Conclusions: A Cosmopolitan Christianity

In 2017, the band decided to go on tour to celebrate the anniversary of *The Joshua Tree*. The tour ran from May to October, bringing in over $300 million in revenue. Writing about the tour, Jon Pareles describes the original album as follows:

> "The Joshua Tree" was worth revisiting. It was a pivotal album for U2, one that announced and then fulfilled grand aspirations. The songs pondered 1980s America as both myth and presence: its landscape, its ideals of freedom and openness, its culture, its sensuality, its violence. The lyrics addressed spiritual and romantic quests along with political and economic predicaments, connecting them with language that drew on the Bible and Beat poetry.[1]

The band decided to engage with America as both myth and presence, as both an idea and a place, again in 2017.

Songs of Experience was finally released on 1 December 2017, a companion to *Songs of Innocence* from 2014. Accompanying the album is a short film called *Liner Notes*. Notably, the film is easily confused with the earlier *Linear*, one letter being different between the two. The monochrome (sepia-toned) film features Bono narrating poetic commentary about the songs over a montage of images – some of the band, some of figures depicting lovers, refugees and others. Bono reveals there that he experienced what he calls "a brush with mortality" the previous winter. He continues, "I won't dwell in it or on it. I don't want to name it. But these songs have that impetus behind them and it would feel dishonest not to admit the turbulence I was feeling at the time of writing".[2]

The first single from the album, 'You're the Best Thing About Me', features Sian Evans (The Edge's daughter) on the cover, in a monochrome photo, light blue and black. Her dark hair flows out and down over her torso to her waist, out from under a combat helmet. The long-time U2 fan will recognize the helmet image: the cover of the collection *The Best of 1980–1990* features a boy in a combat helmet as well (perhaps evoking the original boy on the cover of *Boy* and the same young boy on the cover of *War*). At a more simple level, the combat helmet simply evokes the notion of "war" (and, of course, the band's third album). The fact that the photo depicts Sian Evans links the single to the previous album, *Songs of Innocence*, in that it features Mullen Jr's son in that black and white photo. The cover of *Songs of Experience* features both Sian Evans and Eli Hewson (Bono's son) in black and white. Evans is still wearing the combat helmet and Hewson looks like a young version of his father in a white button-up shirt and dark blazer. The two are holding hands, and seem to evoke the band's early years, with Evans as a stand-in for Bono as "boy" and Evans as a living sign referring to the *War* album and perhaps the sectarian conflict in the Ireland of the band's youth.

About *Songs of Experience*, Calum Marsh writes, "Years in the making, U2's 14th studio album finds the band straining to reassert its relevance in a world where rock music has long since ceded its vanguard status".[3] David Fricke notes the band's sense of urgency: "If *Songs of Innocence* was rock's most persistently hopeful band looking back in wonder at its punk-rock origins and unlimited dreaming in late-Seventies Dublin, *Songs of Experience* is U2 in late-middle age coming to grips with an inevitable reality: They no longer have all the time in the world".[4]

At the centre of U2's project is the idea of cosmopolitanism, a kind of global concern. Much of how U2 approach their social justice campaigns seems to be expressed well by Angela Taraborrelli, Hannah Arendt, Judith Butler, Theodor Adorno and Edith Stein. These are somewhat contemporary conceptions of cosmopolitanism, and they agree with U2's position in relation to the world.

Cosmopolitanism

Angela Taraborrelli suggests that the term "cosmopolitan" is an adjective that refers "more to an attitude of thought, a lifestyle, a general existential thread".[5] She defines the cosmopolitan idea as a "substantive moral and political doctrine capable of offering prescriptions to politics".[6] She suggests that the middle-ages sense of cosmopolitanism as a Christian idea was transformed into that of a political project. An older, and possibly original, conception of cosmopolitanism suggests the idea of being a "citizen of the world". Taraborrelli explains, "This claim was taken to mean not only the perception of a relationship with humankind as a whole but also the pessimistic conviction that civilization was incompatible with true virtue and that it was thus necessary to reject all social ties". This evolved to include all *other* people as "fellow citizens", that is, a global view. These "solidaristic ethics ... represented a moral obligation".[7] Kant further develops the ideal of cosmopolitanism in the direction of the political-legal with the goal of a *Welterepublik*, a cosmopolis: Taraborrelli calls this "a republic of confederated free republics", what Arendt later suggests would be filled with individuals with a "community sense".[8] Drawing from Hannah Arendt's

Lectures on Kant's Political Philosophy, Taraborrelli writes, "We are members of a world community through the simple fact of being human beings and this 'cosmopolitan existence' must be translated into a capacity to judge and act politically that is guided by the notion (not by the effective actuality) of being world citizens and consequently also world spectators".[9] What, though, does being a member of a world community look like? What does having a "community sense" mean?

Perhaps Judith Butler approaches an answer. Butler explores what it means to live in a good way in a world that is fundamentally bad. Butler draws from Theodor Adorno in asking the question, how does one lead a good life in a bad life or context? But she updates Adorno for the contemporary world:

> We have two problems: the first is how to live one's own life well, such that we might say that we are living a good life within a world in which the good life is structurally or systematically foreclosed for so many. The second problem is, what form does this question take for us now? Or, how does the historical time in which we live condition and permeate the form of the question itself?[10]

She then strives to define what constitutes a "good life", and begins with the idea of "the relation of moral conduct to social conditions", and how institutions of power inform how one should live a supposedly "good" life. Adorno states, "it makes absolutely no sense to talk about ethical and moral conduct separately from relations of human beings to each other".[11] In her discussion, Butler points to individual morality being informed by biopolitics, those (often political) powers that organize and manage people's lives. In a biopolitical context, people are forced to ask *which* lives matter, *which* lives are worthy of protection and care. Butler asks, "whose lives are grievable, and whose are not?" She continues, "The biopolitical management of the ungrievable proves crucial to approaching the question, how do I lead this life? And how do I live this life within the life, the conditions of living, that structure us now?"[12] Finally, she asks, "If only a grievable life can be valued ... then only a grievable life will be eligible for social and economic support, housing, health care, employment, rights of political expression, forms of social recognition, and the conditions for political agency".[13] In her exploration of these ideas, she comes to a conclusion, at which she sees in herself the problematic "allocation of value": more (or less) value is placed on her own life than on others. Surely, as a well-known academic, Butler is valued. Her point remains, though: one's perception of being valued or not, and one's eligibility for social and economic support and access to political expression and political agency (among the other rights and privileges above), point to the problematic or unjust allocation of value to people by social and political forces. She calls this unjust allocation of value the "bad life", and thus the title of her lecture.

Phenomenologist Edith Stein considers something she calls "fellow feeling". About celebrating with another person, she writes,

> Should empathy persist beside primordial joy over the joyful event (beside the comprehension of the joy of the other), and, moreover, should the other really be conscious of the event as joyful (possibly it is also joyful for me, for example, if this passed examination is the condition for a trip together so that I am happy for him as the means to it), we can designate this primordial act as joy-with-him or, more generally, as fellow feeling (*sympathy*).[14]

Even with such "fellow feeling", and being sympathetic to the other, what does one do with the other that is fundamentally experiencing a life that is bad? One can be sympathetic and still be "primordial" (to use Stein's language): that is, one might understand expressed joy – and even Stein's "joy-with-him" – without acting. Butler finds herself on one side of this allocation of value, and describes the "bad life" as a state of "unliveability":

> Perhaps we cannot use one word to describe the conditions under which lives become unliveable, yet the term "precarity" can distinguish between modes of "unliveability": those who, for instance, belong to imprisonment without recourse to due process; those living in war zones or under occupation, exposed to violence and destruction without recourse to safety or exit; those who undergo forced emigration and live in liminal zones, waiting for borders to open, food to arrive, and the prospect of living with documentation; those that mark the condition of being part of a dispensable or expendable workforce for whom the prospect of a stable livelihood seems increasingly remote, and who live in a daily way within a collapsed temporal horizon, suffering a sense of a damaged future in the stomach and in the bones, trying to feel but fearing more what might be felt.[15]

U2 tackle some of these issues, and it makes sense that the band would be on board with the other concerns that Butler identifies. Butler makes a startling statement, in that the notion of a "good life" is not only for oneself: morality would suggest otherwise. She states, "under conditions of extreme peril and heightened precarity, the moral dilemma does not pass away; it persists precisely in the tension between wanting to live and wanting to live in a certain way with others".[16] This "wanting to live in a certain way with others" can sound very much like "Living-Together", the Barthesian approach to cohabitation, which consists of a solitude with regular interruptions as a way to live with others.

Butler is also exploring what it means to *act* or *enact* the good life, that is, live it out and make it the case for others. Butler states, "when and where there is suffering or transience, it is there to be transformed into the life of action and thought".[17] And, for Butler, this transformation is a creative act, performative in bringing something new into the world, something that has not existed previously. This is not unlike the band creating a theoretical "new world" through performance. Butler calls this creative and performative body a "political" body. Drawing from Arendt, Butler suggests that the "political" body is the public face of a private experience.

U2 are a sort of "political" body as well: "This well-fed body speaks openly and publicly; this body which spent the night sheltered and in the private company of others emerges always later to act in public".[18] Butler continues,

> When populations are abandoned by economic or political policy, then lives are deemed unworthy of support. Over and against such policies, the contemporary politics of performativity insists upon the interdependency of living creatures as well as the ethical and political obligations that follow from any policy that deprives, or seeks to deprive, a population of a liveable life. They are also ways of enunciating and enacting value in the midst of a biopolitical scheme that threatens to devalue such populations.[19]

This must be part of U2's project, then: the valuing of populations and the bolstering of their worthiness for support, through performativity. And that performativity is enacted by a political body that is well-supported, that is, living a "good life". U2 live a "good life" in order to provide a performative political body in support of those who live the "bad life".

In addition to this, Butler again echoes Barthes' ideas of idiorrhythmy, that idea of living in isolation with regular interruptions. There is a sense that there is an interdependence involved in "Living-Together", an interdependence that recognizes the requirement for independence. Butler states, "no human creature survives or persists without depending on a sustaining environment, social forms of relationality, and economic forms that presume and structure interdependency".[20] And she continues to suggest that being dependent on others means that one is vulnerable to others as well. One of her points here is to call for "an equal distribution of vulnerability", which, in other words, is an equal distribution of interdependency. This is not unlike Barthes' "Living-Together" or U2's "Coexist" (with the crescent, star and cross). Butler states, "I am suggesting that only through a concept of interdependency that affirms bodily dependency, conditions of precarity and potentials for performativity can we think a social and political world that seeks to overcome precarity in the name of liveable lives".[21]

What does this look like, though? Taraborrelli summarizes (from Peter Singer) the "utilitarian framework" as follows: "the only legitimate measure of good and evil is represented by pursuing the greatest possible happiness for the largest number of persons".[22] She understands Singer's moral cosmopolitanism as focusing on how people live or behave rather than on problems inherent in social organization.[23] U2 employ, then, a broader view that aligns with other political philosophies (and Butler), where fairness is a paramount concern. One of these philosophies would be from John Rawls, who emphasizes the idea of social cooperation between members of the same state.[24] U2 would expand this idea to include all of humanity over all of the world, even though their audience would be from a particular socio-economic background. This is assumed simply because of the costs associated with the consumption of recorded popular music, that is, costs for purchase of media or streaming service subscriptions as well as costs for travelling to and attending concerts. Thus, "if economic (and political) interdependence is indicative of a global social cooperation scheme, we ought not to consider national boundaries as morally significant. Since boundaries are not co-extensive with the scope of social cooperation, they do not mark the confines of social obligation".[25]

Within this global view is also the notion of "just membership", referring to the right of citizenship for all people. Seyla Benhabib defines "just membership" as:

> recognizing the moral claim of refugees and asylees to *first admittance*; a regime of *porous* borders for immigrants; an injunction against denationalization and the loss of citizenship rights; and the vindication of the right of every human being "to have rights", that is, to be a *legal person*, entitled to certain inalienable rights, regardless of the status of their political membership.[26]

To conclude, consider Butler:

> If I am to lead a good life, it will be a life lived with others, a live [sic] that is no life without those others. I will not lose this *I* that I am; whoever I am will be transformed by my connections with others, since my dependency on another, and my dependability, are necessary in order to live and to live well.[27]

And, more simply, consider the words of Jesus Christ, in judging the nations: "for I was hungry and you gave me food, I was thirsty and you gave me something to drink, I was naked and you gave me clothing, I was sick and you took care of me, I was in prison and you visited me" (Matthew 25:35-36).

U2 and the Building of a New World

On 16 November 2017, the band performed at the famous Abbey Road Studios in London, the site of many legendary recordings by artists including The Beatles and Adele. The performance, which was globally televised in December 2017, features the band playing songs from their catalogue to a select audience, accompanied by a small orchestra. As a sort of novelty performance – that is, a promotion of a new album and a so-called "intimate" show – the band intersperses the songs (which span their whole catalogue) with references to songs by other artists. During the band's performance of 'Beautiful Day', Bono sings a portion of lyrics from the chorus of David Bowie's 1972 song, 'Starman'. During 'With or Without You', Bono quotes Joy Division's 1979 song, 'Love Will Tear Us Apart'. And in a particularly emotional performance of 'Love is Bigger than Anything in its Way', Bono recites the first verse of Cat Stevens' 1970 song 'Father and Son', before beginning his own "letters … to our daughters". Appropriate for the context, Bono also sings a snippet from The Beatles' 'All You Need is Love', a song that was similarly performed and televised live from Abbey Road Studios in June 1967, complete with a small orchestra. In quoting these tracks by various respected performers, one can assume that U2 are trying to indicate their indebtedness to these bands. Some of the musical or lyrical quotations seem to fit in thematically with the songs by U2, but others do not. Singing a song like 'Love Will Tear Us Apart" only highlights the notion of love in tension that a song like 'With or Without You' seems to espouse. Stevens' 'Father and Son' is a letter upon which Bono's 'Love is Bigger than Anything in its Way' could be modelled. At least the quotation of The Beatles seems to fit because of the physical context – the Abbey Road Studios – if not the implicit tone of the evening. In his introduction to the song 'One', Bono says, "We wrote this in Germany after the [Berlin] Wall came down and, thirty years later, we are singing it as walls are going up". At the end of the song, Bono brings out the megaphone (this time coloured the deep blue of the flag of the European Union, but with the yellow ring of stars that encircles the horn covered, it seems, in black tape) and sings through the megaphone the now-common refrain, "No them, there's only us".

While these sorts of musical quotations make sense thematically, the Bowie reference does not seem to work in the same way. It is quite possible that Bono is trying to do something slightly different. While, of course, paying homage to Bowie as departed artist and cultural icon, Bono quotes 'Starman' just before the middle portion of 'Beautiful Day', in which Bono describes the various wondrous sights of earthly life and activity, seen from a high vantage point (including a look at the diluvial bird, olive branch and rainbow, the start of a new world). 'Starman' evokes Bowie's "cosmic" character Major Tom – incidentally, trapped forever orbiting the Earth – experiencing the wonders of our planet from his place among the stars. Is it that U2 (and Bono) cannot stand on their (or his) own, but must instead be situated among other artists, be it The Beatles, Joy Division or David Bowie? Just as photographs point directly to their referents, so U2 point to those bands that precede them. In a way, like photography, U2 keep their referents alive. Of photography, Walter Benjamin writes,

> No matter how artful the photographer, no matter how carefully posed his subject, the beholder feels an irresistible urge to search a picture for the tiny spark of contingency, of the Here and Now, with which reality has so to speak seared the subject, to find the inconspicuous spot where in the immediacy of that long-forgotten moment the future subsists so eloquently that we, looking back, may rediscover it.[28]

As Steve Edwards explains, in his brief history of photography, "Memory is, after all, a trace or impression of the past that takes place in the present".[29]

As part of the televised special, during the clip in São Paulo, the band are featured in what appears to be an antique shop. While they search among the items for pieces of interest, Bono picks up a rotary phone, taking an imaginary call from the Pope. Bono tells him, "I just had Donald [Trump] on the line", and then turns and says, "He hasn't got time to take his confession". Even with all of the evocations of the past, U2 still have the present in mind.

During the performance of 'Love is Bigger than Anything in its Way', Bono turns to a group of young men and women singing in a chorus behind him, accompanied by the band and orchestra. In return, the young people smile back. They seem to be delighted by the attention paid to them by the celebrity singer. What is striking, though, is not the response by the young people but rather the lyrics that Bono sings to them: he sings of the young people and a "song" that they have. He suggests that the young, though passionate, do not yet have the words to their own song: they do not yet have their own identity perhaps, or their own agency. But he encourages them – those young people in the studio with him and the voices of those in the audience listening – to write or create a theoretical world where people are united to each other, and where people invest in each other. He encourages the choir behind him, through his lyrics, to *sing* this world into being. And they do as they join in the melody of the chorus. In this instance, Bono and the band are not just performing the music, but Bono is performative, that is, he is helping or encouraging others to *create* a world, even if it happens to be a theoretical one that exists only in that place, among those young singers and only for that time. While the world exists only in that place, it is certainly 'even better than the real thing', a *potent* and *potential* world that might inform the *actual* world at large.

Not everything works, though. In an interview with Jonathan Dean in November 2017, Bono says something striking. Dean first sets up the statement:

> When he [Bono] talks about her [Aung San Suu Kyi, the Burmese politician and activist, who was championed by U2 while under house arrest], though, or America, or his dashed hopes after the Arab Spring, it is clear that much he fought for is collapsing around him. He mentions a quote from the activist Wael Ghonim: "The power of the people is so much stronger than the people in power". It is beautiful, he says. His voice trembles. "Turned out not to be true".[30]

In his discussion of what he calls "myth on the left", Roland Barthes writes about language which is the opposite of "myth". This type of language remains political, whereas myth does not. For Barthes, myth is a type of speech (though the idea of myth is not limited to speech) in which the thing that is being talked about refers not only to itself, but is *suggestive* of other things. There is an association – what Barthes calls a "second-order semiological system" – attached to the thing.[31] Further, Barthes explains, "The function of myth is to empty reality: it is, literally, a ceaseless flowing out, a haemorrhage, or perhaps an evaporation, in short a perceptible absence".[32] He considers myth as emptying because of its ability to turn those things which might be thought of as historically or socially informed (say, the idea of national loyalty) into things that are natural: "it has turned reality inside out, it has emptied it of history and has filled it with nature, it has removed from things their human meaning so as to make them signify a human insignificance". Here, Barthes shows his moralist side: he suggests that myth not only depoliticizes, but also dehumanizes.

Barthes continues by defining "political" as "describing the whole of human relations in their real, social structure, *in their power of making the world*; one must above all give an active value to the prefix *de-* [in 'depoliticized']: here it represents an operational movement, it permanently embodies a defaulting".[33]

He writes, "revolutionary language proper cannot be mythical. Revolution is defined as the cathartic act meant to reveal the political load of the world: it *makes* the world; and its language, all of it, is functionally absorbed in this making".[34] The language that Bono uses in songs like 'Love is Bigger than Anything in its Way' is revolutionary. If myth empties reality, its opposite makes reality: it corrects the default.

Bono looking at the young people in the choir is a delightful moment for those young people, whose happiness shows through their facial expressions and reactions. This is a human moment, where the young people are recognized as *people* in the (literal) face of a celebrity who takes a moment to recognize and dwell on their humanness. Bono addresses them as he would address his own children, to encourage them to use their passionate activism to create a new world, and to not let their (current) lack of a voice stop them from considering using their voice in the next moment. And through their voices, through their singing, they create a world. They fill the emptiness of the depoliticized world – the haemorrhaging world – and fill it not only with politics, but also with revolution and, ultimately, humanity.

This ties in with the idea of love as resistance: about *Songs of Experience*, Jon Pareles writes, "It doesn't sound like love – it sounds like resistance".[35] But maybe it's both. In fact, in 'Get Out of Your Own Way', Bono sings explicitly of love as *resistance*: in order for resistance and love to exist, it needs to be engaged and active. Active love equals resistance to the "easy go", a sort of status quo that the band are trying to encourage those same passionate youth to move against in order to create something new. The enemy, so to speak, is there to help, as an element to be overcome with assistance from others, resulting in a resistance of love.

Notes

1. Jon Pareles, "Review: U2 Revisits 'The Joshua Tree' in the Here and Now", *New York Times* (15 May 2017); available from https://www.nytimes.com/2017/05/15/arts/music/u2-joshua-tree-30th-anniversary-tour-review.html (accessed 5 March 2018).

2. When this was mentioned to a colleague, he replied, "That's all rather intriguing. Sounds like something serious there, talking about health and faith at the same time. Hopefully (!) that's the end of the story". But what if that's the end of *Bono's* story? See Brian Boyd, "Bono's Brush with Death: 'I was clinging to my own life'", *The Irish Times* (1 December 2017); available from https://www.irishtimes.com/culture/music/bono-s-brush-with-death-i-was-clinging-to-my-own-life-1.3312042 (accessed 1 December 2017).

3. Calum Marsh, "U2: *Songs of Experience* Album Review", *Pitchfork* (4 December 2017); available from https://pitchfork.com/reviews/albums/u2-songs-of-experience/ (accessed 21 February 2018).

4. David Fricke, "Review: U2 Faces Down Mortality, Reconnects with the Power of Music", *Rolling Stone* (1 December 2018); available from https://www.rollingstone.com/music/albumreviews/review-u2s-songs-of-experience-w513047 (accessed 10 March 2018).

5. Angela Taraborrelli, *Contemporary Cosmopolitanism*, translated by Ian McGilvray (London: Bloomsbury, 2015), xiv.

6. Ibid., x.

7. Ibid., xi.
8. Ibid., xii.
9. Ibid.
10. Judith Butler, "Can One Lead a Good Life in a Bad Life?", *Radical Philosophy* 176 (November/December): 9.
11. Theodor W. Adorno, *Problems of Moral Philosophy*, translated by Rodney Livingstone (Stanford, CA: Stanford University Press, 2001), 19.
12. Butler, "Can One Lead a Good Life?", 10.
13. Ibid.
14. Edith Stein, *On the Problem of Empathy*, translated by Waltraut Stein (Washington, DC: ICS Publications, 1989), 14.
15. Butler, "Can One Lead a Good Life?", 12.
16. Ibid.
17. Ibid., 13.
18. Ibid.
19. Ibid., 14.
20. Ibid., 15.
21. Ibid.
22. Taraborrelli, *Contemporary Cosmopolitanism*, 3.
23. Ibid., 5.
24. Ibid., 5–6.
25. Ibid., 9.
26. Seyla Benhabib, *The Rights of Others: Aliens, Residents, and Citizens* (Cambridge: Cambridge University Press, 2004), 3; original emphasis.
27. Butler, "Can One Lead a Good Life?", 18.
28. Walter Benjamin, "Little History of Photography", in *Selected Writings, Volume 2 (1927–1934)*, edited by Michael W. Jennings (Cambridge: The Belknap Press of Harvard University Press, 1999), 510.
29. Steve Edwards, *Photography: A Very Short Introduction* (Oxford: Oxford University Press, 2006), 120.
30. Jonathan Dean, "U2 Interview: Bono on death, taxes and their new album *Songs of Experience*", *The Times* (19 November 2017); available from https://www.thetimes.co.uk/article/u2-interview-bono-paradise-papers-taxes-new-album-songs-of-experience-hsf7sf25k (accessed 10 August 2018).
31. Roland Barthes, "Myth Today", in *Mythologies*, translated by Richard Howard and Annette Lavers (New York: Hill and Wang, 2012), 223.
32. Ibid., 255.
33. Ibid. Emphasis added.
34. Ibid., 259.
35. Jon Pareles, "U2 Releases 'Songs of Experience'. Cynicism Not Included", *New York Times* (29 November 2017); available from https://tinyurl.com/NYT-2017-11-29-arts (accessed 3 December 2017).

Bibliography

Adorno, Theodor W. *Problems of Moral Philosophy*, translated by Rodney Livingstone. Stanford, CA: Stanford University Press, 2001.

Anderson, Leith Anderson, and Ed Stetzer. "A New Way to Define Evangelicals". *Christianity Today* 60.3 (April 2016): 52–55.

Atkinson, Katie. "U2 & Drake Preach Love amid Tense Political Climate at iHeartRadio Music Festival". *Billboard* (24 September 2016). Available from http://www.billboard.com/articles/columns/music-festivals/7518892/u2-drake-iheartradio-festival-politics-donald-trump (accessed 27 April 2017).

Auslander, Philip. "'Just Be Your Self': Logocentrism and Difference in Performance Theory". In *Acting Reconsidered: A Theoretical and Practical Guide*, edited by Phillip B. Zarrilli, 53–60. London and New York: Routledge, 2002.

Barthes, Roland. *The Pleasure of the Text*, translated by Richard Howard. New York: Hill and Wang, 1975.

—*Sade Fourier Loyola*, translated by Richard Miller. New York: Hill and Wang, 1976.

—"Diderot, Brecht, Eisenstein". In *Image—Music—Text*, translated by Stephen Heath, 69–78. New York: Hill and Wang, 1977.

—*Camera Lucida: Reflections on Photography*, translated by Richard Howard. New York: Hill and Wang, 1981.

—*Michelet*, translated by Richard Howard. Berkeley: University of California Press, 1987.

—"Longtemps, je me suis couché de bonne heure ...". In *The Rustle of Language*, translated by Richard Howard, 277–90. New York: Hill and Wang, 1989.

—*A Lover's Discourse: Fragments*, translated by Richard Howard. New York: Hill and Wang, 2010.

—*Mourning Diary*, translated by Richard Howard. New York: Hill and Wang, 2010.

—*Roland Barthes by Roland Barthes*, translated by Richard Howard. New York: Hill and Wang, 2010.

—*The Preparation of the Novel: Lecture Courses and Seminars at the Collège de France (1978–1979 and 1979–1980)*, translated by Kate Briggs. New York: Columbia University Press, 2011.

—"Myth Today". In *Mythologies*, translated by Richard Howard and Annette Lavers, 215–74. New York: Hill and Wang, 2012.

—*How to Live Together: Novelistic Simulations of Some Everyday Spaces*, translated by Kate Briggs. New York: Columbia University Press, 2013.

Beats 1 on Apple Music. "U2 and Zane Lowe on Beats 1". *YouTube* (20 July 2017). Available from https://www.youtube.com/watch?v=vsKZ3YrF_3Q (accessed 30 July 2018).

Bebbington, D. W. *Evangelicalism in Modern Britain: A History from the 1730s to the 1800s*. London and New York: Routledge, 1989.

Belogolovsky, Vladimir. "Paul Andreu: 'I would only take on a project if the ideas were

mine. Otherwise, I am not interested'". *ArchDaily* (7 March 2017). Available from https://tinyurl.com/DAILY-806698 (accessed 13 July 2018).
Benhabib, Seyla. *The Rights of Others: Aliens, Residents, and Citizens*. Cambridge: Cambridge University Press, 2004.
Benjamin, Walter. "Little History of Photography". In *Selected Writings, Volume 2 (1927–1934)*, edited by Michael W. Jennings, 507–530. Cambridge: The Belknap Press of Harvard University Press, 1999.
—"M". In *The Arcades Project*, edited by Howard Eiland and Kevin McLaughlin, 416–55. Cambridge: The Belknap Press of Harvard University Press, 1999.
Blistein, Jon. "Watch U2 Blast Donald Trump during San Francisco Show". *Rolling Stone* (6 October 2016). Available from https://tinyurl.com/w443707 (accessed 27 April 2017).
Bono. Testimony to the Senate Appropriations Subcommittee on State, Foreign Operations, and Related Programs. "The Causes and Consequences of Violent Extremism and the Role of Foreign Assistance" (12 April 2016). Available from https://tinyurl.com/hyhjd2o (accessed 5 July 2016).
—"Bono: Trump has 'Hijacked the Party'". *Charlie Rose* (20 September 2016). Available from https://www.youtube.com/watch?v=2bY8qGvhIFk (accessed April 27, 2017).
Boyd, Brian. "Bono's Dublin: 'A Long Way from Where I Live'". *Irish Times* (13 September 2014). Available from https://tinyurl.com/1-1927184 (accessed 2 April 2015).
—"U2 Hit 40: The 'Drummer Seeks Musicians' Note that Started It All". *Irish Times* (21 September 2016). Available from https://www.irishtimes.com/culture/music/u2-hit-40-the-drummer-seeks-musicians-note-that-started-it-all-1.2799922 (accessed 18 June 2018).
—"Bono's Brush with Death: 'I was clinging to my own life'". *The Irish Times* (1 December 2017). Available from https://tinyurl.com/1-3312042 (accessed 1 December 2017).
Briggs, Kate. *This Little Art*. London: Fitzcarraldo Editions, 2018.
Briggs, Richard S. "Sarajevo and the Popmart Lemon: The Fractured Form and Function of U2's Walk through the Valley of the Shadow of Death". In *U2 and the Religious Impulse: Take Me Higher*, edited by Scott Calhoun, 75–86. London: Bloomsbury, 2018.
Browne, David. "Original Soundtracks 1". *Entertainment Weekly* (10 November 1995). Available from http://ew.com/article/1995/11/10/original-soundtracks-1/ (accessed 11 February 2018).
Burgoyne, Patrick. "U2 Linear: it's not a music video". *Creative Review* (14 April 2009). Available from https://tinyurl.com/8dcfc8a283b (accessed 21 February 2018).
Butler, Judith. "Can One Lead a Good Life in a Bad Life?". *Radical Philosophy* 176 (November/December 2012): 9–18.
Calhoun, Scott. "Stealing David Bentley Hart's Wisdom for U2's Traveling Show". *@U2* (6 August 2018). Available from https://tinyurl.com/yc8vof6y (accessed 6 August 2018).
Carroll, Jim. "On the Record: U2 'Songs of Innocence'". *Irish Times* (16 September 2014). Available from http://www.irishtimes.com/blogs/ontherecord/2014/09/16/u2-songs-of-innocence/ (accessed 29 September 2018).
Catanzarite, Stephen. *U2's* Achtung Baby: *Meditations on Love in the Shadow of the Fall*. New York: Bloomsbury, 2007.
Clark, Brian. "U2 – Egos and Icons '97 – Part 1 of 7". *YouTube* (9 February 2008). Available from https://www.youtube.com/watch?v=zqIft_5U_IU (accessed 31 July 2018).

Cocks, Jay. "U2: Band on the Run". *Time* (27 April 1987). Available from http://www.u2.com/news/title/rocks-hottest-ticket-time-magazine/news/ (accessed 6 August 2017).

Cohen, Debra Rae. "U2: Boy". *Rolling Stone* (16 April 1981). Available from http://www.rollingstone.com/music/albumreviews/boy-19810416 (accessed 4 July 2016).

Considine, J. D. "Album Reviews: *War*". *Rolling Stone* (31 March 1983). Available from https://www.rollingstone.com/music/music-album-reviews/war-105402/ (accessed 30 July 2018).

Cooper, Julia. "The Essential Mundanity of Grief". *Hazlitt* (17 March 2017). Available from https://hazlitt.net/feature/essential-mundanity-grief (accessed 19 March 2018).

"Cover Story", *U2.com* (25 September 2014). Available from http://www.u2.com/news/title/cover-story/ (accessed 9 October 2014).

Cubitt, Sean. "How to Watch Video Art: My Father Will Heal You with Love". In *Timeshift: On Video Culture*, 86–107. London and New York: Routledge, 1991.

Culler, Jonathan. "Preparing the Novel: Spiralling Back". *Paragraph* 31.1 (2008): 109–120.

Dark, David. "Why Does U2 Irk So Many People? A Look at their Struggle for Pop Hits and Social Justice". *America Magazine* (17 July 2017). Available from https://tinyurl.com/2017-07-17-U2 (accessed 3 August 2017).

Dean, Jonathan. "U2 Interview: Bono on death, taxes and their new album Songs of Experience". *The Times* (19 November 2017). Available from https://www.thetimes.co.uk/article/u2-interview-bono-paradise-papers-taxes-new-album-songs-of-experience-hsf7sf25k (accessed 10 August 2018).

DeCurtis, Anthony. "U2: Rattle and Hum". *Rolling Stone* (17 November 1988). Available from http://www.rollingstone.com/music/albumreviews/rattle-and-hum-19881117 (accessed 9 August 2017).

—"U2: Zooropa". *Rolling Stone* (5 July 1993). Available from https://www.rollingstone.com/music/albumreviews/zooropa-19930705 (accessed 9 February 2018).

—"Zoo World Order". *Rolling Stone* 667 (14 October 1993), 49–54, 130–32.

Dillon, Brian. "Rereading: Camera Lucida by Roland Barthes". *The Guardian* (26 March 2011). Available from http://www.guardian.co.uk/books/2011/mar/26/roland-barthes-camera-lucida-rereading (accessed 29 April 2017).

Dumoucel, Caroline. "The Catastrophes Issue: Paul Virilio". *Vice* (1 September 2010), translated by Pauline Eiferman. Available from https://www.vice.com/en_ca/article/qbzbn5/paul-virilio-506-v17n9 (accessed 1 September 2018).

Dunphy, Eamon. *Unforgettable Fire: Past, Present, and Future—The Definitive Biography of U2*. New York: Warner Books, 1987.

Edwards, Steve. *Photography: A Very Short Introduction*. Oxford: Oxford University Press, 2006.

Egan, Barry. "Bono: 'I still have the rage but I have worked it through: I'm dealing with it'". *The Independent* (17 May 2015). Available from https://www.independent.ie/entertainment/music/music-news/bono-i-still-have-the-rage-but-i-have-worked-it-through-im-dealing-with-it-31228813.html (accessed 26 March 2018).

Eichberg, Henning. "Stadium, Pyramid, Labyrinth: Eye and Body on the Move". In *The Stadium and the City*, edited by John Bale and Olof Moen, 323–47. Keele: Keele University Press, 1995.

Eno, Brian. "Bringing Up Baby: A Behind-the-Scenes Look at the Making of U2's New Album". *Rolling Stone* 618 (28 November 1991), 42–50, 116.

—"Exclusive: Bono Reveals Secrets of U2's Surprise Album 'Songs of Innocence'". *Rolling Stone* (9 September 2014). Available from https://tinyurl.com/U-20140909 (accessed 14 January 2018).

Fallon, B. P. *U2 Faraway So Close*. Boston: Little, Brown and Company, 1994.

Falsani, Cathleen. "Bono's American Prayer". *Christianity Today* (1 March 2003). Available from http://www.christianitytoday.com/ct/2003/marchweb-only/2.38.html (accessed 6 July 2017).

—"Why am I Walking Away". *U2.com* (5 October 2017). Available from http://www.u2.com/news/title/why-am-i-walking-away (accessed 15 March 2018).

Farrell, Nathan. "Celebrity Politics: Bono, Product (RED) and the Legitimising of Philanthrocapitalism". *British Journal of Politics and International Relations* 14 (2012): 392–406.

Flanagan, Bill. *U2 at the End of the World*. New York: Delta, 1995.

Foucault, Michel. "Of Other Spaces". *Diacritics* 16.1 (Spring 1986): 22–27.

Fricke, David. "U2 Finds What It's Looking For". *Rolling Stone* 640 (1 October 1992), 41–48, 83.

—"U2: No Line on the Horizon". *Rolling Stone* (20 February 2009). Available from http://www.rollingstone.com/music/albumreviews/no-line-on-the-horizon-20090220 (accessed 8 August 2017).

—"U2: Songs of Innocence". *Rolling Stone* (11 September 2014). Available from https://www.rollingstone.com/music/albumreviews/u2-songs-of-innocence-20140911 (accessed 10 March 2018).

—"Review: U2 Faces Down Mortality, Reconnects with the Power of Music". *Rolling Stone* (1 December 2018). Available from https://www.rollingstone.com/music/albumreviews/review-u2s-songs-of-experience-w513047 (accessed 10 March 2018).

Galbraith, Deane. "Meeting God in the Sound: The Seductive Dimension of U2's Future Hymns". In *The Counter-Narratives of Radical Theology and Popular Music: Songs of Fear and Trembling*, edited by Mike Grimshaw, 119–35. New York: Palgrave Macmillan, 2014.

Gallix, Andrew. "Roland Barthes' Challenge to Biography". *The Guardian* (14 August 2015). Available from http://www.theguardian.com/books/booksblog/2015/aug/14/roland-barthes-challenge-to-biography (accessed 12 October 2015).

—"The Writer Postponed: Barthes at the BnF". *The Los Angeles Review of Books* (23 August 2015). Available from https://lareviewofbooks.org/essay/barthes-panorama (accessed 12 October 2015).

Gardner, Elysa. "U2: Achtung, Baby". *Rolling Stone* (9 January 1992). Available from https://www.rollingstone.com/music/albumreviews/achtung-baby-19920109 (accessed 1 February 2018).

Ghaly, Adrienne. "Cultural Theory on a Micro-Scale: Roland Barthes's Lectures at the Collège de France". *L'Esprit Créateur* 55.4 (Winter 2015): 39–55.

Gilmour, Michael J. "The Prophet Jeremiah, Aung San Suu Kyi, and U2's *All That You Can't Leave Behind*: On Listening to Bono's Jeremiad". In *Call Me the Seeker: Listening to Reli-*

gion in Popular Music, edited by Michael J. Gilmour, 34–43. New York: Continuum, 2005.
—"'God', 'God Part II' and 'God Part III': Exploring the Anxiety of Influence in John Lennon, U2 and Larry Norman". In *Reception History and Biblical Studies: Theory and Practice*, edited by Emma England and William John Lyons, 231–40. London: Bloomsbury T&T Clark, 2015.
Gleber, Anke. "Flanerie, or The Redemption of Visual Reality". In *The Art of Taking a Walk: Flanerie, Literature, and Film in Weimar Culture*, 151–68. Princeton, NJ: Princeton University Press, 1999.
Graham, Bill. "It's a Celebration!" In *The U2 File: A Hot Press U2 History 1978–1985*, edited by Niall Stokes, 109. Dublin: Hot Press, 1985.
—"Yep! It's U2". In *The U2 File: A Hot Press U2 History 1978–1985*, edited by Niall Stokes, 7. Dublin: Hot Press, 1985.
—"PASSENGERS: ORIGINAL SOUNDTRACKS 1". *Hot Press* (15 November 1995). Available from https://www.atu2.com/news/passengers-original-soundtracks-1.html (accessed 11 February 2018).
Greco, Nicholas. "The Berlin Wall: Bowie, U2 and the 'Urban Real'". In *Culture of Cities: ... Under Construction*, edited by P. Moore and M. Risk, 92–94. Oakville, ON: Mosaic Press, 2001.
Greene, Andy. "Watch U2 Play 'Zooropa' for Syrian Refugees at European Tour Launch". *Rolling Stone* (5 September 2015). Available from https://tinyurl.com/U2-20150905 (accessed 9 February 2018).
—"The Edge Breaks Down U2's Upcoming 'Joshua Tree' Tour". *Rolling Stone* (9 January 2017). Available from https://tinyurl.com/w459473 (accessed 25 April 2017).
—"U2's 'Pop': A Reimagining of the Album 20 Years Later". *Rolling Stone* (14 March 2017). Available from https://tinyurl.com/w471642 (accessed 11 February 2018).
—"Bono Talks 'Joshua Tree' Tour, Trump, Status of U2's Next Album". *Rolling Stone* (30 May 2017). Available from https://www.rollingstone.com/music/features/bono-on-joshua-tree-tour-trump-u2s-next-album-w484398 (accessed 5 March 2018).
Hermes, Will. "U2: The Unforgettable Fire (Deluxe Reissue)". *Rolling Stone* (26 October 2009). Available from http://www.rollingstone.com/music/albumreviews/the-unforgettable-fire-deluxe-reissue-20091026 (accessed 7 July 2017).
"'Herstory'". *U2.com* (29 June 2017). Available from http://www.u2.com/news/title/herstory?hootPostID=d4a02bd7b85ab6fc301ddb756edf601a (accessed 1 August 2017).
Hilburn, Robert. "Far Down the Road, a Sudden U-Turn". *Los Angeles Times* (29 October 2000). Available from http://articles.latimes.com/2000/oct/29/entertainment/ca-43738 (accessed 14 February 2018).
Hirschfeld, Julie, Sheryl Gay Stolberg and Thomas Kaplan. "Trump Alarms Lawmakers with Disparaging Words for Haiti and Africa". *The New York Times* (11 January 2018). Available from https://www.nytimes.com/2018/01/11/us/politics/trump-shithole-countries.html (accessed 9 March 2018).
Hoskyns, Barney. "U2: Pop". *Rolling Stone* (20 March 1997). Available from https://www.rollingstone.com/music/albumreviews/pop-19970320 (accessed 11 February 2018).
Hunter, James. "U2: All That You Can't Leave Behind". *Rolling Stone* (26 October 2000). Available from https://www.rollingstone.com/music/albumreviews/all-that-you-cant-leave-behind-20001026 (accessed 14 February 2018).

Hyden, Steven. "Searching for Sugar Men". *Grantland* (13 May 2013). Available from http://grantland.com/features/a-look-state-rock-documentaries-25-years-u2-rattle-hum/ (accessed 9 August 2017).

Jameson, Frederic. *Archaeologies of the Future: The Desire Called Utopia and Other Science Fictions*. London: Verso, 2005.

Jones, Graham. "Live Aid 1985: A Day of Magic". *CNN.com* (6 July 2005). Available from http://edition.cnn.com/2005/SHOWBIZ/Music/07/01/liveaid.memories/index.html (accessed 4 August 2017).

Joyrich, Lynn. "All that Television Allows: TV Melodrama, Postmodernism and Consumer Culture". *Camera Obscura* 16 (1988): 129–53.

Kärki, Kimi. "The Technological Reach for the Sublime on U2's 360° Tour". In *U2 and the Religious Impulse: Take Me Higher*, edited by Scott Calhoun, 107–119. London: Bloomsbury, 2018.

Kellner, Douglas. "Marxist Criticism". In *Encyclopedia of Contemporary Literary Theory: Approaches, Scholars, Terms*, edited by Irena R. Makaryk, 95–100. Toronto: University of Toronto Press, 1993.

Kracauer, Siegfried. *Theory of Film: The Redemption of Physical Reality*. Princeton: Princeton University Press, 1960.

Light, Alan. "Bono, Behind the Fly: The Rolling Stone Interview". *Rolling Stone* (4 March 1993). Available from https://www.rollingstone.com/music/news/bono-behind-the-fly-the-rolling-stone-interview-19930304 (accessed 7 March 2018).

Loder, Kurt. "U2: The Unforgettable Fire". *Rolling Stone* (11 October 1984). Available from http://www.rollingstone.com/music/albumreviews/the-unforgettable-fire-19841011 (accessed 7 July 2017).

Lotringer, Sylvère. "Barthes after Barthes". *Frieze* (1 January 2011). Available from https://frieze.com/article/barthes-after-barthes (accessed 25 March 2018).

Lynch, Declan. "The Boy Can't Help It". In *North Side Story: U2 in Dublin 1978–1983*, 130–33. Dublin: Hot Press, 2014.

Mackey, Liam. "Light a Big Fire". In *The U2 File: A Hot Press U2 History 1978–1985*, edited by Niall Stokes, 110–11. Dublin: Hot Press, 1985.

—"Blood on the Tracks". In *North Side Story: U2 in Dublin 1978–1983*, 226–29. Dublin: Hot Press, 2014.

MacLeod, Michael R., and Timothy Harvie. "'In God's Country': Spatial Sacredness in U2". In *U2 and the Religious Impulse: Take Me Higher*, edited by Scott Calhoun, 131–43. London: Bloomsbury, 2018.

Marsh, Calum. "U2: Songs of Experience Album Review". *Pitchfork* (4 December 2017). Available from https://pitchfork.com/reviews/albums/u2-songs-of-experience/ (accessed 21 February 2018).

Marstal, Henrik. "'Edge, Ring Those Bells': The Guitar and its Spiritual Soundscapes in Early U2". In *U2 and the Religious Impulse: Take Me Higher*, edited by Scott Calhoun, 11–25. London: Bloomsbury, 2018.

Maslin, Janet. "Review/Film; U2 Hits the Road in 'Rattle and Hum'". *New York Times* (4 November 1988). Available from http://www.nytimes.com/movie/review?res=940DE3DC1639F937A35752C1A96E948260 (accessed 11 August 2017).

Mason, Emma. "Punctive Grace: Reading Religion in Barthes' *Mourning Diary*". *Textual Practice* 30.2 (2016): 327–43.

McCormick, Neil. *U2 by U2*. London: HarperCollins, 2006.

—"U2: Secrets of Stadium Rock". *Telegraph* (17 August 2009). Available from https://tinyurl.com/U2-100002560 (accessed 3 February 2018).

—"Autumn Fire". In *North Side Story: U2 in Dublin 1978–1983*, 172–75. Dublin: Hot Press, 2014.

McEntire, Sandra. *The Doctrine of Compunction in Medieval England: Holy Tears*. Lewiston, NY: E. Mellen Press, 1990.

McGee, Matt. "Directing U2: From Vertigo to Vancouver with Alex & Martin". *@U2* (26 July 2005). Available from https://www.atu2.com/news/directing-u2-from-vertigo-to-vancouver-with-alex--martin.html (accessed 23 March 2018).

McLaughlin, Noel. "Bono! Do You Ever Take Those Wretched Sunglasses Off?: U2 and the Performance of Irishness". *Popular Music History* 4.3 (2009): 309–331.

—"Another Green World? Eno, Ireland and U2". *Popular Music History* 9.2 (2014): 173–94.

McLaughlin, Noel, and Martin McLoone. "Hybridity and National Musics: The Case of Irish Rock Music". *Popular Music* 19.2 (2000): 191–99.

McLuhan, Marshall. "Television: The Timid Giant". In *Understanding Media: The Extensions of Man*, 268–94. New York: McGraw-Hill, 1964.

Merton, Thomas. *Conjectures of a Guilty Bystander*. Garden City, NY: Image Books, 1968.

Mitchum, Rob. "U2: Songs of Innocence Album Review". *Pitchfork* (12 September 2014). Available from https://pitchfork.com/reviews/albums/19816-u2-songs-of-innocence/ (accessed 21 February 2018).

Moberg, Marcus. *Christian Metal: History, Ideology, Scene*. London: Bloomsbury, 2015.

Nabi, Beth. "Every Poet is a Thief: Bono Channels Rilke in 'Oh Berlin'". *BethandBono.com* (1 November 2011). Available from http://bethandbono.com/2011/11/01/every-angel-is-terror-every-poet-is-a-thief/ (accessed 27 June 2018).

—"Dream Out Loud: The Day Beth met Bono". *BethandBono.com* (31 October 2014). Available from http://bethandbono.com/2014/10/31/dream-out-loud-the-day-beth-met-bono/ (accessed 27 June 2018).

Negus, Keith. *Popular Music in Theory: An Introduction*. Hanover: Wesleyan University Press, 1996.

Newcomb, Horace. "Towards a Television Aesthetic". In *Television: The Critical View*. 4th ed., edited by Horace Newcomb, 613–27. Oxford: Oxford University Press, 1987.

NFL Network. "U2's 'Beautiful Day' & Super Bowl XXXVI Halftime Show Helps Heal America after 9/11". *YouTube* (3 December 2017). Available from https://www.youtube.com/watch?v=ZPHGOMXQyDQ (accessed 6 March 2018).

O'Donnell, Chuck. "Bono's Music Fits American Mood". *Ottawa Citizen* (15 February 2002), A13.

Omonira-Oyekanmi, Rebecca. "The Myth and Reality of Brexit and Migrants". In *The Brexit Crisis: A Verso Report*. London: Verso, 2016.

Osborne, Hilary. "Bono Used Malta-based Firm to Invest in Lithuanian Shopping Centre". *The Guardian* (5 November 2017). Available from https://tinyurl.com/u2-paradise (accessed 6 November 2017).

Pareles, Jon. "U2: October". *Rolling Stone* (4 February 1982). Available from http://www.rollingstone.com/music/albumreviews/october-19820204 (accessed 6 July 2017).

—"RECORDINGS; When Self-Importance Interferes with the Music". *New York Times* (16

October 1988). Available from http://www.nytimes.com/1988/10/16/arts/recordings-when-self-importance-interferes-with-the-music.html (accessed 11 August 2017).

—"RECORDINGS VIEW; U2 Takes a Turn from the Universal to the Domestic". *New York Times* (17 November 1991). Available from https://tinyurl.com/NYT-1991-11-17-arts (accessed 1 February 2018).

—"Pop Briefs: PASSENGERS: 'ORIGINAL SOUNDTRACKS 1' Island". *New York Times* (19 November 1995). Available from http://www.nytimes.com/1995/11/19/arts/pop-briefs-048070.html (accessed 11 February 2018).

—"Review: U2 Revisits 'The Joshua Tree' in the Here and Now". *New York Times* (15 May 2017). Available from https://preview.tinyurl.com/NYT-2017-05-15-arts (accessed 5 March 2018).

—"U2 Releases 'Songs of Experience'. Cynicism Not Included". *New York Times* (29 November 2017). Available from https://tinyurl.com/NYT-2017-11-29-arts (accessed 3 December 2017).

Pattie, David. *Rock Music in Performance*. Basingstoke: Palgrave Macmillan, 2007.

Pond, Steve. "U2: The Joshua Tree". *Rolling Stone* (9 April 1987). Available from http://www.rollingstone.com/music/albumreviews/the-joshua-tree-19870409 (accessed 5 August 2017).

—"U2: Now What?" *Rolling Stone* (9 March 1989). Available from http://www.rollingstone.com/music/features/now-what-19890309 (accessed 9 August 2017.

Powell, Mark Allan. "U2". In *Encyclopedia of Contemporary Christian Music*, 978–83. Peabody, MA: Hendrickson, 2002.

Quinn, Steven. "U2 and the Performance of (a Numb) Resistance". *Social Semiotics* 9.1 (1999): 67–83.

Ramert, Lynn. "A Century Apart: The Personality Performances of Oscar Wilde in the 1890s and U2's Bono in the 1990s". *Popular Music and Society* 32.4 (October 2009): 447–60.

Richards, Chris. "U2 Goes MAGA at FedEx Field". *Washington Post* (21 June 2017). Available from https://tinyurl.com/post-style-u2 (accessed 2 August 2017).

Ritzer, George, and Jeffrey Stepnisky. *Sociological Theory*. 9th ed. New York: McGraw Hill, 2014.

Robinson, Valerie. "'I nearly quit U2 before we found fame' says Bono". *Irish Times* (26 June 2013). Available from https://tinyurl.com/IT-2013-06-26-news (accessed 6 July 2017).

Rodriquez, Juan. "Has Bono Sold Out?". *Ottawa Citizen* (11 February 2002): B2.

Rosenfeld, Paul. "Monteverde". In *Discoveries of a Music Critic*, 20–28. New York: Harcourt Brace, 1936.

—*Port of New York: Essays on Fourteen American Moderns*. Urbana, IL: University of Illinois Press, 1961.

—*By Way of Art*. Freeport: Books for Libraries Press, Inc., 1967.

—*Musical Impressions: Selections from Paul Rosenfeld's Criticism*, edited by Herbert A. Leibowitz. London: George Allen & Unwin, 1969.

Rothman, Joshua. "The Church of U2". *The New Yorker* (16 September 2014). Available from https://www.newyorker.com/culture/cultural-comment/church-u2 (accessed 28 August 2017).

Rushdie, Salman. *The Ground Beneath Her Feet*. Toronto: Alfred A. Knopf Canada, 1999.
Saenz, Michael. "Television Viewing as a Cultural Practice". In *Television: The Critical View*, 4th ed., edited by Horace Newcomb, 573–86. New York: Oxford University Press, 1987.
Samoyault, Tiphaine. "Lexique Roland Barthes". In *Roland Barthes: L'inattendu, Le Monde Hors-Série* 26, 113–19. Paris: Société éditrice du Monde, 2015.
—*Barthes: A Biography*, translated by Andrew Brown. Cambridge: Polity Press, 2017.
Scharen, Christian, *One Step Closer: Why U2 Matters to Those Seeking God*. Grand Rapids, MI: Brazos Press, 2006.
Sennett, Sean. "U2: Making Music to Blow their Minds". In *Off the Record: 25 Years of Music Street Press*, edited by Sean Sennett and Simon Groth, 246–52. St Lucia: University of Queensland Press, 2010.
Sheffield, Rob. "U2: How to Dismantle an Atomic Bomb". *Rolling Stone* (9 December 2004). Available from https://www.rollingstone.com/music/albumreviews/how-to-dismantle-an-atomic-bomb-20041209 (accessed 20 February 2018).
Sherwin, Adam. "New U2 album No Line on the Horizon given lukewarm reception". *The Times* (3 March 2009). Available from https://tinyurl.com/TIMES-u2-album (accessed 6 August 2017).
Siegel, Greg. "Double Vision: Large Screen Video Display and Live Sports Spectacle". *Television & New Media* 3.1 (February 2002): 49–73.
Smyth, Gerry. "'Show Me the Way to Go Home': Space and Place in the Music of U2". In *Space and the Irish Cultural Imagination*, 159–97. New York: Palgrave, 2001.
Sontag, Susan. "Remembering Barthes". *New York Review of Books* 27.8 (15 May 1980). Available from http://www.nybooks.com/articles/archives/1980/may/15/remembering-barthes/ (accessed 3 April 2015).
Stein, Edith. *On the Problem of Empathy*, translated by Waltraut Stein. Washington, DC: ICS Publications, 1989.
Stiller, Brian. "To Be or Not to Be an Evangelical". *Christianity Today* (31 March 2018). Available from http://www.christianitytoday.com/edstetzer/2018/march/to-be-or-not-to-be-evangelical.html (accessed 17 April 2018).
Stockman, Steve. *Walk On: The Spiritual Journey of U2*. Lake Mary, FL: Relevant Books, 2001.
Stockman, Steve, and Dermot Stokes. "All Ireland Champions!" In *The U2 File: A Hot Press U2 History 1978–1985*, edited by Niall Stokes, 150–51. Dublin: Hot Press, 1985.
Stokes, Niall. "Boys in Control". In *The U2 File: A Hot Press U2 History 1978–1985*, edited by Niall Stokes, 16–24. Dublin: Hot Press, 1985.
—*Into the Heart*. London: Carlton Books, 1996.
—"Introduction". In *North Side Story: U2 in Dublin 1978–1983*, 9–13. Dublin: Hot Press, 2014.
Taraborrelli, Angela. *Contemporary Cosmopolitanism*, translated by Ian McGilvray. London: Bloomsbury, 2015.
Taylor, W. David O. "Foreword: Bono as the Religious Everyman". In *U2 and the Religious Impulse: Take Me Higher*, edited by Scott Calhoun, xi–xiii. London: Bloomsbury, 2018.
Teeuwen, Rudolphus. "An Epoch of Rest: Roland Barthes' 'Neutral' and the Utopia of Weariness". *Cultural Critique* 80 (2012): 1–26.

Thirlwell, Adam. "My Novel, My Novel". *New Republic* (7 December 2010). Available from http://www.newrepublic.com/article/books-and-arts/magazine/79745/novel-roland-barthes-realism (accessed 26 December 2014).

Thomas, Keith. "Introduction". In *A Cultural History of Gestures*, edited by Jan Bremmer and Herman Roodenburg, 1–14. Ithaca, NY: Cornell University Press, 1993.

Thomson, Iain. "'Even Better than the Real Thing'? Postmodernity, the Triumph of the Simulacra, and U2". In *U2 and Philosophy: How to Decipher an Atomic Band*, edited by Mark A. Wrathall, 73–95. Chicago and La Salle, IL: Open Court, 2006.

Toop, David. *Ocean of Sound: Aether Talk, Ambient Sound and Imaginary Worlds*. London: Serpent's Tail, 1995.

"U2 Perform for Fans at Video Shoot". *RTÉ* (10 January 2007). Available from https://www.rte.ie/entertainment/2005/0429/404017-u2/ (accessed 23 March 2018).

U2. "U2 – Song for Someone (Behind the Scenes)". *YouTube* (12 July 2015). Available from https://www.youtube.com/watch?v=w6jrEtTznYQ (accessed 4 August 2018).

United Nations Refugee Agency. "Will You Stand #WithRefugees?" *UNHCR.org*. Available from http://www.unhcr.org/refugeeday/petition/ (accessed 11 July 2016).

Varèse, Edgard. "Wine of Good Omen". In *Paul Rosenfeld: Voyager in the Arts*, edited by J. Mellquist and L. Weise, 237–38. New York: Creative Age Press Inc., 1948.

Vernallis, Carol. "Music Video's Second Aesthetic". In *The Oxford Handbook of New Audiovisual Aesthetics*, edited by John Richardson, Claudia Gorbman and Carol Vernallis, 437–65. Oxford: Oxford University Press, 2013.

Virilio, Paul. "Speed and Information: Cyberspace Alarm!", translated by Patrice Riemens. *CTHEORY* (27 August 1995). Available from http://www.ctheory.net/articles.aspx?id=72 (accessed 29 April 2017).

—*The Administration of Fear*, translated by Ames Hodges. Los Angeles: Semiotext(e), 2012.

Virilio, Paul, and Sylvère Lotringer. *Pure War: Twenty-Five Years Later*, translated by Mark Polizzotti. Los Angeles: Semiotext(e), 2008.

Wawzenek, Bryan. "Revisiting U2's Unfocused 'How to Dismantle an Atomic Bomb'". *Ultimate Classic Rock* (17 November 2015). Available from http://ultimateclassicrock.com/u2-how-to-dismantle-an-atomic-bomb/ (accessed 20 February 2018).

Wenner, Jann S. "Bono: The Rolling Stone Interview". *Rolling Stone* (3 November 2005). Available from https://www.rollingstone.com/music/news/bono-the-rolling-stone-interview-20051103 (accessed 18 February 2018).

"What is an Evangelical?" *Evangelical Fellowship of Canada*. Available from https://www.evangelicalfellowship.ca/About-us/About-Evangelicals (accessed 23 January 2018).

Williams, Raymond. "The Forms of Television". In *Television: Technology and Cultural Form*, 44–77. Glasgow: Fontana/Collins, 1974.

"With or without EU: U2 Urges UK to Vote Remain". *RTÉ Ten* (22 June 2016). Available from http://www.rte.ie/entertainment/2016/0622/797363-with-or-without-eu-u2-urges-uk-to-vote-remain/ (accessed 12 July 2016).

"Zoo TV Station Talent". *Propaganda* 16 (1 June 1992). Available from https://www.atu2.com/news/zoo-tv-station-talent.html (accessed 5 February 2018).

Zukin, Sharon. *Landscapes of Power: From Detroit to Disneyland*. Berkeley: University of California Press, 1991.

Index

'4th of July' (song) 26
'40' (song) 2
9/11 14, 80–81, 92

Abbey Road Studios 77, 130, 194
Achtung Baby (album) xi, xii, 17, 26, 33, 98, 116–17, 126, 130, 132, 139–40
    and Berlin 18–19, 37–9, 41
    its musical sound 56, 93
'Acrobat' (song) xii, 125, 140–41 *see also* Bono: as Mr MacPhisto
Adorno, Theodor 101, 189–90
aesthetics 14, 104–5 *see also* television
Africa 55, 93, 146–7, 149, 152–3, 156, 163–7
AIDS 10, 55, 64, 93, 102
Åkerlund, Jonas 67, 69
All That You Can't Leave Behind (album) 17, 19, 26, 47–8, 62–3, 67, 96, 117, 145
Andreu, Paul 67–8
Apple (company) 55, 73–4, 105, 140–41, 145–6, 157–8, 171, 180
    Apple Music 73
    iPad 74, 140–41
    iPod 145, 157–8
    iTunes 105, 146, 171, 180, 184
Arendt, Hannah 189, 192
Augustine, Saint 4, 150
"aura of the 'sublime'" 39–41, 42, 68
Auslander, Philip 105–7
autarky 149, 165

'Bad' (song) 28–9
baptism 4, 162
Barthes, Henriette 4, 175, 177, 183, 187
Barthes, Roland xiii–iv, 3–6, 14, 15–16, 53–5, 105, 123, 127–30, 142, 145–69, 171–84, 187, 191–2, 196
Batman 137–8
Batman Forever (film) 137
The Beatles 194–5
Beats (company) 55
'Beautiful Day' (song) 13, 62–75, 194
Bebbington, David 7–11
Benjamin, Walter 41–2, 49, 195
Berlin (city) 37–42, 88, 103

Berlin Wall 18, 37–8, 40–41, 103, 194 *see also* Berlin
The Best of 1980–1990 (album) 65, 77
The Best of 1990–2000 (album) 65
Bible 3–4, 7–10, 188 *see also* Scripture
Birmingham 8, 139
"Black Lives Matter" 95
'The Blackout' (song) 132
Blade Runner (film) 44
"Bloody Sunday" (day) 24–5 *see also* Ireland: "The Troubles"
"Bogside Massacre" 25
Bono
    and Roman Catholicism 11–12
    as dandy 70, 141
    as The Fly xiv, 39, 45, 55, 70–72, 89, 106, 115, 130–2, 137–9, 181
    as Mr MacPhisto xiv, 8, 46, 95, 132–4, 136–41, 172
    as the Shadow Man 141
    his father x, 7, 11, 12, 64, 172, 180–81
    his mother 180–83
    see also "Lypton Village"
Boston 88–9, 92–3, 96 *see also Elevation 2001: Live in Boston*
Bowie, David 25, 38, 194–5
Boy (album) 17, 20–21, 24, 39, 62, 188
'Boy/Girl' (song) 21
Boyd, Brian 11, 13, 180, 184
bread 64, 85, 124–5 *see also* Eucharist
'Breathe' (song) 149
Brexit 98–9
Briggs, Kate 6, 147, 158
'Bullet the Blue Sky' (song) 29, 89–94, 97–8, 103, 133
Bush, George H. W. 18–19, 43, 115
Butler, Judith 101, 189–94

Camera Lucida 54, 176 *see also* Barthes, Roland
Carroll, Jim 180, 183–4
Catanzarite, Stephen 39, 131
'Cedars of Lebanon' (song) 164
'Cedarwood Road' (song) 120
celebrity xiii, 2, 5, 19, 38–9, 97, 106, 117–18, 124, 127, 130–31, 138, 162, 195, 197

Charles de Gaulle airport 67–8 *see also* 'Beautiful Day' (song)
cinema 73, 78, 104–5
'City of Blinding Lights' (song) 79–81, 93
Clayton, Adam 10, 25–6, 30, 32–3, 41–2, 47, 57, 115, 131, 138, 146
   and Shalom Fellowship 21–2
   upbringing 12–13
Clinton, Hilary 108
Cocks, Jay 31, 146
communism 37, 41
community 63, 70, 125–6, 147, 149–51, 154, 163–5, 189–90
"complex" term 53, 55, 60, 168
complicity x, xiii–iv, 13–14, 33–4, 39, 54, 56, 79, 99–101, 105–10, 117–18, 130, 139, 147
"conscience capital" 100
Cooper, Julia 176, 178–9
Corbijn, Anton 41–2, 146–7, 154, 157–8
cosmopolitanism 2–3, 15, 120, 128, 175, 188–94
Cubitt, Sean 69
Culler, Jonathan 174
"cyberpunk" 44

'Daddy's Gonna Pay for Your Crashed Car' (song) 45–6, 136
Dark, David 124
Davis, Angela 108
DeCurtis, Anthony 31, 44–5
Deeley, Cat 77
Derrida, Jacques 106
Derry 6, 25
desire 22, 123, 127–31, 142, 151, 153, 156–7, 165, 176
'Desire' (song) 103, 134
'Discothèque' (song) 19
disreality 123–4, 127–8
"double hermeneutic" 47, 50 *see also* Jameson, Frederic
dromocracy 102–107, 127
dromosphere *see* dromocracy
Dublin 7, 12–13, 24–5, 27, 31, 33, 134, 180, 189
Dunphy, Eamon 12–13, 20–24, 28–9
dystopia 13, 50, 56 *see also* utopia

Eagles of Death Metal (band) 127
Eccleston, Danny 92–3
The Edge 28, 41–2, 57, 102–6, 115–16, 120, 130, 132, 136, 146, 184
   and Shalom Fellowship 20–26
   in performance 79–80, 89–90, 93, 181
   upbringing 12, 20
   see also "Lypton Village"
El Salvador 18, 89, 107, 133
Elevation tour xii, 19, 62, 80, 91–2, 117–19 *see also Elevation 2001: Live in Boston*
Elevation 2001: Live in Boston 14, 17, 65, 88–9, 143
'Elvis Presley and America' (song) 27
empathy 14–15, 63–5, 70, 84–5, 191 *see also* Stein, Edith
Eno, Brian xiii, 17, 25–7, 29–30, 37–9, 43, 46–7, 56, 77
Eucharist 7–8 *see also* bread; wine
Europe 2, 37–8, 45, 49, 95, 97–101, 127–8, 166–7 *see also* European Union
European Union 1, 10, 19, 45, 75, 93, 97–101, 127, 136, 166, 194 *see also* Europe
evangelical *see* Evangelicalism
Evangelicalism 4, 7–11, 15, 21–2, 64, 76, 133, 136
evangelism xii, 11 *see also* Evangelicalism
Evans, Dick 12–13
Evans, Sian 188–9
'Even Better Than the Real Thing' (song) 123–7
'Exit' (song) 141
eXPERIENCE + iNNOCENCE tour 113, 138, 140–41

Facebook 99, 132
Fallon, B. P. 132, 134–5, 181
Fascism 19, 21, 124
fatwa 44, 77
'Fez – Being Born' (song) 155–6
flag 1, 24, 45, 81, 88–96, 98–9, 101, 114, 127, 133–4, 161, 194
Flanagan, Bill 22, 26, 41–3, 115, 135–6
flâneur 41–2, 49 *see also* Benjamin, Walter
Flood (producer) 48
'The Fly' (song) 130
Foucault, Michel 168
Fricke, David 43, 146, 171, 189
Friday, Gavin 77

Gallix, Andrew 183, 187
gaze 155–8, 160–63, 166–7, 170
Germany 18, 37, 41, 51, 56, 194
'Get on Your Boots'(song) 146, 159–62
Gibraltar 156, 164
Gibson, William 44
Gilmour, Michael J. 62, 125–6
Gleber, Anke 42

'God' (song) 125
'God Part II' (song) 124–5
Graham, Bill 20, 27, 46
Grammy Awards 30, 62, 95, 145
Greene, Andy 45, 57, 108, 122
'The Ground Beneath Her Feet' (song) 86, 187
Guggi 12, 22, 24
Gulf War 90, 135

haiku 15–16
'The Hands that Built America' (song) 93
Hansa Studio 37–8, 41
Haring, Keith 57
Harrelson, Woody 81–2
Hart, David Bentley 139
"Heroes" (album) 25, 37–8
'Heroes' (song) 38
"herstory" 107–8, 161
Heston, Charlton 91
heterotopia 168
Hewson, Ali 24, 77, 80, 84, 130, 172
Hewson, Eli 189
Hewson, Eve 77, 181
'Hold Me, Thrill Me, Kiss Me, Kill Me' (song) 137–9
Holy Spirit 9–10, 22–3, 100, 163
How to Dismantle an Atomic Bomb (album) 17, 26, 79, 83, 145
Howard, Richard 174, 179
Howie B 46–7

'I Can't Help Falling in Love with You' (song) 135 *see also* Presley, Elvis
idiorrythmy 147–8, 150–51, 155, 163–5, 192–3
'I Will Follow' (song) 182
'If God Will Send His Angels' (song) 57
Ignatius of Loyola 175
immigration 75, 84, 89–95, 97–103, 127, 136, 149–50, 153, 164–7, 193 *see also* refugees
'In God's Country' (song) 104
incense 23, 64, 85
iNNOCENCE + eXPERIENCE tour 102, 119, 122–3, 180–81
Instagram 98
Intégrales 51–2
intimacy 14, 66, 70, 73–5, 78–9, 83–5, 113, 119, 122, 184
'Into the Heart' (song) 62, 130
Ionization 51–2
Ireland 21–2, 28, 95–9, 102
   and U2 12–13, 88, 95–9
   tensions 3–4, 11, 13, 20, 25, 39, 128, 189

"The Troubles" 6–7, 24–5, 64
'Iris (Hold Me Close)' (song) 175–6, 179–83
Islam 93, 148 *see also* Muslim
   hijab x, 98, 109
Island Records 20–21

Jameson, Frederic 47, 50, 52–6, 168
Jefferson, Thomas 102–3
Jesus Christ xii, 7–8, 10–11, 64, 82–3, 100, 152–3, 174–5, 177, 182, 193–4
   passion 4, 9, 11, 82, 125, 152, 163, 175
Joanou, Phil 31 *see also Rattle and Hum* (film)
The Joshua Tree (album) xi, 17, 20, 26–8, 89
   critical reception 29–33, 37, 145
   its musical sound 104
   themes 18, 96–7, 188
   tour 33, 77, 114
The Joshua Tree 2017 tour 102, 107–9, 113, 122, 141, 161, 188
Joy Division 194–5
Joyrich, Lynn 72
Judaism 93, 148

Kant, Immanuel 189–90
Kellner, Douglas 50, 52
Kennedy, John F. 102–3
Knight, Diana 176
Kracauer, Siegfried 42, 49, 167, 175
Kyi, Aung San Suu 196

Lanois, Daniel 26–7, 37, 77
Large Screen Video Display 116–17
Las Vegas 103, 135–6, 138
Lawless, Terry xi, xiv
Lazarus, Emma 102–3, 109
Léger, Nathalie 174, 179
'Lemon' (song) 182
Lennon, John 91–2, 125–6
Lewis, C. S. 136–8
Lichtenstein, Roy 57, 90
Linear 3, 14, 145–68, 188
"Live Aid" 28–9
London (city) 28, 77, 80, 88, 130, 194
Lotringer, Sylvère 177, 179, 183
'Love is Bigger than Anything in its Way' (song) 94–7
Lovetown tour 33
Lowe, Zane 27, 29–30, 32, 37, 109
"Lypton Village" 20, 24, 35

Mackey, Liam 24, 27
'Magnificent' (song) 157–8
Marxist theory 47, 50, 168

Mary (Jesus' mother) 10, 182
Mason, Emma 3–4, 159, 175–7, 187
McCormick, Neil 21, 23, 140
McEntire, Sandra 175, 185
McGuinness, Paul 20, 29
McLaughlin, Noel 12, 43, 56, 72, 88, 96, 100, 106
McLoone, Martin 88
McLuhan, Marshall 78
mediation xiii, 3, 15, 33, 43, 57, 113, 116, 121–4, 127–30, 157–8, 162, 165
memory 3, 62, 120, 155, 175–81, 184, 195 see also nostalgia
Merton, Thomas 124
Mexico City 83, 91 see also PopMart: Live from Mexico City
microphone 2, 38, 90, 93, 100, 124, 139–40, 162
Middle East 45, 75, 99, 166
The Million Dollar Hotel (film) 86, 96, 187
Mirror-Ball Man 132–6, 141
Moberg, Marcus 99
modernity 54, 67–9, 81 see also postmodernity
'Mofo' (song) 57, 175, 182
'Moment of Surrender' (song) 162–4
Monteverdi, Claudio 49–50
Morocco 163, 167, 174, 184
'Mothers of the Disappeared' (song) 107 see also El Salvador
Mount Temple Public School 11–12
mourning 14, 174–6, 179, 184
Mourning Diary 15, 174–6, 179, 184 see also Barthes, Roland; mourning
MTV 72, 98
Mullen, Aaron Elvis 184, 189
Mullen Jr, Larry 10–13, 32, 37, 41, 115, 118, 138, 146, 158, 184, 189
   playing style 25
   and Roman Catholicism 12
   and the Shalom Fellowship 21–4
Muslim x, 109
'Mysterious Ways' (song) 77
myth 196–7

Nabi, Beth 41, 65
Nazism 1, 19, 38, 101, 165
Negus, Keith 78
neutral 7, 13, 164–5, 176, 184
   "neutral" term 47, 53–5, 60, 147, 154, 159, 168
"The New Colossus" 94–5, 103 see also Statue of Liberty

'New Year's Day' (song) 116
New York (city) 80–81, 83–4, 88, 92–5, 102–3
Newcomb, Horace 73–4, 76, 78
Nike x, 55
No Line on the Horizon 14, 17, 146–7, 155, 166–7
'No Line on the Horizon' (song) 154–5
Norway 95, 136
nostalgia 3, 38, 180, 184 see also memory
novel 6, 14, 54, 76, 123, 147, 154, 171–84

October (album) 17, 21–4, 175, 182
O'Connor, Flannery 141
'Ode to Joy' (song) 1, 93, 98
'Oh Berlin' (song) 41
'One Tree Hill' (song) 33–4, 77
Omonira-Oyekanmi, Rebecca 99
optimism 13–14, 69, 75, 109
'Out of Control' (song) 21
Outside Broadcast 90, 134

Paradise Papers see taxes
Pareles, Jon 23, 31, 39, 47, 188, 197
Paris 2, 41, 67, 83–4, 88, 101, 114, 120, 127–8, 148–50, 165–7 see also U2 iNNOCENCE + eXPERIENCE: Live in Paris
Passengers 17, 47, 49
Passengers: Original Soundtracks 1 17, 46, 105 see also Passengers
Pattie, David 120–2
'Peace on Earth' (song) 63
personae xiv, 5, 14, 45–6, 55–8, 66, 70–72, 95, 105, 113–14, 116, 121, 130–41, 172
"philanthrocapitalism" 55
photography (medium) 54–5, 176–81, 195
Pilieva, Tatia 83–5
'The Playboy Mansion' (song) 57
'Please' (song) 57
The Pleasure of the Text 128–30
"Poème électronique" 47
"poetics of space" 47
Pond, Steve 29, 32
Pop (album) 5, 17, 57–8, 116–17, 145, 175, 182
PopMart: Live from Mexico City 19, 90–91, 94
PopMart tour xii, 19, 57, 71, 78, 90–1, 116–18, 122, 145 see also PopMart: Live from Mexico City
   mirror-ball lemon 19, 117, 145
postmodernity 2, 13, 54–6, 59, 69, 115, 126
The Preparation of the Novel 173, 179 see also Barthes, Roland

Presley, Elvis 39, 71, 134–8
Product (RED) 55, 60
Protestantism 3–4, 6–12, 21, 174
Proust, Marcel 154, 172–4, 184
punk x, 1, 76, 189

Quinn, Steven 106–7, 109

race 9, 30
'Raised by Wolves' (song) 7, 128
Ramert, Lynn 70, 97, 180
Rattle and Hum
　album xii, 17, 97, 124–5, 130
　critical reception 31–3, 37, 39
　film 17, 30, 31–3, 77, 90–91, 133
Reagan, Ronald 18, 102, 109
recording studio xiii, 30, 38, 46–7, 56, 102, 151–2
'Red Flag Day' (song) 166
refugees 2, 10, 45, 75, 78, 84, 97–101, 109, 127–8, 164, 166, 168, 188, 193
Republican (in Northern Ireland) 8–9, 114
Republican (in the United States) 102, 108
Roland Barthes by Roland Barthes 5 see also Barthes, Roland
Roman Catholicism 2, 23, 33–4, 64, 82, 124, 163, 182
　and Roland Barthes 3, 149–50
　in France 3–4
　in Ireland 4, 6–8, 12
　theology 4, 9–11
rosary 2, 31, 124, 182
Rosenfeld, Paul 47–53, 56, 115
Rothman, Joshua x–xi, 140, 180
Rowen, Derek 12 see also Guggi
Rowen, Peter 24
Roxy Music 12, 25
Rushdie, Salman 44, 77, 86, 187

sacraments xiii, 4, 8, 124
Sade Fourier Loyola 183, 187 see also Barthes, Roland
Saenz, Michael 68, 76
Samoyault, Tiphaine 3, 5, 159, 172
São Paulo 77, 195
The Satanic Verses 44 see also Rushdie, Salman
The Screwtape Letters 136–8 see also Lewis, C. S.
Scripture 8, 10, 12, 22, 182
semiotics 3, 14, 114, 117, 153, 196
Shalom Fellowship 9–10, 21–4, 35, 125
Siegel, Greg 116–17
"skyscraper mysticism" 47–56, 115
"Slacktivism" xi, 75, 79 see also "philanthrocapitalism"

Smyth, Gerry 95–7
social justice x–xii, 2–3, 11, 22, 31, 102, 120, 146, 189
'Sometimes You Can't Make It on Your Own' (song) 145
'Song for Someone' (song) 81–3, 175
Songs of Experience (album) 15, 20, 83, 95, 102, 119, 141, 171–2, 188–9, 197
Songs of Innocence (album) 7, 18, 20, 81, 102, 171–84, 188–9
Sontag, Susan 180
'A Sort of Homecoming' (song) xi
Spain 151, 163, 166
'Stand Up Comedy' (song) 158
"star image" 2, 5 see also celebrity
'The Star-Spangled Banner' 93
Starbucks 55
stardom xi, 31, 38–9, 118, 131 see also celebrity
'Starman' (song) 194–5
'Stateless' (song) 96
Stations of the Cross 82, 163 see also Roman Catholicism
Statue of Liberty 94–5, 102–3, 108–9
Stein, Edith 70, 189, 191 see also empathy
Stokes, Niall 20–21, 26–7, 30, 46
'Stories for Boys' (song) 21
"structure of feeling" 66, 75–7
'Summer of Love' (song) 166
'Sunday Bloody Sunday' (song) 24–5, 28, 114
Super Bowl 92–3, 125
swastika 89 see also Nazism
'The Sweetest Thing' (song) 77
Syria 2, 45, 75, 83, 100, 109, 164, 166–7

Taraborrelli, Angela 189–90, 193
Tarifa 156, 162–3, 166
taxes xi, 99, 105–6
Teeuwen, Rudolphus 53, 55, 154, 159
television xiii, 43, 56–7, 66, 68, 89, 104, 116–17, 127, 129, 134, 157–8, 165, 167
　advertising 78–9
　aesthetics 14, 72–7
　television audience 28–9
terrorism 80–81, 96–7, 120, 127–8
Thirlwell, Adam 171, 173, 184
Three (album) 17, 20–21, 24
Tokyo 41–2, 44, 46
'Tomorrow' (song) 175, 182
The Tonight Show starring Jimmy Fallon 93–4
Trump, Donald 93–5, 102–10, 132, 195
Twitter 94, 120, 128

U2 360° at the Rose Bowl xiv, 18, 139, 146
U2 360° tour xiii, 19–20, 118–19, 120, 139 *see also U2 360° at the Rose Bowl*
U2 by U2 80, 181–2
U2 Go Home: Live from Slane Castle, Ireland 18, 65, 77
U2 iNNOCENCE + eXPERIENCE: Live in Paris 18, 99, 127, 171
U2 Live at Red Rocks: Under a Blood Red Sky 25, 114
U218 Singles (album) 146
'Ultraviolet (Light my Way)' (song) 139–40
Under a Blood Red Sky (album) 17, 25, 27 *see also U2 Live at Red Rocks: Under a Blood Red Sky*
The Unforgettable Fire (album) xi, 17, 26–7, 29, 31, 93, 97, 146
'United Colours' (song) 48, 105
United Kingdom 3, 12, 99, 101, 109, 114
University of Notre Dame 2, 124
'Unknown Caller' (song) xiv, 148
'Until the End of the World' (song) 116, 124
utopia 13–14, 16, 47–56, 119, 129, 147–8, 153, 158–9, 163–4, 168 *see also* dystopia

'Van Diemen's Land' (song) 130
Varèse, Edgard 47–8, 50–53, 56
Vernallis, Carol 67, 69, 72, 79
'Vertigo' (song) 119, 145
Vertigo tour xii, 79–80, 118–19, 140, 148 *see also Vertigo 2005: Live from Chicago*
Vertigo 2005: Live from Chicago 2, 18, 91, 93, 124, 130, 146
Vertigo 05: Live from Milan 18, 146
Virilio, Paul 40, 102–5, 127

Visconti, Tony 25
Vita Nova 4, 14, 172–9, 180, 183–4 *see also* Barthes, Roland

'Wake Up, Dead Man' (song) 57
'Walk On' (song) 62–3, 143
War (album) 17, 23–5, 27, 114, 116, 188–9
"War on Terror" 96, 110
Washington 92, 109
Wenders, Wim 47, 96
'When I Look at the World' (song) 63–5, 124
'Where the Streets Have No Name' (song) 29–30, 80, 92, 125, 133–4
'White as Snow' (song) 152
Williams, Raymond 75–6
Williams, Willie 107–8, 116
wine 51, 64, 85, 124–5 *see also* Eucharist
'Winter' (song) 150–2
Wise Blood (book) 141
'With or Without You' (song) 194

'Yahweh' (song) 83
'Your Blue Room' (song) 47
'You're the Best Thing About Me' 83–5, 94, 188
YouTube 73, 79

'Zoo Station' (song) 1, 45, 115
Zoo TV: Live from Sydney 1, 19, 44–5, 89–90, 99, 115–16, 133–4
Zooropa (album) 17–18, 26, 39, 44, 46–7, 117, 126, 146, 182
'Zooropa' (song) xiii, 44–5
Zukin, Sharon 40, 68

www.ingramcontent.com/pod-product-compliance
Lightning Source LLC
Chambersburg PA
CBHW062025220426
43662CB00010B/1475